BEARDLESS IRISES

A Plant for Every Garden Situation

KEVIN C.
VAUGHN

Schiffer Publishing Ltd

4880 Lower Valley Road • Atglen, PA 19310

Other Schiffer Books on Related Subjects:

All the Garden's a Stage: Choosing the Best Performing Plants for a Sustainable Garden
by Jane C. Gates, ISBN 978-0-7643-3979-0

Creating Ponds, Brooks, and Pools: Water in the Garden
by Ulrich Timm, ISBN 978-0-7643-0915-1

Geraniums: The Complete Encyclopedia
by Faye Brawner, ISBN 978-0-7643-1738-5

Designed by Justin Watkinson
Cover by Danielle Farmer
Type set in Weidemann Bk BT/Minion Pro

ISBN: 978-0-7643-4906-5

Printed in China

Published by Schiffer Publishing, Ltd.
4880 Lower Valley Road
Atglen, PA 19310
Phone: (610) 593-1777; Fax: (610) 593-2002
E-mail: Info@schifferbooks.com

For our complete selection of fine books on this and related subjects,
please visit our website at www.schifferbooks.com. You may also write for a free catalog.

This book may be purchased from the publisher. Please try your bookstore first.

We are always looking for people to write books on new and related subjects.
If you have an idea for a book, please contact us at proposals@schifferbooks.com.

Schiffer Publishing's titles are available at special discounts for bulk purchases for sales promotions
or premiums. Special editions, including personalized covers, corporate imprints, and excerpts
can be created in large quantities for special needs. For more information, contact the publisher.

CONTENTS

PREFACE

PREFACE

*Essentially I have been gardening
with beardless irises almost my entire life.*

I grew up in Massachusetts and my neighbor Polly Bishop gave me my first named Siberian iris, 'Gatineau', when I was nine years old. The density of blooms and the clump habit of this Siberian iris immediately impressed me, and they became my pets. Thanks to the generosity of Sarah Tiffney, Dorothy Spofford, and Bee Warburton I obtained an impressive collection for that time, and the first Siberian iris test garden was established in my parents' yard when I was but fourteen. Louisiana, spuria, and Japanese irises also graced beds around my parents' home. It was a love affair with beardless irises that I never lost. Although I couldn't grow Siberian irises well when I lived in Mississippi, the Louisiana, spuria, and water irises not only filled the void but added new interests and hybridizing fun for me. It's been a wonderful fifty-year adventure!

When I moved from Mississippi to Oregon in September 2010, I was confronted with a piece of property with many differing gardening aspects. Within my three acres, I had dry and wet shade, a meadow with both wet and dry sites, a traditional mixed perennial border, a neglected water feature, and a nearly bone-dry area next to a porch, made more alkaline by a concrete base. Amazingly, for every one of these sites I could find a beardless iris type that would not only grow but burgeon. It was something that I found I must share with gardeners faced with similar planting dilemmas, and is the reason for the title of this book.

Compared to their bearded iris cousins, the beardless irises have remained a secret to many gardeners, and I'm hoping that this book will introduce you to the wide variety of beardless irises that are available and to the improvement in these groups that hybridizers around the world have brought to the horticultural table. In this book, I cover not only the basics a beginner needs to know, but also include information that more sophisticated beardless iris aficionados will appreciate.

In each chapter, you will note areas of interest to a beginner (garden uses, culture, a history of hybrids, favorite cultivars), and other areas that definitely require previous experience with irises, genetics, or other phases of botany.

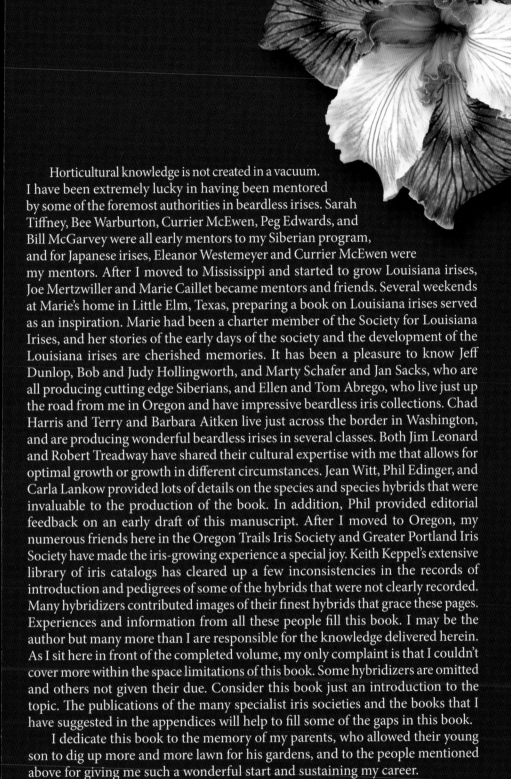

Horticultural knowledge is not created in a vacuum. I have been extremely lucky in having been mentored by some of the foremost authorities in beardless irises. Sarah Tiffney, Bee Warburton, Currier McEwen, Peg Edwards, and Bill McGarvey were all early mentors to my Siberian program, and for Japanese irises, Eleanor Westemeyer and Currier McEwen were my mentors. After I moved to Mississippi and started to grow Louisiana irises, Joe Mertzwiller and Marie Caillet became mentors and friends. Several weekends at Marie's home in Little Elm, Texas, preparing a book on Louisiana irises served as an inspiration. Marie had been a charter member of the Society for Louisiana Irises, and her stories of the early days of the society and the development of the Louisiana irises are cherished memories. It has been a pleasure to know Jeff Dunlop, Bob and Judy Hollingworth, and Marty Schafer and Jan Sacks, who are all producing cutting edge Siberians, and Ellen and Tom Abrego, who live just up the road from me in Oregon and have impressive beardless iris collections. Chad Harris and Terry and Barbara Aitken live just across the border in Washington, and are producing wonderful beardless irises in several classes. Both Jim Leonard and Robert Treadway have shared their cultural expertise with me that allows for optimal growth or growth in different circumstances. Jean Witt, Phil Edinger, and Carla Lankow provided lots of details on the species and species hybrids that were invaluable to the production of the book. In addition, Phil provided editorial feedback on an early draft of this manuscript. After I moved to Oregon, my numerous friends here in the Oregon Trails Iris Society and Greater Portland Iris Society have made the iris-growing experience a special joy. Keith Keppel's extensive library of iris catalogs has cleared up a few inconsistencies in the records of introduction and pedigrees of some of the hybrids that were not clearly recorded. Many hybridizers contributed images of their finest hybrids that grace these pages. Experiences and information from all these people fill this book. I may be the author but many more than I are responsible for the knowledge delivered herein. As I sit here in front of the completed volume, my only complaint is that I couldn't cover more within the space limitations of this book. Some hybridizers are omitted and others not given their due. Consider this book just an introduction to the topic. The publications of the many specialist iris societies and the books that I have suggested in the appendices will help to fill some of the gaps in this book.

I dedicate this book to the memory of my parents, who allowed their young son to dig up more and more lawn for his gardens, and to the people mentioned above for giving me such a wonderful start and sustaining my career.

Kevin C. Vaughn
Salem, Oregon
August 2014

1 WHAT ARE BEARDLESS IRISES?

Iris flowers vary tremendously in size and shape from the tiny *I. cristata* and miniature forms of Siberian irises with narrow petals and 2–3" flowers to the 10–12" dinner-plate style Japanese irises. Despite these differences, they all share one common structural format: each flower has six segments in two sets of three (with the exception of a few mutations to more petals). The three innermost or uppermost parts are called standards and the three lower portions are called falls. The size and extent of these two petal types vary dramatically from each type of iris, making for a huge variety of lovely forms. The sexual parts of the flower, the pollen bearing anthers, and the styles, are relatively minor portions of the flower but of course are critical in the sexual reproduction of the iris.

All of the irises I will describe in this book are rhizomatous, that is, they have a more or less prominent rhizome, a highly modified underground stem. Rhizomatous irises include both the familiar bearded irises (such as the most well-known tall bearded irises), and the lesser known beardless irises. The bearded irises were originally included in the subgenus *Pogon* and most of the beardless irises were included in the subgenus *Apogon*.

To know what a beardless iris is we must actually know what a bearded iris and its beard are. In bearded irises, an area on the falls (lower portions of the blossoms) contains a collection of unicellular hairs that resemble a moustache more than a beard. Often these beards are of bright colors, and the iris uses these beards as a method of attracting would-be pollinators. Beardless irises lack these structures, although often beardless irises have a strong signal of lighter or darker colors that serves as the same sort of pollinator attractant. A third type of iris, the crested iris, has crests, small linear ridges of tissue that occupy the place of the beard in bearded irises. Although the crested irises are now known to be more related to the bearded irises (see below), many of the hardy members of this group grow under the same conditions as beardless groups and are covered in this volume.

A beardless iris: a Vaughn bright gold spuria seedling

RECENT TAXONOMIC DECISIONS

In the 1950s, the classification system that we used was fairly simple (Lawrence 1953). The genus iris was divided easily into bearded (*Pogon*) and beardless (*Apogon*) types, with the crested irises as a subgroup of the beardless types. Although this was an easy system for horticulturists, it was an artificial system, based upon a single criterion: whether an iris had a beard or not. Even as gardeners, we knew that this system was artificial. For example, the crested iris, *I. tectorum*, could be crossed with bearded irises and gave hybrids such as 'Paltec' but other beardless irises could not be crossed with bearded irises. Rodionenko (2008) expanded the classical taxonomy of the genus, by examining a series of morphological characters—such as nectaries, growth of the seedlings, and rhizome characteristics—that gave better clues as to the interrelationships between the various iris types, but were still based upon relatively few characters.

Classical taxonomy is based upon morphological criteria. We are biased by the very obvious characteristics such as beards, flower color, size of the plant, or rhizome type. Although obvious, these very salient differences may in fact be due to relatively few genetic changes. In contrast, other characters, even some perhaps not as salient, may represent much more radical changes in terms of DNA changes that have occurred. By using analysis of DNA sequences and examining a number of clones of bearded and beardless iris species, we can develop a system of classification free of the morphological bias of classical taxonomy. Several groups have examined a variety

of irises, including both bearded and beardless irises (Wilson 2004; 2009; 2011; Tillie et al. 2000; Wheeler and Wilson 2014) and the results point in general towards the same trends, despite differences in sequences used for the analysis. The data from these studies give us a much better understanding of the interrelationships between the various tribes, and they also produce a number of surprises.

Within the beardless irises, the phylogenetic analysis has revealed a clear separation for the core group of beardless irises known as *Limniris* (Pacific Coast Native, Siberians, Japanese, and Louisiana classes plus a few other related species) from other iris types, although the spuria irises appear to be more distantly related to this core group. This separation of the spurias from the other groups has also been supported by more classical morphological criteria such as the presence of nectaries (Rodionenko 2008) and the linking of this group with the bulbous irises that are of similar floral morphology. Crested irises show stronger affinities with bearded irises. Surprisingly, the very ancient blackberry lily (*I. domestica*), which has been placed in a separate genus by some taxonomists, showed close affinities to the bearded irises.

Despite these changes in our understanding, I have retained discussions of several groups that are outside of the core beardless iris groups in this text that have traditionally been considered as "beardless." For example, the hardy crested irises are often grown under similar garden situations as other true beardless iris groups and *I. tenuis* was even once considered a Pacific Coast Native iris. These are covered in this text.

I. cristata 'Precious Pearl', a crested iris with prominent crest

HORTICULTURAL CLASSIFICATIONS

Within the beardless irises, five major groups of irises have been developed. The Siberian, spuria, and Japanese irises are derived from Old World species, whereas the Pacific Coast Native and Louisiana irises are derived from New World species. Each of these has a chapter devoted to them in this book. Species that are not included in any of these groups are classified by the American Iris Society in the general "species" class. The species class also includes collected variants and garden crosses of species that are included in other groups but are more akin to the ancestors of these groups than modern hybrids. For example, the collected *I. fulva* 'Bayou Bandit' (Weeks '97) is a species clone even though *I. fulva* is involved in the Louisiana iris group. Hybrids between these species or any hybrid that exhibits more species-like characteristics are lumped into the "species hybrid" class. An example would be the so-called "CalSibes" that are the result of crosses between the Pacific Coast Native Irises and the 40-chromosome Siberian irises. The Species Iris Group of North America has done much to promote the introduction of outstanding clones of species and their use in creating novel garden hybrids, greatly expanding our options as to beardless irises. Moreover, many of these hybrid types are able to grow in climates and conditions in which neither parent will grow.

For each of these horticultural groups, the American Iris Society has established an awards system. Three years after introduction, a cultivar is eligible for an honorable mention (HM). Only ten percent of the available plants win this award. Two years later, the cultivars that have won honorable mentions are eligible for the award of merit (AM). Generally, only two cultivars win this award in any year. Cultivars that have won an AM are eligible for the top award of their class, such as the Nies Medal for spurias. All the medal winners in all of the iris classes, bearded and beardless, are eligible for the Dykes Medal, the top award for all irises. No beardless iris has won this award in America but in England both Pacific Coast Native and Siberian irises have won the Dykes Medal, and in Australasia both Louisiana irises and a Siberian iris have won the highest awards. A list of these award winners can be found on the website www.wiki.irises.org. Generally irises that have won the special award of their type are proven performers and offer the gardener some assurance that they are garden-worthy. However, many very worthy plants have never won any awards. Some of these gems are listed in the "A few favorites" section at the end of each chapter.

Because of the diverse climates, soil types, and precipitation levels in areas where the parental species of these groups grow, there is literally some beardless iris type that will grow in virtually any gardening situation. For those in relatively temperate climates, the choices of beardless iris types that may be grown are almost limitless.

In the following chapters, each of these beardless classes will be described in terms of the species involved, the development of hybrids, their culture, and hybridization. Although no treatise can be encyclopedic, it is hoped that this book will answer many questions on these fascinating plants. As I researched these plants, it became obvious how the hybridizers have capitalized on the work of previous hybridizers. It is a marvelous story of cooperation and collaboration of breeders from around the world to create the wonderful variety of beardless iris hybrids that are available today. In my fifty years of growing and hybridizing beardless irises, it has been my pleasure to watch many of these developments unfold.

When I started to write this book, I realized that the way in which horticulturists designate a hybridizer and year of introduction are identical to the way in which citations of the literature are made. To separate these I have made a distinction in the text.

References that are citations of publications are listed in this format: "Wilson (2004)" or "(Wilson 2004)." These refer to a journal article, with the full details of that reference listed at the end of the chapter.

When the name and date in parentheses follows a cultivar name, then this is the year the hybridizer introduced that particular cultivar into commerce. For example, a listing such as "'Red Velvet Elvis' (Vaughn '97)" in the text means that this cultivar was hybridized by Vaughn and introduced into commerce in 1997. The standard way cultivars are designated is with a single quote, an exception being those that are not officially registered with the American Iris Society. They are in double quotes.

In this book, I have left out the designation *Iris,* or its shortened form *I.,* because this book is about irises and would have made the text flow less smoothly. When I have mentioned other perennials or cultivars of these perennials, the genus named is always spelled out fully. Hopefully this will eliminate some confusion over these two designations.

REFERENCES

Lawrence, G.H.M. (1953) A reclassification of the genus *Iris. Gentes Herbarium* 8(4): 346–371.

Rodionenko, G. (2008) *A New System of the Genus* Iris. Special book, published by Species Iris Group of North America.

Tillie, N.M., M.W. Chase and T. Hall (2000) Molecular studies in the genus *Iris* L.: a preliminary study. *Annali di Botanica* 58: 105–114.

Wheeler, A.S., and C.A. Wilson (2014) Exploring phylogenetic relationships within a broadly distributed, Northern Hemisphere group of semi-aquatic *Iris* species. In press.

Wilson, C.A. (2004) Phylogeny of *Iris* based on chloroplast *matk* gene and *trnK* intron sequence data. *Molecular Phylogenetics and Evolution* 33: 402–412.

Wilson, C.A. (2009) Phylogenetic relationships among the recognized series in *Iris* section *Limniris. Systematic Botany* 34: 277–284.

Wilson, C.A. (2011) Subgeneric classification in *Iris* re-examined using chloroplast sequence data. *Taxon* 60: 27–35.

Vaughn yellow tall bearded iris with prominent tangerine beard

2 SIBERIAN IRISES

In climates and gardens that offer the conditions that Siberian irises prefer (cooler, acid soil, moisture), there is almost no easier garden plant. They survive in some of the coldest climates as they are completely dormant in the winter. Siberian irises appear delicate but are anything but! From dense clumps of relatively narrow leaves comes a virtual bouquet of stalks. In some cases, the density of blooms obscures the underlying foliage and, in many cultivars, the flowers flutter in even the slightest breeze. Although bloom season for a given cultivar of many varieties is 2 to 3 weeks, there are recurrent blooming sorts that bloom for much longer. The erect beautiful foliage provides a strong vertical accent from spring to fall, much as do ornamental grasses. Moreover, unlike many irises, Siberian clumps do not require frequent division and actually become more attractive with age. I have seen clumps that are 20+ years old with hundreds of bloomstalks that are true garden statements. There aren't many plants of any kind that have that sort of sustained performance.

Although my description of the beautiful clump-forming nature of these plants makes it sound as though there is little variety, nothing could be further from the truth. Early on in the establishment of judging standards for Siberian irises, diversity was cherished, so that flower forms that range from classic pendant forms to a very compact forms with wide petals, flat forms in which all the petals are the size and shape of the falls, and multi-petal types are all accepted as long as they create a pleasing effect (Warburton 1973). Heights range from 6″ (dwarfs, such as 'Baby Sister') to approximately 4′ ('High Standards' and 'Tall Dark and Handsome'). Foliage also differs greatly in thickness, from the grass-like foliage of cultivars closely related to *I. sibirica* to thicker foliage from *I. sanguinea*, and spiraled foliage in cultivars derived from *I. typhifolia*. Add to that the fact that there are flower colors from white through all shades of blue to dark-violet, plus shades more towards red and pink and yellow. Although there are self-colored blossoms, many varieties exhibit intriguing bold signal patterns, contrasting colors in the style arms, and

'Bluebird Kisses'

Field of Siberian irises at Ensata Gardens

bicolors in many combinations. Forms vary from the classical pendant shape to the now more popular highly flared compact form typical of descendents of 'White Swirl', to true flat types, and multipetal types. Truly, the gardener today has a fairly broad palette of colors, sizes, and shapes from which to choose that were not available to gardeners even as recently as the 1980s. Luckily the Siberian breeders have taken multiple approaches, and each year we see new examples of each type of form, color, height, and foliage coming to the market.

There are two groups of Siberian irises. Those derived from the 28-chromosome species are sometimes called "garden Siberians" and are the group to which most of this chapter is dedicated. They are the kinds sold by most nurseries, and are ones that grow most easily in most of the United States. A second group of Siberians, sometimes designated as "Sino-Sibes," is derived from 40-chromosome Siberian irises from China. In general, they are more difficult to grow, especially in warmer, drier areas of the United States, with good growth reported only in the Pacific Northwest and in New England. It is a pity, as they are charming garden plants and have very interesting patterns of colors in the blossoms.

GARDEN USES AND CULTURE

Siberian irises "play very well" with other plants! They work well in a mixed sunny perennial border and not only add blooms during the bloom season, but also the upright clumps of leaves have the effect of an ornamental grass when not in bloom. Siberian are especially good in combination with peonies, true lilies, daylilies, hardy geraniums, garden phlox, Oriental poppies, and a variety of other perennials that require moderately acid soil and an average to greater-than-average amount of water. A garden where the plants receive ½ to 1" of water per week during the growing season is ideal for Siberian irises and many other perennials. Siberian irises are not water plants, however. Siberians may be grown besides pools but must not have their roots continually wet. Taller sorts may be used at the back of the border, while miniature cultivars may be used as edging plants. In the Northern United States, Siberians must receive at least a half day of sun to grow and bloom properly, and the more sun the better. In the Southern United States, high shade is very effective for the growth of these plants. Years ago, Mildred Johnson planted the cultivar 'Mandy Morse' in three locations that varied in sun exposure. By planting in three locations, the blooms of that cultivar started blooming over the period of a month, greatly extending the bloom season.

'Fisherman's Fancy'

In my garden in Oregon, I use Siberian irises as occasional accents in the perennial borders but also do a massed planting that provides for a colorful display for 4 to 8 weeks, by using cultivars that vary in bloom season and have the ability to repeat bloom. In my parents' garden in Massachusetts, we planted a 100' border solidly with Siberian irises which was backed by a low brick wall; they literally stopped traffic when in bloom. The addition of summer annuals between the clumps kept the color in the bed for the remainder of the summer. Siberians do resent transplanting, so you should consider their locations as permanent positions for these plants.

Although plants may be grown without mulch, the addition of mulch seems to be very effective in keeping the Siberian irises growing to their full potential. Mulches like pine needles, salt marsh hay, or ground pine or fir bark keep the soil moist, protect young plants, and suppress the growth of weeds. Fertilizers such as 5-10-10 should be applied early in the season to promote growth and bloom. Well composted manures and alfalfa meal are also excellent additions to the soil and seem especially to benefit growth of Siberian irises. Slow-release fertilizers are also a useful and easy way to apply fertilizer, although I tend to use them as a supplement to other fertilizers in the Siberian iris planting. Siberian irises are deciduous and thus must make a complete new set of leaves and produce bloom stalks in the spring, making a large available source of nutrients critical at this time. In addition, if spring rains are not usual, then water should be applied to the plantings to allow for maximal growth and optimal bloom.

In areas of the country where the soil is not acid, Siberian iris growth is definitely much less satisfactory. Any way that the soil pH may be lowered, such as with the addition of compost, animal manures, peat moss, or soil sulphur, are all effective in making Siberian irises grow better. In addition, mulching with fir or pine bark or pine needles (so-called "pine straw") is a good way to maintain soil acidity, as well as suppressing weeds and retaining soil moisture.

'Hooked Again'

Most Siberian irises set seed readily and form an abundance of pods. Some gardeners use these pods for dried arrangements. The branched stalks of *I. sibirica* and cultivars derived from it have unusual acorn-shaped pods that are especially lovely in arrangements. However, if you do not want to use pods for dried arrangements or to grow seedlings, all the pods should be chopped off the plants while still green. This reduces the burden of the plant to produce seed and allows the plant to invest itself in the growth of the plant rather than the seed. In addition, seed spilled from the pods can grow up within the clump and contaminate the clump with seedlings that are not the same as the parent.

After the season is over, the Siberian foliage will begin to yellow and eventually turn brown and lay flat on the ground. At this time, trim the foliage to ground level—but not before. Nutrients from the leaves flow to the rhizomes, and cutting leaves before they have fully senesced will stunt the plants. Siberian iris leaves are tough and a mechanical trimming device is useful for cleaning off the old foliage, especially if you have a large planting.

Clumps may be left in the same place for many years and will continue to produce blooms without dividing. Indeed, the clump aspect of the Siberian with its multitude of flowers is one of the best garden aspects of these plants. However, if the center of the clump seems to be dying out or the center is hollow, then the clump should be dug and divided or portions of the clump removed to start a new clump. A spading fork or a pair of spading forks positioned back to back is useful for teasing apart the clump. An established Siberian clump is a formidable opponent! By the time a Siberian iris clump needs to be divided, the plant is deeply rooted and will require some muscle to remove pieces to start a new clump. Cut the leaves of the divisions down to about 3 to 4" tall before putting them in a new location, to reduce transpiration and reduce transplant shock. An alternative approach is to remove portions of dead rhizomes and replace the dead center of the clumps with fresh soil, keeping the clump in the same location but refreshing its soil conditions. In time, the rhizomes will grow back into the dead areas, although the symmetry of the clump is often compromised.

Transplanting Siberians is one of the most difficult aspects of their culture. Plants that are received from mail order nurseries are most frequently shipped as bare root plants with their roots wrapped in peat moss or moist toweling. If new roots aren't showing, soaking the plants up to the foliage bases in a bucket of water for 24 hours will often stimulate new root production. Dig a hole that is slightly deeper than the length of the roots, so that the rhizomes will sit 1 to 2" below the soil level. Place the plant in the hole and fill the hole with water. Allow the water to drain and fill in the soil around the plant. Tamp the soil around the rhizomes and apply a quantity of

water to eliminate air pockets in the soil. Keep the plants moist for several weeks until new growth is apparent. Applying mulch above the plants soon after planting also enhances the survival of the plants. Some nurseries sell Siberians that have been grown and are shipped in pots. These plants are very easy to transplant as you simply pop the plant from the pot, dig a hole large enough to allow for the contents of the pot, put the plant and soil into the hole, water heavily, and fill in any gaps with more soil. Easy! If you have had trouble with transplanting Siberians otherwise, try this as a method before giving up on these plants.

Opinions vary greatly about spring planting compared to fall planting. Traditionally, plants were shipped in the fall. However, a number of nurseries are shipping plants in the spring as well. If you live in a climate similar to the nursery shipping the plant, this gives you an opportunity to obtain the plants months earlier and allow the plants to establish long before winter. I have found that plants shipped in the spring seem to catch on more quickly and frequently will even bloom the first season. If your climate is warmer and dry, then fall planting is probably best for Siberian planting.

As mentioned above, culture of the 40-chromosome Siberian irises is more difficult than the Garden Siberians. First of all, they have a more limited range of climates in which they grow easily. The Pacific Northwest and New England and New York are the chief areas where they are successfully grown. Even in these areas, the 40-chromosomes require more moisture than the garden Siberians. Supplementing with more water, planting in small depressions in the flower bed, and mulching heavily are helpful in the success of these plants. I have had good luck planting these irises at the bottom of a hillside, where the plant receives extra moisture from rain and irrigation water uphill from the plant. Unlike the Garden Siberians, the 40-chromosome Siberians need to be dug and divided more regularly or else the plant declines. Generally, removal of a portion of a clump to a new site and leaving a portion at the original site is a good strategy to maintain cultivars. In this way, if the transplanted division fails to grow, there is a chance to take a division from the parent clump in the next season. Transplanting techniques and other cultural conditions are the same as those for Garden Siberians.

Growing Siberian irises in arid and warm climates is not easy. Although certain cultivars like 'Caesar's Brother', 'Ruffled Velvet', 'Velvet Night', and 'Lights of Paris' grow and bloom well in warm climates, many do not. Plants stay very dwarf and produce short bloomstalks. Generally this is followed by an increasing senescence of the plant and ultimately death. Some of the symptoms of the demise remind one of the so-called Southern blight that attacks a number of species. Growing the plants in high shade and applying additional moisture during the dry summers can extend the list of survivors. When I lived in Mississippi, I crossed 'Velvet Night' with 'Ruffled Velvet' and obtained hundreds of seedlings that prospered in that environment, so it is possible to select for plants that are suited to that climate.

PESTS AND DISEASES

In general, Siberian irises are free of pests and diseases. However, there are some problems in some areas of the country that range from minor annoyances to severe problems.

Iris borers, the larval stage of the moth *Macronoctua onusta*, are ubiquitous on the East Coast and throughout the Midwest. The iris borer mainly attacks bearded iris rhizomes and in these species the larva will damage a single fan and the attached rhizome. Because the Siberian iris rhizome is so much smaller than the bearded iris rhizome, the borer tends to invade a greater number of rhizomes, causing dead portions of the clump. Borers tend to be solitary so that if the borer damage (chiefly bits of eaten foliage and stunted leaves) is noted early, the fans can be examined and the small borer destroyed. Systemic insecticides remain the best alternatives to control, especially the insecticides containing dimethoate as the active ingredient. It is imperative that all labels on these insecticides are adhered to strictly. If borers are controlled for several seasons, generally the pests do not return unless there are wild irises in the same area or infected garden populations in close proximity.

Perhaps the most discouraging Siberian iris pest is the iris bud fly, *Orthochaeta dissimilis*. The iris bud fly attacks developing flower buds. The grub is a small (3 to 4 mm in length) white insect with a prominent black spot at one end, and attacks chiefly the reproductive organs of the flower. When the flower opens, the style arms are a gnarly mass of chewed and deformed tissue. Although some spraying programs have proven effective for controlling this pest, a more benign approach has come through the use of yellow sticky cards that are used for control of greenhouse insects. Yellow cards are positioned near plants about the time that stalks are becoming visible in the clump. The fly is attracted to these cards and sticks to them before it can deposit eggs in the developing stalks. If infestations are light, a good way of ensuring fewer problems in the next season is to manually inspect the flowers and destroy the grub. The grub is generally solitary and shies from light. If the grub is not still in the flower, it generally hides in the leafy spathes that surround the developing blossom. Careful elimination of infected flowers will severely lower or eradicate this pest from your planting.

Vaughn 40-chromosome Siberian iris seedling

Hollingworth seedling 10K8B3

Siberian irises are occasionally attacked by *Botrytis,* and occasional plants will show scorch-like symptoms. Both of these diseases are much less frequent on Siberian irises than they are on bearded irises and generally they only affect a few fans in a portion of the clump. The 40-chromosome Siberians are much more often affected by disease. Occasionally a whole clump or even areas of a bed will die. Many theories have been put forward as to the cause. Some speculation is that it is some sort of water mold. One possible solution is to remove portions of a clump to new soil every several years to keep these plants going. Amazingly, plants can be grown from seed relatively easily and most of the seedlings from these plants are pleasing plants, worthy of garden space.

DIPLOIDS AND TETRAPLOIDS

Besides the two groups of Siberian irises, there are also two ploidy levels for these plants, diploid and tetraploid. All of the wild plants are diploids, that is, containing two sets of chromosomes, as are most of the cultivars. However, due to the work of Currier McEwen, Robert Hollingworth, and Thomas Tamberg and more recently John White, Jeff Dunlop, and Dean Cole, a number of tetraploid cultivars have been produced. To produce tetraploid plants, young seedlings are treated with colchicine, a drug derived from the autumn crocus, that arrests cells in mitosis, but after they have duplicated their DNA before entry into mitosis. The colchicine is then washed out of the seedlings, and the cells are now able to divide, but the affected cells continue to have the higher amount of DNA. The diploid plants have two copies of each chromosome but the tetraploids have four copies. Tetraploid

'Paprikash'

small segregant out of crosses of the Wiswell reds and 'Little White' (McEwen '71) out of 'Gatineau' breeding, both very happy accidents. Currier McEwen started a serious program of producing consistently miniature Siberians, using his 'Little White' and other smaller Siberians to create a line of miniatures. However, even he found that many of the miniatures, after several years of staying small, would grow 24" to 30" stalks and produce larger flowers. McEwen did produce some very consistent miniatures though, and his 'Baby Sister' (McEwen '86), 'Annick' (McEwen '86), and 'Sassy Kooma' (McEwen '93) are very consistent miniature cultivars that stay miniature even as clumps. Other small ones that stay consistently small are yellow amoena 'My Little Sunshine' (Schafer-Sacks '11), clear blue 'Blue Hyacinth' (Bush '87), bright red 'Paprikash' (Schafer-Sacks '12), pinkish 'Precious Doll' (Varner '88), and

plants tend to be larger and of stiffer substance and often exhibit an exaggeration of the traits found in the diploid clones, such as ruffling and style ornamentation. Early tetraploid conversions of the pendant-form diploids tended to give a sort of a rather unpleasant propeller-shaped flower, but later hybrids have more attractively formed flowers. Tetraploids do not have the fluttery characteristics of many diploids, but they do tend to have greater substance and are a little more resistant to adverse weather conditions. Hybridizers are working at both ploidy levels and are producing lovely and distinctive plants that are useful to gardeners.

Another virtue of tetraploid Siberians is that they may be crossed with other tetraploid beardless species to produce fertile amphidiploids hybrids. The hybrids inherit two sets of chromosomes from the Siberian parent and two from the other, enabling chromosome pairing within the sets of chromosomes from each parent. This chromosome arrangement (essentially amphidiploids) allows for very stable hybrids with normal levels of fertility.

MINIATURE CULTIVARS

Although the dwarf cultivar 'Acuta' has been available since the 1800s, progress in the development of dwarf and miniature Siberians has not been a priority of Siberian breeders. With most of the progress centering on larger flowers, the miniatures fall out of these programs as lucky accidents (Edwards 1964; Walkup 2002). These miniature Siberians are especially good to be used in the front of mixed perennial borders or at the front of an all-Siberian iris planting. Some cultivars tend to produce shorter progeny more consistently, such as 'Gatineau' (Preston '32), 'Carrie Lee' (Wiswell '63), and 'Claret' (Wiswell '66). As examples, Vaughn's 'Little Red' ('77) was a single very

'It's Delightful'

'Love Always'

grape-colored 'Little Papoose' (Varner '92). Several other Siberian cultivars are small, but not quite miniature in all proportions, such as 'Sweet Little Susy' (Schafer-Sacks '10) and 'Pixie Preview' (Hollingworth '09). These might be termed "intermediate" or "median" Siberians and are similarly useful in facing down taller types or as edging plants.

REPEAT BLOOM

Reblooming bearded irises are well known, but most of these don't rebloom until the autumn months. Siberian rebloom is different, and Currier McEwen used the term "repeat bloom" to distinguish it from the more familiar bearded iris rebloom. When Siberians repeat bloom, the repeat bloomstalks come in immediately after the first bloomstalks have finished. Elizabeth Scheffy was the first to introduce a true repeat bloomer, her 'My Love' (Scheffy '49), a very well-branched clear blue. Repeat bloom on this cultivar extends the blooming period for nearly two months. 'Salem Witch' (Spofford '62), a tall purple with white signals, is a very strong repeat bloomer, although it was registered as having an extremely long bloom period, not as a rebloomer. Not much activity occurred in this breeding area until Currier McEwen began using 'My Love' in crosses. Now there are quite a number of Siberian irises that have been registered as rebloomers and the latest checklist from the Reblooming Iris Society (2012) lists over one hundred cultivars known to repeat bloom. Bee Warburton noted that the ability to repeat bloom was associated with *I. sibirica* characteristics whereas breeders had selected more for *I. sanguinea* traits such as wider petals and lower bloomstalks, which accounts for its relatively low occurrence. Terry Aitken noted that the ability to repeat bloom was much greater in the Pacific Northwest on the west side of the Cascades as soil temperatures stayed cool for a longer period of time. Repeat bloom ceased when the soil temperatures reached 60° F. Thus, both climate and genetics will influence whether a given cultivar will show repeat bloom. Besides 'My Love', there are several other cultivars that show repeat bloom in a number of different climates, including 'Exuberant Encore' (McEwen '85), 'George

'Solar Energy'

Henry' (Warburton '83), 'Lavender Bounty' (McEwen '83), 'Mad Magenta' (Warburton '87), 'On and On' (McEwen '77), 'Reprise' (Warburton '87), 'Soft Blue' (McEwen '79), 'Welcome Return' (McEwen '81), and 'White Encore' (McEwen '81). These cultivars are a fairly complete mix of colors, so one is not limited to the blue of 'My Love' in a patch of repeat blooming Siberian irises.

GROWING SIBERIAN IRISES FROM SEED

Growing Siberian irises from seed is relatively easy and, for the difficult-to-transplant 40-chromosome Siberians, is a good way to obtain these plants and to determine whether they will be happy in your garden. A technique that works well for me is to plant seeds in the fall of the year, in 6- to 8"-diameter pots that are filled with a good sterilized potting mix. Plant the seed about 1" deep, planting approximately 25 to 30 seeds per pot, spread evenly throughout the pot. Water the pot and make sure that the pot stays wet through the winter. In my garden, I keep my pots in an area near my garage that is protected from severe cold but still exposed to the elements. In colder climates, delaying the planting to later or planting in protected locations seems to ensure good germination.

Carefully examine the pots for signs of germination, and protect any pots with young seedlings from severe freezing weather. In the spring, the bulk of the seed will germinate and seedlings can be rowed out in garden beds when they are about 2" tall and all danger of frost has passed. Plant the seedlings 6" apart in rows 10" apart, in any good garden soil. Full sun is best, but part shade will also grow fine Siberian iris seedlings. To keep the seedlings actively growing, water the seedlings with a water soluble fertilizer every couple of weeks and keep the seedling bed itself moist during the growing season. Seedlings benefit from mulching but the mulch should be increased in depth gradually during the season rather than applied all at once. With this care, the seedlings should produce increase by the fall and most will bloom the following spring. Any seedling that doesn't bloom by the second season is too weak a plant and should be discarded.

The garden Siberians are 28-chromosome sorts derived from *Iris sibirica, I. sanguinea,* and, more recently, *I. typhifolia.* These species are native to Europe and Asia, and come from some of the more inhospitable climates for gardening, making them ideally suited for cold climate–challenged areas in the United States and Europe. Each species has contributed unique aspects to the hybrids in this group. *I. sibirica* is a very tall plant with narrow, grasslike foliage. The stems have six to eight flowers per stalk that rise well above the foliage, and frequently the flowers occur in a pattern of dark blue standards over white falls veined all over in the darker blue of the standards. Pods are produced in abundance and have a distinct acorn shape. My most vivid memory of this species is of a clone being grown by a woman from my hometown in Massachusetts that reached nearly 6' in height and had 18 buds and flowers of a softer blue than typical of the species. The clump was a sea of blooms. Various white variants of this species have been registered as 'Caesar's Ghost', 'Snow Prince', and 'Sea Turn'. These whites are milk whites infused with pale lavender. Generally *I. sibirica* and its cultivars bloom early in the season but continue blooming through at least mid-season because of their copious buds. In contrast, *I. sanguinea* is a much shorter plant, at approximately 24", with larger flowers than *I. sibirica* and stems that barely reach over the top of the foliage and generally only two to three buds, clustered in the terminal, and peaking later in the bloom season. Older collected cultivars of *I. sanguinea* include the dark purple 'Emperor', dark blue 'Blue King', and the clear white 'Snow Queen'. All of these cultivars would be important parents in supplying both dark colors but also bluer and lighter blues from crossing 'Snow Queen' into blue-violet cultivars. In Japan, a number of other wild forms with double or flat-formed flowers have been found that are also seeing their way into the breeding of modern cultivars. *I. typhifolia* is the most recently described species and occurs over a restricted area of northeast China. Plants are similar in size to *I. sanguinea* but the bloom season is much earlier, as much as a month before *I. sanguinea,* and the foliage forms neat mounds of twisted foliage. Most flowers are in the blue-violet range. Although this species was only available to hybridizers in the late 1980s, it was quickly used to create a number of very early blooming plants that greatly extend the Siberian iris season. Several clones of *I. typhifolia* have been registered, such as 'Caitlin's Smile', that are better selections of this species.

It is unfortunate that the so-called "Sino-Siberian" or "40-chromosome Siberian" irises are so much more difficult to grow in most climates, as they are most charming subjects in areas where they can be grown successfully. These species originated generally from the southeastern provinces of China and require more uniform moisture and temperature requirements than those in the "garden Siberian" group. As a group they tend to bloom after the garden Siberians. *I. chrysographes* is a 2' species, and features unbranched stems with maroon to dark violet velvety flowers with a prominent gold-braided signal, the source of its name, which is Latin for "gold writing." Almost any form of this species is an attractive one but they tend to be non-persistent. McGarvey's near-black clone 'Id' was especially dark but also especially difficult to grow. *I. clarkei* is a bit taller-branched blue violet with a prominent white signal that appears in many of its hybrids. It is also distinct from all other Siberian irises in having solid stems. The tallest accepted species, *I. delavayi,* grows 3 to 4' tall and occasionally as tall as 5'. The stalks are well-branched. Among the 40-chromosome Siberian irises are the yellow-flowered species, *I. forrestii* and *I. wilsonii,* that add these colors to the group, and are similar with unbranched stems in shades of lemon yellow. The falls often have brown penciled signals. Several other species have been described but there is far less certainty that they are valid species as they have been found infrequently (*I. dykesii*) or the progeny from these plants do not breed true (*I. bulleyana*), making the clones currently distributed under these names suspect as true species. Even a variant of *I. sibirica* was distributed as an example of this species! However, recent collections of *I. bulleyana* in China produce uniform lavender flowering progeny, indicating that it is a good species.

THE DEVELOPMENT OF GARDEN HYBRIDS

The history of Siberian iris breeding is an interesting one since so many hybridizers were able to build upon the work of others to create the Siberian iris we know today. Moreover, many of these older Siberians are still wonderful garden plants and offer unique combinations of colors, sizes, and forms. Fortunately, many of these cultivars are still commercially available.

Many of the early named cultivars (pre-1900 to 1910) had no published pedigrees and may have been simple selections of the species from Japan and elsewhere, such as 'Emperor' (Barr '14) and 'Snow Queen' ('00) that are cultivars of *I. sanguinea* or 'Grandis' (Farr '12), a selection of *I. sibirica.*

Other early hybridizers appeared to have made deliberate crosses or at least raised seed from selected varieties. English breeder Amos Perry, a prolific breeder in many genera, was one who turned his attention to irises early on and his 'Perry's Pygmy' ('12), 'Mrs. Rowe' ('16), 'Sibirica Nana Alba' ('40) and 'Perry's Blue' ('12) are still available commercially. Perry was also the first to make a cross between a 40-chromosome Siberian and a Pacific Coast Native iris that resulted in the first English Dykes Medal for the lovely 'Margot Holmes' ('27). A number of 40-chromosome hybrids were registered but it is unlikely that any are still extant.

Vaughn pink
6-fall seedling

Although Perry gave the English a great start to Siberian hybridization, the next great push of Siberian hybrids would be from North America. Isabella Preston was employed by the Canadian government to produce horticultural plants that would survive the brutal Canadian climate and developed not only Siberian irises, but lilacs and true lilies as well. Crossing 'Sibirica Maxima' × 'Snow Queen' gave Preston a large series of hybrids that combined the best qualities of both parents and combinations of characters that would help to popularize Siberian irises greatly. These are the first hybrids which are from documented crosses of *I. sibirica* and *I. sanguinea*. 'Gatineau' ('32) is probably the most famous and well-distributed of these clones, a very clear blue with wide petals and very good growth habits. It has been one of the most important parents as it carries the recessive white gene from 'Snow Queen' and often its seedlings, even from self-pollinations, are much better than itself. 'Rimouski' ('37) was for years the white Siberian with the most yellow on the petals. 'Ottawa' ('30) is a much darker flower than 'Gatineau' and with a bold white signal.

Perry's fellow Canadian, the renowned plantsman F. Cleveland Morgan, also turned his attention to Siberian irises, producing the famous trio of 'Caesar', 'Caesar's Brother', and 'Tropic Night' with the latter two winning the Morgan Award, the top award for Siberian irises. 'Caesar' ('24) and 'Caesar's Brother' ('31) are from 'Blue King' × 'Nigrescens', so are predominantly (perhaps totally) of *sanguinea* blood, and 'Tropic Night' ('37) is from a bee pod on 'Caesar'. All three are various shades of dark purple with 'Tropic Night' being one of the darkest. 'Caesar's Brother' may be the most distributed

Siberian iris of all. Its vigor and ability to grow in much warmer climates have made it a perennial favorite. Both Preston and Morgan were awarded the American Iris Society Hybridizers Medal for their careful work with the Siberian irises.

Unlike the detailed cross records kept by Preston and Morgan, a number of hybrids that were produced in two Northeast US nurseries during the 1930s and '40s are without

'Tycoon' was used extensively as a parent, consistently gave high quality seedlings, and won the very first Morgan Award in 1951.

pedigree. It is not known whether these were from intentional crosses that were not recorded with the registrar, bee set seed, or hybrids that appeared spontaneously in a larger planting from spilled seed. A large number of the 40 Siberians introduced by Frances Cleveland of New Jersey are still available today. 'Silvertip' ('39) is a clear blue with near-white styles that is very distinctive, as is the cute arranger's iris 'Summer Sky' ('39), a *sibirica* type in pale blue with white styles. One of the first quality lavender-pink cultivars, 'Morning Magic' ('39) was also one of the Cleveland Siberians. The lovely 'Turquoise Cup' ('27) was the first Siberian to show the wider form and it was coupled with a blush of turquoise on its style arms. Perhaps the most important of the Cleveland Siberians is 'Tycoon' ('38). For many years 'Tycoon' was the largest of all Siberian irises. It was used extensively as a parent, consistently gave high quality seedlings, and won the very first Morgan Award in 1951. The very distinctive 'Cool Spring' ('39), a blue with textured veins all over, was introduced by Willard Kellogg from the "Over the Garden Wall" nursery in Connecticut which he ran with his mother Grace. It very belatedly was awarded the Morgan Award in 1966, twenty-seven years after appearing on the market, and it is still being offered in catalogs today.

Charles Gersdorff, a scientist with the US Department of Agriculture in Beltsville, Maryland, and a long-time registrar for the American Iris Society, registered a number of Siberian cultivars from planned crosses in the 1930s and '40s but only the clear sky blue 'Mountain Lake' ('38), medium blue 'Skyblue Water' ('39), and dark purple 'Night Sprite' ('39) were marketed. 'Mountain Lake' is a lovely flower and widely grown. Fred Whitney introduced two of the more popular early reddish-toned Siberians in the 1940s: 'Helen Astor' ('38) and its seedling 'Eric the Red' ('43). 'Helen Astor' is a pale red, nearly pink, and shorter in stature than many Siberians, whereas 'Eric the Red' is a dark magenta of much larger size and wider petals. 'Eric the Red' won the Morgan Award in 1953 and was used extensively as a parent. A lone Siberian introduction from L.

Merton Gage, 'Snowcrest' ('32), is a direct cross of the two *I. sanguinea* selections 'Emperor' and 'Snow Queen'. It won the Morgan Award in 1963, thirty-one years after it was introduced.

The period of breeding from the late 1940s through mid-1950s was a slow time for Siberian introductions. In this period, however, there was an outstanding group of hybrids produced by Elizabeth Scheffy and introduced through her Lark Meadows Nursery in Mansfield, Massachusetts (Tiffney 1967). Scheffy had one of the largest collections of Siberians of her day and many of these hybrids appear to have been spontaneous seedlings found amongst her collection. Of these introductions, the short magenta 'Towanda Redflare' (Scheffy '49), the huge flat-formed navy blue 'Blue Moon' (Scheffy '52), and the dainty pink amoena 'Fairy Dawn' (Scheffy '53) are among those that played a part in further hybrids and are still widely grown plants. Perhaps the most surprising Scheffy introduction was her 'Tunkhannock' (Scheffy '44). For many years this was the largest white and it had the wide compact form that was typical of 'White Swirl' long before that cultivar existed. It proved to be an outstanding parent as well, siring several future Morgan Award winners. Another innovation of the Scheffy Siberians was the first truly reblooming cultivar 'My Love' (Scheffy '49). This cultivar would put up as many as three sets of bloomstalks, with some of the later bloomstalks actually exceeding the height and branching of the first. 'My Love' would prove to be an important parent for reblooming types.

In this same era, several outstanding darker Siberians appeared. Louise Marx, wife of famed Japanese iris breeder Walter Marx, introduced 'Seven Seas' (Marx '56) and 'Congo Drums' (Marx '56), the latter from seed of 'Caesar's Brother'. Interestingly, Peg Edwards's sultry and extremely vigorous 'Velvet Night' (Edwards '61) resulted from the second generation of bee seed purchased from the Marx nursery and may be related to those of Louise Marx, as there is a strong family resemblance. 'Velvet Night' won the Morgan Award in 1969. 'Royal Ensign' (Hall-Nesmith '51) was the darkest of the reds to that time and would soon find use as an important breeder of red and pink Siberians.

Fred Cassebeer took the production of new Siberians seriously. In the early 1950s, he harvested four coffee cans full of bee set seed from his best Siberians and raised thousands of seedlings, which were winnowed down to about 150 selections of which five were subsequently introduced, four of which won the Morgan Award. The most important of these cultivars is 'White Swirl' (Cassebeer '57), which in itself created high interest in the class and made an impression on many bearded-iris-only gardeners at the 1958 American Iris Society Convention. 'White Swirl' had a new look. The lightly ruffled falls were flared horizontally and the standards were wide and filled in the gaps between the falls, creating a relatively solid flower of large size and flat form. Plants were vigorous and most stalks had a branch. 'White Swirl' caused a revolution in Siberian iris breeding and virtually everything produced from this time on had 'White Swirl' somewhere in the pedigree. It was honored by the AIS by receiving not only the newly re-initiated Morgan Award in 1962 but also the American Iris Society Board of Directors Award to recognize a significant development in irises that did not win the Dykes Medal. Among the other selected seedlings were three outstanding blues with the new type of form but each of quite different character: 'Blue Brilliant' (Cassebeer '60) is a navy blue, an improved 'Mountain Lake' type; 'Placid Waters' (Cassebeer '62) is a mid blue blend; 'Pirouette' (Cassebeer '64) a navy blue with nearly white styles. 'Blue Brilliant' and 'Pirouette' both won the Morgan Award. 'Violet Flare' (Cassebeer '60) had the same horizontal falls as the blues but was in a clean violet with minimal signal. It was also a Morgan Award winner. That was quite a good result from four coffee cans of bee-set seeds! Seed from 'White Swirl' gave the lovely blue violets 'Clear Pond' (Cassebeer '69) and 'Ausable River' (Cassebeer '69), the latter an especially valuable parent.

Another interesting crop of Siberian hybrids appeared spontaneously on the Spofford property on the northeast shore of Massachusetts. Mildred Peck Spofford had planted a collection

'White Swirl' had a new look. It caused a revolution in Siberian iris breeding and virtually everything produced from this time on had 'White Swirl' somewhere in the pedigree.

of Siberian irises and the conditions were so ideal for their growth (moderate climate, constant moisture from mist and fog) plants seeded about and many new colors and forms appeared on the property and that of her daughter-in-law Dorothy. Amongst these spontaneous finds were the darkest lavender-pink of its day 'Mildred Peck' (Spofford '62), the dark purple with white blaze 'Salem Witch' (Spofford '62), and the extremely vigorous and showy blue with white styles 'Mandy Morse' (Spofford '65). 'Mandy Morse' makes extremely large clumps quickly and hundreds of bloomstalks would be produced in each clump. 'Salem Witch' is a tall *I. sibirica* type of plant with up to 18 buds on a stalk and a flower that is incredibly showy, and it also blooms from early to late. It remains one of my favorites even though I saw this for the first time in 1966!

While some Siberians were becoming taller, Gladys Wiswell had a different vision of the ideal Siberian iris (Wiswell 1971). She wanted clumps that had shorter bloomstalks (approximately 2' high) but produced a high density of blooms creating a living bouquet. Her 'Carrie Lee' (Wiswell '63; light red with a large white signal), 'Claret' (Wiswell '66; dark magenta) and 'Sapphire Bouquet' (Wiswell '66; sapphire blue) reflect this choice and all are still available commercially. The clump effect of these plants is outstanding and their vigor is unmatched, making them ideal plants for the mixed perennial border.

After a long hiatus of great British breeders, three hybridizers, Maurice Kitton, Philip Hutchinson, and Marjorie Brummitt produced a number of significant cultivars in the late 1950s and 1960s. Brummitt imported 'White Swirl' early on and was quick to use it in crosses. The cross of 'White Swirl' and 'Gatineau' resulted in 'Cambridge' (Brummitt '64), for years one of the truest blues. 'Cambridge' was the first full Siberian to win the British Dykes Medal. Crosses of the large-flowered 'Tycoon' with 'White Swirl' resulted in the lovely dark violet 'Dreaming Spires' (Brummitt '64) and the turquoise-shaded 'Sea Shadows' (Brummitt '64). The first improved white from 'White Swirl' breeding resulted from the rare 'White Swirl' pollen on 'Wisley White' and was named 'Anniversary' (Brummitt '65). It would be the top white Siberian for many years and earned Brummitt her second Dykes Medal in 1979. All of these Brummitt hybrids were fine parents and vigorous plants. Maurice Kitton (1964) experimented with both the 28- and 40-chromosome groups, as well as producing some of the first hybrids between these two groups, 'Moonscape' (Kitton '64). His 'White Magnificence' (Kitton '67) is a huge well-formed flower that was very popular and used much in crossing. In the 40-chromosome Siberians, Kitton produced a number of unusual colors that result from overlaying the anthocyanin pigments from *I. bulleyana* over the base yellow flowers from *I. forrestii*, resulting in apricot-flowered 'Yellow Apricot' (Kitton '64) and copper-toned 'Copper Elf' (Kitton '63). Hutchinson's hybrids are from a very straightforward breeding program, combining the best of the classic Siberians like 'Caesar' and 'Eric the Red'. These resulted in a series of mostly dark violet offspring, of which 'Purple Mere' (Hutchinson '62) and 'Violet Mere' (Hutchinson '71) are the most well known.

D. Steve Varner had an illustrious career as a plant breeder of irises, peonies, and daylilies and, unlike many others, used planned and protected crosses to produce his hybrids. His first Siberian introduction came from self-pollinating 'Caesar's Brother' (the only Siberian he owned at the time!) and one of the seedlings was the velvety flat-formed hybrid 'Tealwood'. It was introduced for the then-princely sum of $25.00 per division and quickly garnered the Morgan Award in 1964. Not surprisingly, Varner's line was based upon 'Tealwood', but he also made extensive use of a series of seedlings from Cloyd Sensenbach (Varner 1971). These Sensenbach seedlings had many unusual combinations of color and arose spontaneously in the Sensenbach garden, similar to the Spofford cultivars (Sensenbach 1967). Only one of these, 'Little Tricolor', was introduced but the others, especially #6 and #12, were used by Varner to create a unique series of hybrids. From crosses of Sensenbach seedlings with 'Tealwood' and other Varner Siberians gave directly 'Wine Wings' (Varner '77), 'Showdown' (Varner '76), 'Rejoice Always' (Varner '75), 'Illini Charm' (Varner '75), 'New Wine' (Varner '79) and 'Maranatha' (Varner '74). One of my favorite of Varner's Siberian introductions is 'Pirate Prince' (Varner '77), from crossing 'Maranatha' with Brummitt's 'Dreaming Spires', which is a dark purple that is virtually a self-colored flower. A cross of 'Tealwood' and the flat 'Blue Moon' gave the popular navy-blue flat 'Steve'. Unlike many hybridizers, he did not dip significantly into 'White Swirl' as a breeder but the 'White Swirl' seedling 'Dreaming Spires' (Brummitt '64) was used often (Varner 1971) and led to the dappled 1983 Morgan Award winner 'Ann Dasch' (Varner '78). Another couple of 'White Swirl' derivatives, 'Ausable River' and 'Dreaming Yellow', combined with the Varner white lines resulted in the large white Morgan Award winner 'King of Kings' (Varner '83), one of the most popular of the Varner Siberians.

Bill McGarvey was fascinated in the genetics of irises and used the diploid Siberians to pursue these studies. He used relatively few parents, chiefly 'Royal Ensign', 'Gatineau', 'Caesar's Brother', and 'White Swirl'. McGarvey was one of the first to use 'White Swirl' in this country and his first two introductions, 'Ego' (McGarvey '66) and 'Super Ego' (McGarvey '66), sold for $50 a division and they were worth it! Bill once confided to me that he offered them at this high price so that people would think they were worth $50! Certainly people took notice of these hybrids. These took the 'White Swirl' form and expanded them with greater size or ruffling. 'Ego' is a blue self with a very compact form and 'Super Ego', a lighter blue with a beautiful veined pattern in the falls. 'Dewful' (McGarvey

'67) and 'Blue Burn' (McGarvey '68) rounded out these first generation 'White Swirl' blues. 'Dewful', 'Ego' and 'Super Ego' all won the Morgan Award and 'Dewful' was the first Siberian iris to win the President's Cup for the favorite iris from the host region of an American Iris Society convention. Subsequent generations of this line gave rise to the yellowish 'Earthshine' (McGarvey '75), and the whites 'Wing on Wing' (McGarvey '72), 'Gulls Way' (McGarvey '82) and 'Esther C.D.M.' (McGarvey '82). As much as these McGarvey blue and white irises did for the popularity of Siberian irises, his progress in the red and pink Siberians was perhaps more important in terms of the future development of Siberian irises. A self pollination of the maroon-red 'Royal Ensign' gave not only the expected maroon reds, but also 25 percent pinks, some as near amoenas (McGarvey 1961). Combining this group with the 'White Swirl' line a group of beautifully formed pinks and reds were created, including the Morgan Award winners 'Augury' (McGarvey '73) and 'Pink Haze' (McGarvey '80) and the reds 'Temper Tantrum' (McGarvey '86) and 'Jamaican Velvet' (McGarvey '85). McGarvey also hybridized with the 40-chromosome types and introduced the yellows 'King's Forrest' (McGarvey '69) and 'Forrest Scion' (McGarvey '70) out of *I. forrestii* breeding and the near black 'Id' (McGarvey '69) from *I. chrysographes* breeding. 'Id' finished out the Freudian trio with 'Ego' and 'Super Ego'. McGarvey was a professor of psychology and the names of these irises were his nods to his professional life. Another significant development was the production of 'Foretell' (McGarvey '71), the first fertile hybrid between 28- and 40-chromosome Siberian irises. It grows as easily as the 28-chromosome hybrids.

The owners of Melrose Gardens, Ben Hager and Sid DuBose did much to promote Siberians, including introducing Peg Edwards's 'Velvet Night' and Rich's Southern-adapted 'Lights of Paris' (Rich '67), but they also produced a number of fine Siberians themselves. Most of Hager's introductions were in red shades, including his first two introductions 'Ruby Wine' (Hager '68) and 'Sparkling Rose' (Hager '68), in dark and light magenta respectively. Further generations of this line gave the more well formed 'Cabernet' (Hager '82), 'Chilled Wine' (Hager '81) and 'Rose Quest' (Hager '83). Hager's one Morgan Award winner, 'Swank' (Hager '69), was a result of combining 'Bluecape' with 'White Swirl'. 'Swank' has an unusual pebbled texture and made a lovely clump. Crossing 'Swank' with McGarvey's 'Ego' gave the striking blue 'Jaybird' (Hager '82), still one of the closest to true blue Siberians.

DuBose's two Siberian introductions, 'Vi Luihn' (DuBose '74) and 'Savoir Faire' (DuBose '74), were the result of a single cross of 'Tunkhannock' × 'Swank'. Both are blue violet and of fine form, with 'Vi Luihn' winning the Morgan Award.

Forrest McCord used Elizabeth Scheffy's fine white 'Tunkhannock' and crossed it with 'Tycoon' to produce the wide and bright blue 'Grand Junction' (McCord '69). A back cross of 'Grand Junction' to 'Tycoon' would result in the very vigorous blue-violet 'Halcyon Seas' (McCord '72). Both 'Grand Junction' and 'Halcyon Seas' would win the Morgan Award, a 100 percent success rate!

George Bush was a hybridizer and dealer of many beardless irises and was a true character in real life. His crowning achievement was the appropriately named 'Frosty Rim' (Bush '79), a dark blue with a very thin edge of white. His rosy orchid 'Spirit of York' (Bush '85), named to honor his home town of York, Pennsylvania, is a very good garden performer. 'Blue Hyacinth' (Bush '87) is one of the smallest Siberian irises at 15" tall and is also one of the first to bloom, sometimes with the standard dwarf irises, 2 to 3 weeks before the peak Siberian iris bloom.

Vaughn seedling with sibirica pattern

Bee Warburton had already created an outstanding array of median and dwarf bearded iris creations when she turned her attention to Siberian irises. Warburton was enamored with 'White Swirl' and her initial intention in a cross to 'Eric the Red' was in an effort to produce a red with the form of 'White Swirl'. However, the seedlings from this cross were all blue-violet, although one with turquoise style arms gave her the immediate goal of putting these styles into more flowers. The backcross of that seedling to 'White Swirl' produced an outstanding series of hybrids, including the blue with white styles 'Deep Shade' (Warburton '72), clear blue with fringed styles 'Blue Song' (Warburton '73), and gently dappled and edged 'Shadow Lake' (Warburton '72). Warburton began a series of backcrosses of these and sibling cultivars, especially those with lighter petal centers, back to 'White Swirl' resulting in a number of outstanding cultivars, with the appropriately named 'Atoll' (Warburton '75) being the most significant. In the 'Atoll' pattern, the petal edges are distinctly rimmed in dark blue-violet and the centers much lighter blue, marbled deeper. At this point Warburton made a series of outcrosses of 'Atoll' to other fine Siberians, such as 'Ruffled Velvet' and 'Wing on Wing', with the seedlings from the 'Ruffled Velvet' cross being exceptional. 'Percheron' (Warburton '82) really startled her and she was initially revolted by its large size and bold mottling/dappling of very dark violet on light. However, iris growers loved the flower and it became one of her most favorite flowers. Besides 'Percheron', two other siblings from this cross are excellent repeat bloomers, the white with orange signals 'George Henry' (Warburton '83), named for Warburton's cat with a similar coloring, and the rose bitone 'Silver Rose' (Warburton '85). Combining siblings from the 'Atoll' × 'Ruffled Velvet' cross, gave 'Reprise' (Warburton '87), a very unusual silvery-lavender with strong repeat blooming tendencies, and the bright magenta 'Mad Magenta' (Warburton '87). Warburton went back to line breeding and crossed a sibling to 'Percheron' back to 'Ruffled Velvet' and the bright purple with magenta undertones 'Purple Prose' (Warburton '86) and the very ruffled white 'Belissima' (Warburton '86) were the results. Crossing 'Belissima' with 'Butter and Sugar' gave the pinnacle of Warburton's line, the ruffled yellow amoena 'Isabelle' (Warburton '89). Warburton named this iris for her mother, certainly a nod to her estimation of the plant. Warburton would pass her line onto Marty Schafer and Jan Sacks, who would take it to new levels of excellence.

Dale Johnson made a quick flash onto the Siberian iris scene when his 'Silver Illusion' (Johnson '87) was one of the stars of the Indianapolis American Iris Society convention. 'Silver Illusion' is a different sort of color application, basically a white flower shot through with greyed lavender, giving an overall silver effect. Despite being a beautiful flower it was a miffy grower in many areas of the country, although it turned out to be an interesting parent for many other breeders. The blue seedling of 'Silver Illusion', 'Cathy Childerson' (Johnson '88) was a fine grower and inherited the fine form of its parent as well. Both 'Silver Illusion' and 'Cathy Childerson' would win Awards of Merit from the American Iris Society.

Anna Mae Miller was a good friend of Bill McGarvey and she used many of his hybrids to start her strain. 'Aqua Whispers' (Miller '88) stems from both 'Pink Haze' and 'Temper Tantrum' and is a pinkish amoena with a flush of aqua near the signal area, inspiring the name. 'Frosted Cranberry' (Miller '91), from tight inbreeding of 'Pink Haze', is well named as the color is a cranberry pink with prominent white styles that adds to the frosted look of the flower. I think Bill McGarvey would be pleased of the work of Miller in improving upon his classic pink Siberians. Both of these pink Siberians would go in to win the Morgan-Wood Medal. Her pinkest Siberian, 'Mary Louise Michie' (Miller '96), combines 'Aqua Whispers' with Currier McEwen's 'Lavender Bounty' as does its very

'Believe in Angels'

pretty pink sibling 'Cheery Lynn' (Miller '91). Other favorites from Miller include bright blue repeat bloomer 'Dancing Nanou' (Miller '83), blue with a darker violet blaze 'Liberty Hills' (Miller '89), and rose-violet 'Forever Remembered' (Miller '04). The latter is in memory of her deceased husband Ronald and its pedigree combines the marvelous McGarvey white 'Esther C.D.M.' with Miller's pink lines.

Sarah Tiffney was one of the founding members of the Society for Siberian Irises and crossed Siberians partly out of scientific curiosity as well as to produce beautiful blossoms (Tiffney 1971). She maintained a large collection and always enjoyed the fluttery types of blooms more typical of *I. sibirica*. Her two introductions, 'Snow Prince' (Tiffney '90) and 'Little Blue Sparkler' (Tiffney '96), represent excellent forms of this species, in near white and with the typical blue-veined pattern of *I. sibirica*, respectively. Both of these are excellent plants for the perennial border as they make very tight clumps and have high densities of blooms over ornamental grassy foliage. Marty Schafer and Jan Sacks would make quick use of 'Snow Prince' in their program, with startling results.

Although Currier McEwen is certainly most known for his tetraploid Siberians, his work in diploid Siberians was extensive and covered several colors and patterns as well as repeat bloom. McEwen's work in the dark purples gave an outstanding trio of garden plants. 'Ruffled Velvet' (McEwen '73), was the first of these a lightly ruffled dark-violet with a small signal. It proved to be not only an outstanding garden plant but also an amazingly fine parent, especially for reds and dark purples. 'Ruffled Velvet' won the Morgan Award in 1980. From a cross of 'Tealwood' × 'Ruffled Velvet' came 'Shirley Pope' (McEwen '79), a much darker version of 'Ruffled Velvet' and from the reciprocal cross, 'Teal Velvet' (McEwen '81), also a dark purple but with more of the influence of 'Tealwood' in form and signal pattern. 'Pansy Purple' (McEwen '71) is one of my favorites of McEwen's work, a clear deep purple with no signal, although there are a couple of small lines where the signal should be. The clump effect of 'Pansy Purple' is outstanding with a high density of blooms and very vigorous growth. McEwen also did wonderful work in several other areas in the diploid Siberians, approaches to yellow, clearer blues, miniatures, and repeat bloomers (the latter two described above). McEwen often described his hybridizing a bit of skill and a lot of "the McEwen luck." Although that was a bit of modesty on his part, the beginnings of his yellow lines were pure luck. Marjorie Brummitt had sent McEwen bee set seed from her 'Dreaming Spires' and 'Cambridge'. Along with the blues and violets that he expected, two of the whites had a more extensive yellow signal than most Siberians. These were named 'Dreaming Yellow' (McEwen '71) and 'Floating Island' (McEwen '73). A cross between the two gave a significant advance in yellow color and was named 'Butter and Sugar' (McEwen '77). The plant quickly went on to win the Morgan Award and the newly-instituted Morgan-Wood Medal in 1986. 'Butter and Sugar' was named to honor the superb butter and sugar corn that Frank Warburton raised and that was a highlight of the beardless iris auctions of the 1970s and '80s in the Warburton garden. 'Butter and Sugar' is certainly the most popular of the McEwen Siberians and has been widely distributed in general perennial catalogs for decades.

McEwen was fascinated with the blue flowers and went on a quest to produce spectrum blue Siberians. His first two blues were crosses of 'White Swirl' onto his two favorite blues of the time. The cross of 'White Swirl' × Simonet's 'Grey Dove' gave the lovely pastel blue 'Sally Kerlin' (McEwen '70) and the cross of 'White Swirl' × 'Blue Brilliant' gave the rich navy blue 'Marilyn Holmes' (McEwen '72). The quest for the true blue started with 'Dear Delight' (McEwen '75), a very true blue that was from highly inbred breeding of the very blue 'Cambridge'. 'Dear Delight' used again with a 'Cambridge' seedling gave the blue with deeper intensification in the signal area 'Signals Blue' (McEwen '82). 'Signals Blue' crossed with another seedling involving 'Blue Brilliant' and 'Cambridge' gave the lovely violet blue 'Kenabee' (McEwen '82). This flower was named for three of its chief admirers, Ken Waite, Agnes Waite, and Bee Warburton, who strongly persuaded McEwen it should be marketed, even though it was not an improvement towards McEwen's goal of a true blue.

McEwen's lavender line started out partly in his frustration of attending American Iris Society conventions and not seeing Siberian irises in bloom so he began crossing the very early lavender varieties. 'Lavender Light' (McEwen '74) was the first of these, a direct cross of two of the better pink Siberians of their time 'Morning Magic' × 'Fairy Dawn'. A cross of 'Lavender Light' with 'Augury' gave the much improved 'Lavender Bounty' (McEwen '81), a much larger and extensively branched lavender pink that reblooms easily as well. One of McEwen's last hybrids is the long-blooming and wide-petaled 'Little Centennial' (McEwen '02) which is out of lavender breeding, combining Johnson, McEwen and McGarvey pinks. It is turning out to be an interesting parent too. The name celebrates McEwen's hundredth birthday, certainly a ringing endorsement for what gardening with beardless irises can do for you!

As much as McEwen's contributions are to diploid Siberian irises, he will forever be known as the father of tetraploid Siberian irises. McEwen was inspired by the success of Orville Fay in creating tetraploid daylilies and set out to produce them. Fred Cassebeer supplied McEwen with bee set seed from the better plants in his garden for this project. Treating the seedlings with colchicine would kill or fail to convert a majority of the seedlings, so that large amounts of seed were required for the project. Several seedlings from these first groups of seedlings were partially converted chimera plants and intercrosses between two of these seedlings gave the first fully tetraploid garden Siberian iris, the blue 'Orville Fay' (McEwen '70). 'Orville Fay' would receive the Morgan Award in 1976. Fertility of these early tetraploid Siberian irises was much reduced compared to the diploids so that persistence was required to produce seedlings from these plants. 'Silver Edge' (McEwen '74), a seedling of 'Orville Fay', has a distinctive white edge around the falls and had a more attractive form than most of the earlier generation tetraploids. 'Silver Edge' would win the Morgan Award in 1978 and would prove to be a useful parent. The sister seedling 'Navy Brass' (McEwen '74) would be the first tetraploid or any Siberian to show a gold petal edge. McEwen continued to convert other diploid material to expand the genetic base of the tetraploids. Seed from a cross of 'Tealwood' and 'Ruffled Velvet' converted to tetraploid level by colchicine would give the velvety tetraploid 'Teal Velvet' (McEwen '81). Peg Edwards supplied seed from a cross of 'White Swirl' and 'Turquoise Cup' that would be used to produce a large blue with turquoise influence that he named 'Peg Edwards' (McEwen '75). McEwen continued to develop the tetraploid Siberians right to the end of his over one-hundred-year life and continued to produce breakthrough plants in a number of colors and patterns. These served as the basis for virtually all the other tetraploid programs in the country. Some of these more important accomplishments include the siblings orange-yellow-tinged 'Dreaming Orange' (McEwen '87) and cream nicely edged with bright gold 'Golden Crimpings' (McEwen '85), cream whites 'Ivory Creme' (McEwen '87), 'Currier's Choice' (McEwen '06) and 'Harpswell Happiness' (McEwen '83), blue violets 'Circle Round' (McEwen '83), 'Harpswell Prelude' (McEwen '94) and 'Dear Dianne' (McEwen '79), dark purples 'Harpswell Velvet' (McEwen '91) and 'Midnight Purple', clear and true blue 'Pride in Blue' (McEwen '00), yellow amoena 'Butter and Cream' (McEwen '99), and the approaches to green in 'Dreaming Green' (McEwen '88) and 'Merryspring' (McEwen '04). Besides creating this wonderful series of plants McEwen was extremely generous in sharing seeds and plants of his hybrids with other hybridizers from all over the world. Certainly Siberian breeding is far ahead because of his generosity.

'Judy, Judy, Judy'

Kenneth Waite was inspired by the hybridization of fellow New Englanders Bee Warburton and Currier McEwen although his introductions involve other hybridizers' work. All of his are blues, which were his favorites. 'Harbor Mist' (Waite '83), a very light blue, is a prodigious bloomer and judges in New England really coerced him to introduce his flower after getting local accolades. They were right. It won an Award of Merit, as did the dark blue-purple 'Laughing Brook' (Waite '84). 'Serenade in Blue' (Waite '88) is the bluest of the Waite

introductions and has the unusual habit of transforming its form each day, each an interesting variation.

Robert Hollingworth had a distinguished career as a pesticide scientist. While a professor at Purdue University, he became interested in breeding irises and saw a future in Siberian irises. Since then, Hollingworth has introduced an amazing array of both diploid and tetraploid Siberians and has produced smaller cultivars, flat types and multi-petal forms, over 60 introductions in all. His first introduction, 'Forrest McCord' (Hollingworth '83), was from a bee pod on Cassebeer's 'Ausable River', and is a nicely formed blue-violet with a good white rim around the falls. The iris honors the person who gave Hollingworth many bee pods for use in his projects to convert diploids into tetraploids. Hollingworth made what must be the most productive cross ever made by a Siberian iris, crossing McEwen's superb purple 'Ruffled Velvet' with Steve Varner's 'Showdown'. From that one cross came three Morgan-Wood Medals, the red diploids 'Lady Vanessa' (Hollingworth '86) and 'Sultan's Ruby' (Hollingworth '88), as well as the tetraploid 'Jewelled Crown' (Hollingworth '87). The latter was the basis of a wonderful series of tetraploid Siberians that have that very distinctive white signal patch that was first noted in 'Jewelled Crown'. If all crosses could be that good!

'Rigamarole'—with no two flowers alike

Hollingworth used 'Jewelled Crown' to create a wonderful line of tetraploids that showed his determination of purpose with two color lines coming out of this work. The red line led to 'Coronation Anthem' (Hollingworth '90) and in another generation gave rise to 'Currier' (Hollingworth '03), an homage to Currier McEwen who guided Hollingworth in his tetraploid Siberian breeding. The next generation produced two *amazing* offsprings, both of these are wine reds with bold white signals on the falls, abundant ruffles and a very starchy flare: 'Judy Judy Judy' (Hollingworth '10), which honors his equally gardening-crazed wife Judy, and 'Something Shocking' (Hollingworth '13) with an even broader white blaze on the falls and a good rebloomer in the Pacific Northwest. 'Judy Judy Judy' won the Walther Cup for the most Honorable Mention votes of *any* iris in 2013, a rare feat for any iris except for the very popular tall bearded iris. 'Coronation Anthem' would lead to another line of blue-violet Siberians that include the extremely ruffled and round flower 'Blueberry Fair' (Hollingworth '96) and its seedling the gold edged blue 'Neptune's Gold' (Hollingworth '13). Besides these tetraploids Hollingworth has done some outstanding work in diploid Siberians as well. One of my favorite smaller Siberian iris is the very ruffled lavender blue 'Pixie Preview' (Hollingworth '03) and its dark purple seedling 'Petite Purple' (Hollingworth '12). Hollingworth was one of the first to use the double flowered Siberians from Japan and his breeding with 'Parasol' gave the wide-petaled six-fall type called 'Six Love' (Hollingworth '05). Three very distinctive whites are also products of his breeding: very ruffled and compact 'Galadriel' (Hollingworth '02), lemon-tinted white 'Lemon Mousse' (Hollingworth '12) and the *huge* 'Swans in Flight' (Hollingworth '06). 'Swans in Flight' won the Morgan Wood Medal in 2013 and a very worthy winner it is. Anyone considering Siberian iris breeding should study the pedigrees of Hollingworth irises as they show clearly how breaks are used to create even more exciting irises and how careful line breeding can produce quality offspring.

Bob Bauer and John Coble were surrounded by Siberian enthusiasts Bob and Judy Hollingworth, Anna Mae Miller and Hal Stahly and not surprisingly became fascinated with them as well as with their favorite Japanese irises. Bauer and Coble's Siberian choices oftentimes *look* like Japanese irises. They had early access to the *I. sanguinea* selections from Japanese hybridizer Ho Shidara and they proceeded to cross these with the best modern Siberians. The results were startling with 'Shebang' (Bauer-Coble '99) and 'Kabluey' (Bauer-Coble '99), so named because it looks as though things went kabluey in terms of forming petals! Lavender-pink 'Rigamarole' (Bauer-Coble '00) is one of the most elegant of these multipetal forms in a lovely shade of pink. Some of these multi-petal Siberians were converted to the tetraploid level leading to 'Bundle of Joy' (Bauer-Coble '00) and 'Kaboom' (Bauer-Coble '01). My favorite of the Bauer-Coble doubles is the *huge* 'Imperial Opal' (Bauer-Coble '00) that has lovely pink over lemon yellow flowers with many petals. People often ask "Why is that Japanese iris blooming so early?" It really looks so like one. Bauer and Coble bred a number of more traditional Siberian irises as well. The clear blue 'Lee's Blue' (Bauer-Coble '94), silvery lavender 'Mesa Pearl' (Bauer-Coble '94) and all-over dotted pink on a lighter background 'Sprinkles' (Bauer and Coble '94) were their first three introductions and remain popular. 'Lemon Veil' (Bauer-Coble '00) represents one of the first examples of the overlay effect of pink over yellow and has been a tremendous parent for this type of flower.

Jim Copeland and his wife Jill are both avid hybridizers of beardless irises. Jim is the Siberian iris hybridizer in the family. Besides his interest in irises, Jim is also an avid fisherman and often throws fish fries for visiting gardening groups, and

'Kaboom'

'Mesa Pearl'

'Lemon Veil'

the names of his hybrids reflect this other interest. 'Fisherman's Fancy' (Copeland '12) is a lavender pink with a flush of turquoise in the signal area and in the styles. It is descended from the McGarvey lines of whites and pinks, and has the very wide wavy form of the McGarvey whites and the unusual lavender shades from the McGarvey pinks. It is one of my favorite flowers and I use it heavily, as was apparent in my gardens last spring. An even more amazing flower may be 'Fisherman's Twilight' (Copeland '14) which looks like a more intense version of 'Fisherman's Fancy' but with all the same good qualities of form and plant habit. The signal flash of turquoise on this flower is almost neon.

After a career in animal husbandry, Dana Borglum started planting and hybridizing irises. A cross of McGarvey's 'Gulls Way' × Varner's 'Outer Loop' gave the round and ruffled blue 'Lake Keuka' (Borglum '94). This iris was a star at the 1994 American Iris Society Convention in Portland and went on to win the Morgan-Wood Medal in 2002. A cross of 'Lake Keuka' × its sibling 'Seneca Feather Dancer' gave the heavily ruffled blue bitone 'Seneca Moodstone' (Borglum '00). My favorite of the Borglum introductions is 'Seneca Colorplay' (Borglum '03), which has rims of red on a bluish dappled flower and nearly white styles. What a unique color combination!

Calvin Helsley started breeding bearded irises but became interested in Siberians in the early 1970s. 'Blue Kaleidoscope' (Helsley '82) combines 'White Swirl' with Bill Peck's very floriferous volunteer seedling 'Sky Wings' and is, as the name suggests, a mixture of different blue tones. His first Siberian that became popular on the national scene is the lightly fragrant (a character rare in Siberian irises) medium blue 'Mabel Coday' (Helsley '85). 'Mabel Coday' combines two great breeders, 'White Swirl' and Varner's red 'Showdown'. 'Mabel Coday' turned out to be a fine breeder too and crossed with a Varner seedling S060: ('Maryla' × 'Steve') gave the very branched and floriferous 'Where Eagles Dare' (Helsley '95), a dark blue violet. 'Where Eagles Dare' would win the Morgan-

'My Bubba'

'Reeda Jo'

'Black Garnet'

One of the true characters of the iris world was the ebullient Louise Bellagamba. She hybridized many types of irises and produced several nice Siberian irises. Her short blue with nearly white styles 'Rill' (Bellagamba '92) was her most widely distributed and earned an award of merit. Her red-purple 'Harry Truman' (Bellagamba '84) and its seedling 'Handsome Harry' (Bellagamba '05), an improved version of its parent, are also well-loved Bellagamba Siberians.

Unlike many other hybridizers, Lorena Reid decided to specialize in the 40-chromosome Siberian irises as they grew so well in her Springfield, Oregon, garden. Although most hybridizers have centered their work on red-purple *I. chrysographes* and the yellow *I. wilsonii* and *I. forrestii*, Reid used more *I. clarkei* and *I. delavayi* in her crosses. These species transferred height, vigor and branching to the progeny. The progeny from *I. clarkei* also inherited a unique pattern on the falls in which a bold white signal is bordered by a nearly black band, formed by coalescing spots. Reid's triumph in this pattern is the beautiful 'Dotted Line' (Reid '92), a strong lavender blue with a bold white blaze edged in black dots. Other fine examples of Reid's hybridizing include the very deep purple with darker signal 'Black Garnet' (Reid '96), dark and clear navy blue 'McKenzie Bruiser' (Reid '01), beautifully patterned 'Butterfly Mode' (Reid '91) and light blue with a dark violet thumbprint 'Pacific Dark Eyes' (Reid '91). Even in the ideal climate of the Pacific Northwest Reid began losing many of her 40-chromosome Siberians because of a water mold that had infected her plantings. Luckily most of the more choice clones had been shared with others so they are still available.

It has been my privilege to watch the hybridizing career of Marty Schafer and Jan Sacks start and take flight. For many years, we would gather at Barbara and David Schmeider's house to present slides (and then digital images) each July or August to show what interesting seedlings had occurred in our seedling patches. It was such fun seeing the flowers of the future before everybody else and to watch the evolution of this line! Marty and Jan are a team, with Marty making the crosses and Jan taking the photos and assisting in the evaluations. Bee Warburton had Marty and Jan introduce her last Siberian

Wood medal in 2005. After that success with the cross that gave 'Where Eagles Dare', Helsley repeated the cross and introduced a whole series of light to darkish blue-violets: 'Festival Prelude' (Helsley '92), 'Shadowed Eyes' (Helsley '95), 'Carmen Jeanne' (Helsley '96), 'Navy Trim' (Helsley '02), and 'Night Knight' (Helsley '02). Wouldn't it be nice if all such matings were as productive! Of these 'Carmen Jeanne' is the most popular, a wide dark blue violet with a white signal. 'Navy Trim' is one that has performed particularly well for me, making a large clump of blue-violet blossoms on stalks that are impressively branched. One of my favorites is the *intense* red-purple 'Then Sings My Soul' (Helsley '05), which has outstanding branching and growth habits. Helsley's 'My Bubba' (Helsley '10), a very dark and full-formed dark blue violet is named for his dog, but this flower is no dog! 'My Bubba' is from a cross of two Morgan-Wood Medal winners, 'Ships Are Sailing' and 'Where Eagles Dare' and combines the best properties of both lines. Helsley's premier red Siberian is the well-formed rosy-orchid 'Reeda Jo' (Helsley '11), which honors his sister.

iris and it is from these lines that Marty and Jan developed their strain. 'Isabelle', 'Mad Magenta' and several other cultivars that were the last of Warburton's creations served as the basis of Schafer and Sacks's lines. 'Forrest McCord' and 'Silver Illusion' were early additions to this hybridizing stew. These crosses led to a number of fine blues, whites, and magentas, some with much improved form. Dark wine-red 'Devil's Dream' (Schafer-Sacks '90), blue purple edged white 'Trim the Velvet' (Schafer-Sacks '95), and one of my favorites, the pale blue with dark blue petal edges 'Turn a Phrase' (Schafer-Sacks '00) typify the hybrids that are extensions of Warburton's line. However, it was 'Snow Prince' that really opened up new vistas for this hybridizing team. Schafer noted that the bud backs of 'Snow Prince' were yellow and a different shade than that of the yellows derived from the expansion of the throat yellow in *I. sanguinea* bloodlines. 'Snow Prince' is an *I. sibirica* white which, instead of creating blues in crosses to red and pinks, allows for the production of reds and pinks in crosses to that type (see hybridizing chapter for more details). To say 'Snow Prince' caused a revolution in the Schafer-Sacks breeding program is an understatement! The crosses involving 'Snow Prince' produced several exciting things: examples of the veined-falls *I. sibirica* pattern but in more modern forms such as 'Banish Misfortune' (Schafer-Sacks '99); blue standards/yellow falls as in 'So Van Gogh' (Schafer-Sacks '05) and 'Tips of Blue' (Schafer-Sacks '10); golden-browns such as 'Humors of Whiskey' (Schafer-Sacks '07), 'Ginger Twist' (Schafer-Sacks '09) and 'Drink Your Tea' (Schafer-Sacks '14); very branched yellows and yellow blends such as 'Tree of Songs' (Schafer-Sacks '06) and 'Colonel Mustard' (Schafer-Sacks '13); clear and much more true pinks such as 'Careless Sally' (Schafer-Sacks '96), 'Sandy River Belle' (Schafer-Sacks '11), and 'Fancy Me This' (Schafer-Sacks '12); vivid red-blends such as 'Miss Apple' (Schafer-Sacks '09), 'Sugar Rush' (Schafer-Sacks '08) and 'On Mulberry Street' (Schafer-Sacks '12). Besides these advances in colors, the influence of *I. sibirica* has strong influence on the plant habits. Most of these hybrids have very good bud counts and branching and the foliage is narrower than most Siberian irises with very tight clumps. In the Pacific Northwest almost all of these show some rebloom. Not all of the Schafer-Sacks hybrids are tall and several such as orange-

red-violet 'Paprikash' (Schafer-Sacks '12), white standards/yellow falls 'My Little Sunshine' (Schafer-Sacks '10) and black bitone 'Black Joker' (Schafer-Sacks '13) would be classified as miniatures. These are superb plants for the front of the border and lovely flowers too.

Schafer and Sacks did not ignore the wonderful blues that were the legacy of Warburton's line either. Morgan-Wood Medal winner 'Riverdance' (Schafer-Sacks '97) in rich blue flowers with rolling ruffles, ruffled blue bitone Morgan-Wood Medal winner 'Ships are Sailing' (Schafer-Sacks '98), dappled blue

'So Van Gogh'

'Cape Cod Boys' (Schafer-Sacks '09) and blue with white signals 'Jolly Young Man' (Schafer-Sacks '13) are outstanding examples and all great garden plants. I think Bee Warburton would be very happy with where Schafer and Sacks took her line.

Three hybridizers from Maine, John White, Jeff Dunlop, and Dean Cole, were disciples of Currier McEwen and many of their hybrids descend directly from their mentor's lines. As is the case with Schafer-Sacks taking over Bee Warburton's line, these hybridizers have done much to pursue the original goals of McEwen and have extended this in new directions as well. John White hybridized both diploids and tetraploids and had success in both ploidy levels. Many of these carry the "Dirigo" stable name that is from the motto of the state of Maine. In the diploids, White's 'Neat Trick' (White '97) is the most unique, a purple self but shot through all over with white splashes in the manner of the broken color bearded irises. This is a most unique iris but unfortunately not an easy parent. Two of White's other notable diploids include the lavender pinks 'Dirigo Lavender Fountain' (White '06) and 'Dirigo Tiffney Pink' (White '05), the latter one of the pinkest available. White's tetraploids include two of the very darkest ones available, 'Dirigo Black Velvet' (White '99) and 'Dirigo

'Miss Apple'

Black Knight' (White '05), the latter with a narrow white rim. Other tetraploids include the blue with white edge 'Dirigo By Design' (White '06), indigo blue 'Dirigo Indigo' (White '07) and the pair of riffled blues, 'Dirigo Ruffled Feathers' (White '01) and 'Dirigo Valiant' (White '03).

Jeff Dunlop and Dean Cole work as a team, although they have separate lines of breeding and each introduces his own hybrids. Unlike many of the earlier tetraploids that were two-budded, the work of these breeders contains at least a branch and many will have five buds per stalk, and the flowers lack all of the "propeller shapes" but are lovely rounded and ruffled flowers. Colors on these show some of the promise of tetraploidy,

including more intense colors. Cole's tetraploids include the ruffled white 'Joyce Cole' (Cole '06), curly-styled blue 'Great Falls Love' (Cole '07), plum magenta 'My Girl Emily' (Cole '08), ruffled magenta red 'Say Please' (Cole '09), blue with red edge 'Pool Party' (Cole '10), and lavender-pink 'Baby Steps' (Cole '10). Dunlop named his triumph in yellow tetraploid Siberian iris 'Currier's Dream' (Dunlop '10) as it was a color that McEwen himself had worked on for years but never obtained anything with the depth or form of this beauty. Other fine creations from Dunlop include the blue violet 'Another Pretty Face' (Dunlop '09), blue bitone 'Dear Currier' (Dunlop '05), bright yellow amoena 'Dreaming of You' (Dunlop '08—the name a nod to Currier's "Dreaming" series of Siberian irises), intensely grape 'Grape Truffle' (Dunlop '07), and one of the finest reds 'Crimson Fireworks' (Dunlop '12). This dynamic pair of hybridizers has many great things in the works and I'm sure that Currier McEwen is happy to see his legacy carried on so well.

Two iris hybridizers whom we generally associate with their quality median and dwarf bearded irises, Terry Aitken and Marky Smith, also have produced some very nice Siberians. Smith has named several of hers with Hawaiian names, far from what we associate with Siberian irises! Her 'Ali'i' (Smith '05) is a very wide and ruffled mauve-violet with darker veins and signal whereas 'Kilauea' (Smith '07) is a dark burgundy and 'Star Lion' (Smith '06) is a lavender/blue bicolor with wine hafts and rim. 'Haleakala' (Smith '06) is one of the strongest yellow diploids with primrose yellow standards and mimosa yellow falls. As in several others of his lines, Terry Aitken is fascinated with repeat blooming plants and his Siberians are no exception as the blue-violet 'Majestic Overtures' (Aitken '06) and lavender/burgundy bicolor 'Burgundy Fireworks' (Aitken '13) are strong rebloomers, especially in the Pacific Northwest. Aitken also named an outstanding red tetraploid, the white edged 'Crimson Cloisonne' (Aitken '05).

Siberians have attracted breeders in the United Kingdom, Germany, and the Pacific Rim as well. Unfortunately because of quarantine laws and the sensitivity of many beardless irises to transplant, many of these have not been grown in the United States although seed from the British Iris Seed Exchange has at least allowed some of this germplasm to come to the United

States. The biggest of these groups of Siberian iris hybridizers is in the United Kingdom (Hewitt 2011). Jennifer Hewitt has hybridized both diploid and tetraploid Siberian irises but it is her tetraploids that have brought her the most fame with the British Dykes Medal for navy blue 'Peter Hewitt' in 2008 and for wide and ruffled magenta 'Stephen Wilcox' in 2011. Cy Bartlett had a prolific career as a hybridizer of bearded irises and was awarded the British Dykes Medal (for two of my favorite bearded irises, 'Orinoco Flow' and 'Alexia', both

'On Mulberry Street'

'Flight of Butterflies' and 'Summer Skies'. Wells has used the stable name "Wealdon" for this strain, with striped fall types 'Wealdon Mystery' (Wells '05), 'Wealdon Butterfly' (Wells '05) and 'Wealdon Carousel' (Wells '08) and fluttery pale to mid-blue 'Wealdon Skies' (Wells '08) and 'Wealdon Summer' (Wells '05) being ones presently named. After many years of round and ruffled types, it is a pleasure to see these forms making a resurgence.

German Tomas Tamberg has been a prolific hybridizer of beardless irises of all types and his work with Siberians includes diploids, tetraploids, 40-chromosome types and even tetraploid versions of the 40-chromosome Siberians. Many of these have been used in further crosses to produce an amazing number and variety of SPEC-X hybrids. Most of his tetraploid Siberians are derivatives of the McEwen tetraploids, with some of the Hollingworth hybrids in later introductions. Among the pure tetraploid Siberians, navy blue tetraploid 'Prussian Blue' (Tamberg '93), wide medium blue 'Berlin Ruffles' (Tamberg '93), and wide lavender 'Berliner Ouverture' (Tamberg '03) are his best known. Two small Siberians from Tamberg include the pair of ruffled white 'Berlin Little White' (Tamberg '88) and light blue 'Berlin Little Blue' (Tamberg '93) that are around 20" tall and with smaller flowers. Seedlings from Tamberg's tetraploid 40-chromosome work bloomed in my yard this spring and were impressive in that the normally floppy-standards of the 40-chromosome hybrids were now stiffly held and the flowers were half again as big as the largest diploids. This is a big improvement and hopefully these can be used to create hybrids for sale in the United States.

Iris sanguinea is a native of Japan but it has not excited the Japanese to work with this plant in the way that they have with the Japanese irises and to a lesser extent *I. laevigata*. Ho Shidara is an exception to this. He discovered a double form of *I. sanguinea* and set about breeding with this form with other Siberian irises in his garden. This breeding produced not only six-falled types of doubles but also flowers with multiple petals. The first two of these hybrids were introduced by Ben Hager, the dark purple 'Helicopter' (Shidara '88) and the lavender pink 'Rikugi Sakura' (Shidara '88), both six-petal types. Other six-fall types include the dark purple 'Nagaraboshi' (Shidara '99) and lavender-pink 'Parasol' (Shidara '99). Most interesting are the multipetal pink 'Ranman' (Shidara '97)

of which I'm still using in my bearded iris breeding) as well as the 2000 medal for his blue bitone Siberian iris with lighter style arms called 'Perfect Vision' (Bartlett '96). Harry Foster's hybridizing career was cut short by his early death but he had very active programs in both tetraploid and 40-chromosome Siberian irises. Foster's tetraploids were derived from the McEwen tetraploids and his 'Glanusk' (Foster '90) represents an improvement upon McEwen's 'Silver Edge'. Olga Wells likes the fluttery type of Siberian iris that is closer to *I. sibirica* in form so that the falls are more down-hanging, the standards erect and the flowers carried on tall, well-branched stems that arise over grassy foliage. Many of these descend from two classic Siberian irises that are much in character with *I. sibirica*,

'Joyce Cole'

SIBERIAN IRISES

'Burgundy Fireworks'

and blue-violet 'Uzushio' (Shidara '00). All of these irises have been used by breeders here in the United States and have produced a number of outstanding hybrids. We all owe Mr. Shidara our thanks for bringing this interesting bit of germplasm to breeders.

Many hybridizers are just starting to develop Siberian iris breeding programs and some exciting things are coming from many parts of the world. Czech hybridizer Zdenek Seidl has produced some very interesting hybrids including the lavender with strong veins 'Purple Web' (Seidl '11) and pink amoena with sprinkles of darker pink 'Colours of Ostrava' (Seidl '12). He is selecting for cultivars with good branching and bud count (Seidl 2014). Brian Wendel introduced his first Siberian iris in 2014, 'Simply Delightful' (Wendel '14), that was one of the favorites at the recent Siberian and Species Convention in Michigan. As the name implies, it is a more simply formed flower, belying its heritage from *I. typhifolia*, and is incredibly floriferous. Even in far away New Zealand, the blue with light style arms Siberian iris 'Emma Ripeka' (Love '90) not only won the Australasian Dykes Medal but actually appeared on a postage stamp!

A FEW FAVORITES

Of course everybody's tastes differ but there are a few older Siberians that I will probably always grow. I grew them as a kid and adored them. Surprisingly American Iris Society judges that visit my yard remark on how beautiful and unique these cultivars are and "where did you get that?" is often the question. These cultivars also seem to be interesting parents when mated with more current hybrids. My choices among the newer ones might change each season, but these older favorites are sort of classics.

OLDER FAVORITES

'Summer Sky' (Cleveland '39). A very delicate blue flower of the fluttery type, with prominent clear white styles that almost make the flower appear as an amoena because the styles are so prominent. Totally unique! Lots of buds ensure a long season. I am not alone in my opinion of this plant as it regularly appeared in the Society for Siberian Irises' popularity poll into the 2000s long after other cultivars no longer made these polls.

'Salem Witch' (Spofford, registered '62 but never officially introduced). I first saw 'Salem Witch' in 1966 and have never lost my love for this flower. A tall fluttery type with dark purple standards and styles and white falls boldly striped dark purple. Stalks may have up to 18 buds and a very reliable repeat bloomer so often 'Salem Witch' is the first Siberian to bloom and the last to stop blooming. A garden treasure.

'Carrie Lee' (Wiswell '63). This was another "love at first sight." 'Carrie Lee' produces these low clumps in which the density of blooms is so great as to obscure the foliage. The low mound of bloom makes this perfect to place in the perennial border. Has the pendulous form that shows off the prominent white signal and the soft frosted raspberry pink flower so well. 'Carrie Lee' was named for Gladys Wiswell's mother, who lived well over one hundred years. This Siberian iris has similar staying power!

'Blue Moon' (Scheffy '52). For some reason we have very few quality six-fall Siberians. This was one of the earliest and in some ways still one of the best. This is a very large flower on a tall stalk with all petals in a bright blue violet with a signal on both standards and falls and the standards and falls lying in the same plane. A robust plant that makes a dramatic landscape statement.

'Velvet Night' (Edwards '61) and 'Congo Drums' (L. Marx '56). These two flowers are similar and you need not own both, although I do. Both are a deep purple with velvety falls and both have very small to no signals. Both are very vigorous and

extremely floriferous. 'Velvet Night' is a little shorter and may have the extra branch at times. 'Congo Drums' is a more rounded flower. If you have grown and liked 'Caesar's Brother' you will like these better.

'Flight of Butterflies' (Witt registered 1972 and released by White Flower Farm). This is the classic *I. sibirica* type flower but on a shorter, more restrained plant that fits in well in the perennial border. Standards and styles are blue violet and the falls are white veined in a butterfly wing pattern the same shade of blue as the standards. Neat smaller, almost spatulate flowers. A clump in bloom looks like a sea of butterflies.

'Illini Charm' (Varner '74). Steve Varner produced many fine Siberians. This is one of his earlier hybrids. A rosy magenta flower with a peacock flash of teal on the falls near the white signal that sets the flower apart. Makes neat lower clumps and is extremely floriferous.

'Blue Song' (Warburton '73). A lovely round flower of a clear blue violet that makes a very neat garden clump. The unique feature is the on the style arms that have the most beautiful frills and enhanced by shots of a real turquoise blue. This was a star in the Siberian border at my parents' garden in Massachusetts.

'Pirate Prince' (Varner '74). Although I normally like strong signals, patterns or contrasting styles on my Siberians, this one is almost a perfect self. A very rich dark purple flower with nice shape and a plant that grows vigorously. This is one that looks great planted in masses.

'Mandy Morse' (Spofford '65). In my parents' garden in Massachusetts, the clump of 'Mandy Morse' would have several hundred flowers and was a landscape spectacle. The followers are medium large and a clear shade of hyacinth blue with long, prominent white style arms and a matching white signal spot on the falls. A clump two feet across could have as many as one hundred stalks, obscuring the foliage when in bloom. The pendant form allows the styles to really show off in the clump.

'Salem Witch'

NEWER FAVORITES

'Then Sings My Soul' (Helsley '05). Calvin Helsley has produced many very nice Siberian irises. This one is a darker red-violet with a brilliance of color I've not seen in others in this class. In the sun it glistens. Moreover, it has lots of buds and branching that allow for a very long bloom season. My first results from using it as a parent have been interesting too.

'Swans in Flight' (Hollingworth '05). Great name for this flower as the large ruffled white blooms perched above the foliage resemble a flock of swans or egrets. Very floriferous and with great plant habits make this one a sure winner. It is like 'White Swirl' on steroids!

'Sugar Rush' (Schafer/Sacks '10). Marty and Jan have produced a number of lovely Siberians with the overlay pattern of red-purple over yellow. 'Sugar Rush' has one of the cleanest of these overlay colors with pinkish standards and quite red falls. The shape is wide but the flowers are more vertical than many current Siberians, allowing for a better landscape value as well.

'Sweet Little Susy' (Schafer/Sacks '03). This is certainly not the flashiest flower but it just *screams* cute. The plant is shorter but it is still very well branched, with five to seven flowers per stalk. The flowers are almost round and very ruffled and a pleasing shade of light lavender. An excellent plant for the front of a border as it has excellent plant habits.

'Sandy River Belle' (Schafer/Sacks '10). A lovely flower in an odd shade of quite true pink with a more yellow flush towards the signal area. Lots of buds and branching and a very happy plant. My clump is growing in a bit of dappled shade and it just glows when in bloom.

'Neat Trick' (White '00). Every collection of irises needs a conversation piece. This is it. Flowers are a nice dark purple but the "trick" is the marbling of white on the falls. No two flowers are alike so that the clump produces a wonderful variety of blossoms.

'Imperial Opal' (Bauer/Coble '06). Okay, maybe you need two conversation pieces! This flower is *huge*. Normally I prefer smaller flowers to huge, but this one somehow works. It looks like a Japanese iris and you can fool visitors with its size and multitude of petals. The color is also unusual, an odd shade of pinkish lavender with an opalescent cast.

'Turn a Phrase' (Schafer/Sacks '06). We need a good blue but this is not just blue but a wonderful mélange of shades of blue. The petals are light blue with heavy texture veins and then edged a much darker shade of blue. Nicely branched and with lots of buds.

'Sandy River Belle'

'Something Shocking' (Hollingworth '13). Here's a tetraploid to round out the list. I prefer the diploids but this tetraploid is nothing short of spectacular. A huge flower with very strongly flaring ruffled falls in a rich magenta-maroon with a bold white signal that has become a Hollingworth trademark.

'McKenzie Bruiser' (Reid '09). This is one 40-chromosome hybrid that is also a wonderful garden plant and a fairly easy grower. A delicious navy blue with a much darker signal. Stalks are tall and branched making for a long bloom season.

Almost every 28-chromosome Siberian iris will be a wonderful garden plant. The ones listed above would give you a good mix of types although I noticed that I have not listed a single yellow in my favorites even though I grow many. Try a bunch from different nurseries and you will not be disappointed.

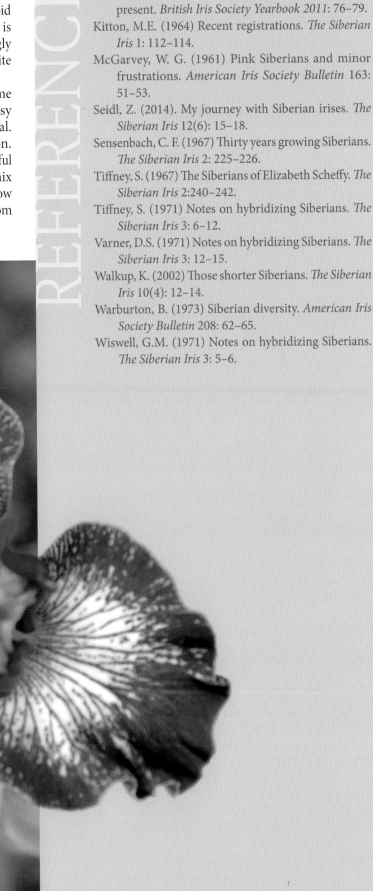

'Something Shocking'

REFERENCES

Edwards, P. (1964) Small Siberians. *The Siberian Iris* 1(7): 119–120.

Hewitt, J. (2011) Siberian irises in Britain, past and present. *British Iris Society Yearbook 2011*: 76–79.

Kitton, M.E. (1964) Recent registrations. *The Siberian Iris* 1: 112–114.

McGarvey, W. G. (1961) Pink Siberians and minor frustrations. *American Iris Society Bulletin* 163: 51–53.

Seidl, Z. (2014). My journey with Siberian irises. *The Siberian Iris* 12(6): 15–18.

Sensenbach, C. F. (1967) Thirty years growing Siberians. *The Siberian Iris* 2: 225–226.

Tiffney, S. (1967) The Siberians of Elizabeth Scheffy. *The Siberian Iris* 2:240–242.

Tiffney, S. (1971) Notes on hybridizing Siberians. *The Siberian Iris* 3: 6–12.

Varner, D.S. (1971) Notes on hybridizing Siberians. *The Siberian Iris* 3: 12–15.

Walkup, K. (2002) Those shorter Siberians. *The Siberian Iris* 10(4): 12–14.

Warburton, B. (1973) Siberian diversity. *American Iris Society Bulletin* 208: 62–65.

Wiswell, G.M. (1971) Notes on hybridizing Siberians. *The Siberian Iris* 3: 5–6.

3 JAPANESE IRISES

Japanese irises are the most spectacular of the beardless iris groups with relatively flat flowers up to a foot across on stalks 3 to 4' tall. Among the major beardless iris groups, the Japanese irises are the latest to bloom, starting with the late spurias and blooming for nearly a month afterwards. Although the color range of Japanese irises is limited to white, lavender, blue, purple (to near black), and wine-red, the patterns of the colors are almost infinitely varied. Most recently hybridizers have extended the color range by producing much closer to true pinks and blues without obvious violet overtones. Besides self-colored blossoms, patterns of darker or lighter edges, darker or lighter veins, all-over dappling of darker or lighter colors, and all combinations of these are available in the Japanese iris cultivars. Signals are generally small and bright yellow but the yellow does not in general extend further into the petals, although a few cream colored Japanese irises are available. Bicolors are fairly rare except in the single forms. In these, the three small standards are often much darker than the falls, creating a good contrast.

Forms are also quite diverse among the Japanese irises. Although the species has relatively simple pendant flowers with three falls and small standards, Japanese iris hybridizers have created six-fall types that are probably the most prevalent among the named hybrids and 9- to 15-petal multipetal types or so called "peony formed" flowers (Ackerman and Williams 1982). Style arms in many of the hybrids have become intensely frilled and widened and standing up to create what appears

'Amethyst's Sister'

'Dragon Tapestry'

'Japanese Plum'

to be a crown above the petals. The clustering of elaborate stamens on the six-fall types is among the most popular of the forms as the appearance of these flowers resembles a highly decorated crown.

GARDEN USE AND CULTURE

In Japan, Japanese irises are grown in large numbers in public gardens. At peak bloom, the fields are flooded and create a glorious display. Unfortunately, this has created one of the myths of Japanese iris culture that they must be grown in constantly flooded conditions. Nothing could be further from the truth. Although Japanese irises prefer moist roots, covering the crown with water will result in the death of the plant. Save these constantly flooded spots to some of the water irises described in the species and species hybrid chapter and the Louisiana irises. These types do grow well in a constantly flooded situation. Rather, Japanese irises are probably best grown in beds with other plants that enjoy moist soil and full sun to partial shade and well-mulched with pine or fir bark. Flower beds containing Siberian irises, daylilies, Heleniums, Louisiana irises and Japanese irises, for example, would give a long and continuous season of bloom from late April through September here in the Pacific Northwest. Early daylilies that have yellows, melons and peach tones are the perfect complement to the blues, violets and orchids of the Japanese irises as they are colors not found in the Japanese iris.

For many years another myth was being perpetuated about Japanese irises: that they actually poisoned their soil after several years. Luckily, we now know what causes this decline in plant growth. Chad Harris has done much to further our understanding of Japanese iris culture (Harris 2012) and his garden in the Columbia Gorge is a testament to his techniques in growing these beauties; it is a spectacular display that is truly breathtaking. His most important observation concerns the way in which Japanese iris rhizomes grow. Unlike other irises, in which the increases grow *out* from the center of the clump, Japanese iris rhizomes grow *up*. Because of this the rhizomes pile on top of each other and the rhizomes are lifted higher and higher until the crowns are above the soil line. This situation causes the clumps to become weaker because the rhizomes have no soil in which to form roots, so that after 3 to 4 years the clump has degenerated. Digging the clump and replanting the irises after 3 to 4 years of growth is essential to maintain high bloom quality. Incorporating compost or other organic material and adding new soil further enhances the growth of these plants.

Japanese irises are heavy feeders. They go completely dormant in the winter so they must produce a huge plant and those extremely large flowers. In the spring, side-dress the plants with a balanced fertilizer such as 10-10-10. Well composted cow

'Foolish Fantasy'

manure appears to be a good addition both to the soil when reworking the soil prior to transplanting as well as a side dressing. After bloom, addition of a high nitrogen fertilizer appears to be beneficial to sustained plant growth. However, if you live in an area of high temperatures and humidity, this should be done with some restraint as the plants can be burned by this treatment. Alternately, a time-released general fertilizer is a more safe addition, even in high humidity areas.

One thing critical in Japanese iris culture is an acidic pH. Lime can be lethal to Japanese irises so if you grow bearded irises, and have applied lime to these areas, make sure the soil pH is tested before planting Japanese irises in these same areas. I never plant Japanese irises near concrete sidewalks nor in raised beds that are constructed from concrete paving stones. Both increase the soil pH and can harm Japanese iris growth or at worse result in death of the plant. Many years ago, German Max Steiger set out to produce a strain of Japanese iris that are resistant to the effect of lime by rowing out seedlings in higher pH soils and selecting the survivors. He did create a strain called "CARE" (Calcium Resistant) that tolerated higher pH but these plants were lost during an illness of the hybridizer.

Japanese irises can be grown in containers using good moisture-retentive potting mix. The same rules that apply to not flooding the crown in the garden situations can be applied to the container culture. *Never* submerge the crown. Groups of pots may be assembled in shallow kiddy wading pools and 2 to 4" of water maintained constantly during the growing season. In winter it is best that the pots be heeled into a vegetable garden or other unused area of the garden as there would be a good chance the pots would freeze and kill the rhizomes.

'Rivulets of Wine'

In the northern United States, Japanese irises are best grown in full sun or at best some dappled shade. In the South and other hot and humid climates, the blooms look their best in at least dappled shade if not partial shade. The blooms in these climates can wilt quickly and look more like rags on a stick than a beautiful garden flower. Additionally, early cultivars are definitely preferred as they bloom before the worst of the summer heat. For example Chad Harris's fine 'Pleasant Earlybird' blooms several weeks before the main groups of Japanese irises and did very well for me when I gardened in Mississippi. Ken Durio found that the tetraploid Japanese irises were best suited to his conditions in Opelousas, Louisiana. There the heavy substance of the blossoms were a great aid in not wilting too quickly.

Transplanting techniques are similar to Siberian irises. Care should be made that the rhizomes are planted deeply enough and kept watered and mulched until well established. Plants are generally obtained as bare-root divisions from nurseries in the fall, although some nurseries do sell them in the spring as well. Spring plantings should only be tried from nurseries approximately the same climate as yours. Wait until fall if ordering from a nursery in a cooler climate than yours.

Despite many who think of the Japanese as temperamental garden subjects they are actually bothered by relatively few pests. Thrips can sometimes attack the blossoms and borers may sometimes attack the rhizomes but even these are rather rare events.

SPECIES INVOLVED IN JAPANESE IRISES

Unlike other beardless iris groups, in which a number of related species have been intercrossed to produce the group, only one species is involved in the creation of Japanese irises, *I. ensata*. In the past this species was known as *I. kaempferi* and it is sometimes referred by this illegitimate name in general gardening catalogs. This species has a wide range of distribution including areas of Siberia. Collections from these very cold areas by colleagues of Rodionenko have provided important germplasm for gardeners in severely cold climates such as northern Russia and Scandinavia. Some authorities had assumed that Japanese irises may have had the other water iris of Japan, *I. laevigata*, but hybrids between these two species are sterile and thus it is unlikely that any other species is involved in the Japanese irises.

HISTORY OF HYBRIDIZING

Japanese irises have the longest history of hybridizing of any group, starting in the 16th century (McEwen 1990). This early hybridizing work resulted in three distinctive strains: Edo, Ise, and Higo.

The Edo strain was the earliest of these strains and was developed around present day Tokyo; the name "Edo" refers to the old name for Tokyo. The most prominent of the early hybridizers of the Edo strain was Matsudaira Sadatomo. His father had collected many variants from around Japan, but the seed from these cultivars produced nothing unusual. However, seeds obtained from the Asaka marshes produced outstanding single dark purples. He continued to raise seedlings and subsequently produced the first double or six-petal type blossom. Subsequent hybridization work by Matsudaira and prominently Rokusaburo Mannen, produced a strain of Japanese irises known as the Ise strain. Amazingly, these contained most of the colors and patterns that are found in the present-day Japanese irises. The first peony, or multipetal type, was also produced by these early hybridizers. The Edo strain differs from the Ise and Higo strains in their generally more simple form. Petals do not overlap and there may be even gaps between the petals. Styles are small and never have the elaboration of tissue seen in the Higo strain but in the single flowers, the standards are fairly prominent and held stiffly erect. Flower stalks are branched and the flowers are positioned well above the foliage mound.

'Second Wave'

The Ise strain was created in Ise, a city fifty miles south of the ancient capital of Japan, Kyoto. It is likely that the wild variants used in the development of this strain were different than either the Edo or Higo strains. The most prominent of the hybridizers was Sadagoro Toshii, with later developments by Saikichi Noguchi and Kenzaburo Nagabayashi. Flowers of the Ise strain are mostly single types with the falls wider but often pendulous rather than stiffly flared. Plants produce stalks that rise only slightly above the foliage mound. Unlike the Edo strain, the Ise strain was bred for pot culture so that the production of one or two perfect blossoms was more important than having branched stalks. Flowers tend to be pastel, pinks and pale blues and without sharp contrasts or patterns.

'John's Fancy'

The Higo strain was developed from varieties selected from the Edo strain. Junnosuke Yoshida apprenticed under Shoo and brought back selected cultivars to Kumamoto Prefecture then known as Higo to develop a distinctive strain of Japanese iris. Higo types are found in all types of flower form and color patterns and the flowers are very large, up to a foot in diameter, on unbranched stalks. The Higos were bred for pot culture, so that a single large flower could be observed

in close proximity and from its opening until its senescence. Flowers were produced on tall stalks that stood well above the foliage, like the Edo strain.

For many years, the export of Japanese irises to the West was prohibited. However, in the late 1800s and early 1900s these hybrids were exported to America. Probably the biggest of these importers was the Childs nursery (Swearengen 1969). This nursery also named some cultivars although it is unclear if they were hybrids produced by that nursery or renamed hybrids from the Japanese. Childs also listed a number of hybrids produced in this country, including 'Gold Bound', 'Mount Hood', 'T.S. Ware', and 'Templeton'. The plants from the Childs Nursery would be the basis for many other American hybridizers, such as Arthur Hazzard. Other important importers include Bertrand Farr, who introduced 20 irises from "the gardens of the Mikado," F.B. Meade, who introduced a similar numbers of varieties, and the Hobbs Nursery that introduced "standard varieties." The popularity of Japanese irises was quite high at that time with nurseries listing up to four hundred cultivars. The introduction of all this breeding stock ushered in the phase of extensive hybridization in the United States. The American hybridizers had very different hybridizing aims than the Japanese hybridizers, selecting for more branching, ruffling, improved substance and new colors and patterns.

W.A. Payne is the father of the Japanese iris hybridizers in the United States. His hybrids are primarily derived from ten cultivars of the Edo strain from plants obtained from Hobbs and Meade. In the course of the years of his hybridizing he raised over 100,000 seedlings. These are extensively line bred for over forty years, resulting in 180 named varieties. Although there are many outstanding varieties, 'Dancing Waves' (Payne '64), a blended violet with a narrow white edge, 'Immaculate Glitter' (Payne '64), a dark purple double with all parts neatly bordered in white, 'Wounded Dragon' (Payne '64), a purple all-over heavily dappled white, 'Blue Nocturne' (Payne '59), a six-falled blue violet, 'Fashion Model' (Payne '50), a fluorite violet self with six to nine petals, 'Rose Adagio' (Payne '69), a pale flower with broad edges of rose-pink, and 'Orchid Majesty' (Payne '53), a pale lavender with a bluish halo, are among the most distinctive and important of these

Payne introductions. These and many others have been used extensively in hybridizing by others.

Walter Marx of Boring, Oregon, was one of the pioneers in breeding Japanese irises in the United States and his elaborate color catalog was a great promotion for these irises. Marx imported a number of the best Higo varieties from Japan such as 'Karahashi', 'Hisikata', and 'Miyuki Guruma' and worked these varieties into a strain he called "Marhigos" that indicate their origin from the Higo strain but selected in the Pacific Northwest for plants more adapted to the United States. Initially the Marx plants were offered as strains of irises. That is, these were not cultivars per se but rather groups of seedlings that had similar colors and patterns. This allowed for quicker distribution of new varieties but a good bit of variability in quality. However, starting in 1953, cultivars were registered and introduced: 'World's Delight' (Marx '53), the first really good quality lavender-pink double; 'Summer Storm' (Marx '55), a quality dark purple; the huge and tall white six-fall type 'Snowy Hills' (Marx '55); 'Vain Victor' (Marx '57) a bold white strongly edged a bright red-violet; 'Blue Lagoon' (Marx '55), a clear gentian blue; and one of my favorites 'Frilled Enchantment' (Marx '59), a six-falled white with a narrow rim of rose around each petal. Each of these cultivars would be used in breeding of others.

When Walter Marx was ready to retire, there were still many fine seedlings in the Marx fields that had not been introduced. Dorothy and Al Rogers bought the Marx stock and introduced several varieties using the "Caprician" stable name for some of these plants, for their Caprice Farms Nursery. 'Caprician Butterfly' (Marx by Rogers '85) is the most outstanding of these, with dark purple standards and white falls dramatically veined purple. This cultivar won the Payne Medal in 1994. Ben Hager also registered one of the nicest Marx seedlings as 'Flashing Koi' (Marx by Hager, '78), a white both splashed and edged in a bright red-violet, even surpassing the patterns found in some fancy koi types.

In the 1950s and '60s, there was a new center of JI hybridizing in California (Hager 1969). Violet Worley grew seed of the Marhigos from Marx. Two very outstanding cultivars came from this seed: 'Worley Pink' (Worley '66), a vast improvement on the classic Marx Japanese iris 'World's Delight' and Payne Award winner in 1970, and 'My Heavenly Dream' (Worley '65), a rose-red with deeper veining and almost pink edges. Fred Maddocks made planned crosses for over 30 years but did so for his own enjoyment until his garden was discovered by Jonnye Rich. His lines were derived from some of the older imported varieties and early Marx cultivars. After this discovery a number of cultivars were selected from his seedling patch including the Payne Award winner, 'Leave Me Sighing' (Maddocks '64), patterned dark purple on white 'Geisha Gown' (Maddocks '64) and bold white with broad petals of navy blue 'Time and Tide' (Maddocks '68) and the stunning red boldly veined white 'Hue and Cry' (Maddocks '70). Seedlings from both the Worley and Maddocks programs were incorporated into the program of Jonnye Rich. Perhaps

'Kimono Silk'

selecting in a hotter, drier climate made her select for flowers that would hold up better to adverse weather conditions. Outstanding among the Rich cultivars are: 'Star at Midnight' (Rich '64), a dark violet-purple with a small white patch on the falls, the huge lavender pink 'Enchanting Melody' (Rich '68), 'Tuptim' (Rich '74), a large light blue veined deeper with prominent much darker styles. One of Rich's last introductions, 'Center of Attraction' (Rich '86), is a very wide petaled violet veined darker. Her 'Geisha Obi' (Rich '88) combines the Maddocks and Worley irises and is a rich mulberry strongly veined with white and edged with bright mulberry. It went on to win the Payne Medal in 1999. Melrose Gardens introduced these cultivars to the market and owner Ben Hager also introduced a number of Japanese irises. His 'Stranger in Paradise' (Hager '70), a bold fuchsia with a white blaze is his best, and won the Payne Award in 1976. It is a combination of the best Japanese imports and Maddock's 'Time and Tide'.

Art Hazzard used a number of the varieties from the Childs Nursery to develop his strain of Japanese irises. Despite this, what might be considered a relatively ancient genetic base, Hazzard received three Payne Awards/Medals for his hybrids, many of which have the stable name of "Prairie." The white self 'Prairie Love Song' (Hazzard '70) and deep purple 'Prairie Velvet' (Hazzard '72) won the Payne Awards in 1975 and 1979, respectively. After Hazzard's death a very interesting seedling, a blue-violet with a broad but jagged white edge, was selected for naming by Robert Bauer and John Coble, and named 'Kalamazoo' (Hazzard by Bauer & Coble '89). This flower was extremely popular and went on to win the Payne Medal in 1996. Hazzard was a tireless promoter of Japanese irises and in the early 1970s distributed seed to virtually everyone in the American Iris Society to try and enhance the popularity of these irises. I grew a crop of seedlings from this seed and was impressed at the beautiful colors and patterns that came from that nice gift of seed.

Adolph Vogt didn't introduce many Japanese irises, but those he did were breakthroughs in the class. He introduced two of the very few what might be called miniature Japanese irises, the white with green veining 'Little Snowman' (Vogt '90) and its ruffled white seedling 'Little Snowball' (Vogt '90). Two others of the Vogt Japanese irises would go on to win the Payne Award, the white with violet veins 'Lilac Peaks' (Vogt '87) and the light violet with prominent dark lavender centers to the falls 'Oriental Eyes' (Vogt '84). This darker center on the falls of 'Oriental Eyes' gives the impression of an eye. 'Oriental Eyes' would win the Payne Medal in 1993 and still remains a popular Japanese iris.

Currier McEwen was the first to develop tetraploid Japanese irises. He had already successfully converted Siberian irises but the Japanese irises proved a bit more difficult and it took eight years before the first fully tetraploid Japanese iris was produced. As in the early tetraploid Siberian irises, producing seed on these plants was difficult, and some of the flowers had so much substance that they tended to flip their falls up or not open properly. McEwen did not flinch from this challenge, however, and success came in the next generation. This work resulted in two Payne Award winners: white edged raspberry purple 'Raspberry Rimmed' (McEwen '79), and its seedling, the white edged blue 'Blueberry Rimmed' (McEwen '83). The two rimmed cultivars greatly increased interest in the tetraploid Japanese irises. The most popular of the early McEwen tetraploids is the magnificent red-purple with white edge 'Japanese Pinwheel' (McEwen '88), which won McEwen his only Payne Medal in 1992. It still remains popular as it performs well over a large

'Rings A Bell'

section of the country and has a distinct jaunty flare. McEwen continued on his quest for more perfect tetraploid Japanese irises throughout his life and Sharon Whitney continues to grow and select the McEwen Japanese irises for sale. Among these more recent tetraploids, pink with white blaze 'Fourfold Pink' (McEwen '96), red-purple 'Centenary' (McEwen '02), double tetraploid white with blue edge 'Maine Elegance' (McEwen '09), delicate lavender pink 'My Elisabeth' (McEwen '08), and one of the few repeat blooming tetraploids, the dark purple with white edges 'Thoroughbred' (McEwen '99). McEwen's work with diploid Japanese explored some less traveled waters, including strong repeat bloomers in 'Returning Tide' (McEwen

'76) and 'Exuberant Chantey' (McEwen '90), variations on the pink colors such as the violet blue and pink 'Easter Pastel' (McEwen '03) and clear pink 'Honour' (McEwen '01), and species-looking rose-pink 'Joan Trevithick' (McEwen '92). McEwen's Japanese irises were a tremendous boost to the Japanese iris breeding pool and of course served as the nucleus for all of the future tetraploid Japanese hybridizing.

Fellow Maine resident John White was impressed with McEwen's work on Japanese irises and produced many irises that I'm sure his mentor approved of most heartily. All of White's introductions are diploids. Many of White's irises carry the stable name of "Dirigo" from the motto of the state of Maine. 'Dirigo Debutante' (White '94), a white veined and

'Sugar Dome'

sanded violet was the first of these. Two of his most famous introductions are the gorgeous true-pink 'Dirigo Pink Milestone' (White '00) and red-violet 'Dirigo Red Rocket' (White '01); both of these flowers won the prestigious Warburton Medal for best introduced iris originating in New England. 'Evelyn White' (White '08), a white flower narrowly edged red-violet, and its seedling 'Dirigo Editor' (White '10), a white flower narrowly edged blue, both honor White's wife Evelyn, who was for many years editor of the Society for Japanese Irises publication *The Review*.

Sterling Innerst was a renowned hybridizer of bearded irises having won the Dykes Medal for his near black tall bearded 'Before the Storm'. Innerst also became interested in breeding Japanese irises and had similar success despite picking

out some of the worst iris names ever! Even the nursery that introduced his plants asked him to "pick out better names." Oddly his bearded irises generally had very nice names. Two of Innerst's Japanese irises won the Payne Award or Medal, the wine purple with splashes 'Epimethus' (Innerst '92) and the pale violet veined and sanded deep blue violet 'Iapetus' (Innerst '99). Other great Innerst irises are the white veined and boldly edged violet 'Jocasta' (Innerst '87) and the velvety wine red with blue peacock flash 'Capaneus' (Innerst '88).

Lorena Reid worked with beardless irises for many years and hybridized 40-chromosome Siberians, CalSibe hybrids, *I. laevigata* and Japanese irises and sold them through her nursery Laurie's Gardens. It was a great source for unusual beardless irises. Reid and I also share something in that we are the only living charter members of the Species Iris Group of North America. She created a unique series of very early flowering Japanese irises with stable name of "Springtime" as they bloom 2 to 3 weeks before the main Japanese iris bloom. White 'Springtime Snow' (Reid '84) and red-violet marbled white and different shades of violet 'Springtime Showers' (Reid '86) were the first two of these early blooming Japanese irises introduced by Reid and a cross of these two varieties gave the other extra early mauve-pink 'Springtime Melody' (Reid '94) and splashed mauve-wine 'Springtime Prayer' (Reid '94). One of Reid's finest hybrids is her Payne Award winner, 'Freckled Geisha' (Reid '81), a seedling of Marx's 'Frilled Enchantment' and an improvement upon that classic with many more spots (the freckles) that add so much to the flower. Very subtle 'Picotee Princess' (Reid '92), a white with a sanded light orchid border, won the Payne Medal in 2001. Her greatest triumph in Japanese iris breeding is her 'Sings the Blues' (Reid '97), a blue-violet boldly edged in white that gives a very blue garden effect. 'Sings the Blues' won the Payne Medal in 2006 and is a very popular iris. Reid has retired from the nursery business but she is still a very active iris society judge. It was a pleasure to have her in my garden this last spring to evaluate the 40-chromosome Siberian iris seedlings.

Jill and Jim Copeland both breed beardless irises but Jim confines his hybridizing to Siberians. Jill plays the field a bit more and is a major hybridizer of Japanese irises. An early success was 'Blue Marlin' (Copeland '81), a wide and clear navy blue seedling from the Payne Award winner 'Star at Midnight'. It would follow its mother and win the Payne Award in 1985. Pink irises were a serious pursuit and 'Pink Dace' (Copeland '83) and its grandchild 'Pink Puffer' (Copeland '06), the latter an unusual violet-toned pink double, having both been well received. Two "Christina's," 'Christina's Gown' (Copeland '06), a blue with broad white edges, and 'Christina's Sister' (Copeland '09), a white with strong veining and deeper styles, are both big doubles. Jill produced one of the rare tetraploids, and even more amazing a white double one called

'Alexisaurus' (Copeland '12), that comes from the McEwen bloodlines but also contains a new tetraploid seedling of hers in the mix. The tetraploid gene pool is rather limited so this is a most welcome accomplishment.

Terry Aitken is a truly addicted hybridizer, working in all the bearded iris classes and nearly all of the beardless ones as well. His work on Japanese irises has been sterling, and has taken different paths than many others, including repeat blooming Japanese irises. This repeat blooming line started with Aitken's first introduction, the very dark purple 'Midnight Stars' (Aitken '90). Breeding from this plant, the seedlings showed an amazing ability to repeat bloom with 'Midnight Fireworks' (Aitken '14) the strongest of these rebloomers, blooming for months here in the Pacific Northwest. Other important Aitken Japanese irises include the Payne Medal winning duo, 'Electric Rays' (Aitken '90), a violet with lighter veins, and the light violet with prominent blue purple crested styles 'Cascade Crest' (Aitken '88) and the lovely white all over veined blue-violet with darker styles 'Butterflies in Flight' (Aitken '91). Two of the "Glow" series were also Payne Medal winners, a bright raspberry wine with blue veins 'Raspberry Glow' (Aitken '92) and blue-purple 'Electric Glow' (Aitken '92). Aitken also has a line of "Tessas" with the dark purple styles on a light lavender blossom 'Tessa Dark Eyes' (Aitken '95) and the reddish toned seedling 'Red Tessa' (Aitken '07).

Bob Bauer and John Coble garden in Michigan and their garden is a showplace for Japanese irises including gardens with the traditional Japanese style raked sand areas. Their nursery is called Ensata Gardens, honoring the species *I. ensata* that is the species that gave rise to the Japanese irises. Their hybridizing program started off just with some curiosity. A bee set seed pod on 'Prairie Chief' gave rise to a very vigorous and beautiful blue violet single flower that was named 'Bellender Blue' (Bauer-Coble '93). Amazingly this very first offering went on to win the Payne Medal in 2000. A very good start to a hybridizing program! Several other Payne Medals would follow. 'Lion King' (Bauer-Coble '96), a seedling of 'Frilled Enchantment' takes the white edged rosy violet pattern to new extremes with a broad red-violet edge and rolling ruffles make for a truly outrageous flower. 'Raspberry Candy' (Bauer-Coble '99) takes the classic 'Geisha Gown' pattern but converts it into much deeper shade of red-violet with vivid veins, giving a vivid garden effect. 'Raspberry Candy' would win the Payne Medal in 2009. 'Lake Effect' (Bauer-Coble '04) is an amazing flower, a white with a large blue "blot" on the falls that pales as it approaches the petal edge, leaving the edge white. It is an improvement upon and seedling of Lorena Reid's Payne Medal winner 'Sings the Blues'. Besides these sterling introductions the Bauer-Coble hybridization program has made strides in many areas, but especially in the pinks and flowers with contrasted or dark frilly styles gathered into a crown-like structure. In the pinks, very clear pink 'Pinkerton' (Bauer-Coble '99), pale pink with darker pink styles 'Peak of Pink' (Bauer-Coble '99), and lavender pink with lighter edges 'Rafferty' (Bauer-Coble '00) are all popular flowers with wide ruffled form. The flowers with big contrasted styles are spectacular flowers and are guaranteed to wow garden visitors. Favorites of these include near white with prominent purple styles 'Crown Imperial' (Bauer-Coble '01), 'Sapphire Crown' (Bauer-Coble '96), a white veined violet with prominent purple styles, and the 'Sapphire Crown' child 'Indigo Angel' (Bauer-Coble '11), a white with blue veins and dark blue-violet petal edges and prominent dark blue-purple styles. The ultimate in this crown line might be 'Enchanted Island' (Bauer-Coble '13) in white with fine dark purple veins and petal edges plus a cluster of deep purple style arms. All of the Bauer-Coble plants are fine garden plants as well as having spectacular flowers. These even grew well

'Alexisaurus'

'Midnight Fireworks'

'Indigo Angel'

'Dalle Whitewater'

'Coho'

in Mississippi for the author, before moving to the more Japanese iris-friendly growing areas in Oregon.

Chad Harris has one of the most beautiful pieces of property on a steep hillside overlooking the Columbia Gorge. This unique piece of property has wonderful cold springs that allow for irrigation of his plantings. That, coupled with his impeccable horticultural techniques, produces a sea of blooms on his Japanese irises. I feel privileged to have visited this lovely garden on several occasions. Harris's first introductions had the stable name of "Pleasant" and indeed they were quite pleasant. 'Pleasant Earlybird' (Harris '96) is one of my favorites; a single flowered lavender pink that blooms weeks before the main Japanese iris bloom and is a vigorous grower that works in well in beds with other perennials. The duo of 1997 introductions includes two variations on the sanded pattern. 'Pleasant Sandman' (Harris '97) is a white with a broad edge of violet and sanding of the same color throughout the white areas of the petal. This seedling inherits many of the attributes of its fine parent 'Dancing Waves'. 'Pleasant Starburst' (Harris '97) is a white that is both veined and sanded in blue-violet but leaving a clear edge of white around the petals. The newer 'Dalle Whitewater' (Harris '11) brings the sanded pattern to a high level of sophistication in white so finely sanded in blue as to give an ice blue effect in the landscape. Harris has worked especially hard in producing clear pinks and has utilized a lot of approaches towards this goal. Many flowers are being evaluated now but the lovely hybrid 'Coho' (Harris '04), named

to honor our locally famous Coho salmon, in a very clean and fairly true pink. It went on to win the Payne Medal in 2012. Harris's 'Bewitching Twilight' (Harris '00) is a gorgeous ice blue garden effect caused by fine blue lines on a white background. 'Bewitching Twilight' won Harris his second Payne Medal in 2013. By crossing two 'Dancing Waves' seedlings, Harris created what I think may be his best Japanese iris to date, 'Celestial Emperor' (Harris '11), a complex pattern of silvery lavender with a bold edge of mulberry and then that edged silvery lavender. A simply gorgeous flower and a good grower and garden plant too.

Lee Walker is a man with ambition. Walker lives in an area of Oregon that is quite dry and with rather alkaline water. In order to water the Japanese irises he must truck in the water to use on his massive seedling fields. He has worked extensively with both diploids and tetraploids although his most well known hybrids are from the "Craola" series which have very intense (like an iris colored by crayons) that give these flowers lots of visual impact. 'First Strike Craola' (Walker '05) and 'Kool Craola Ice' (Walker '06) have similar patterns of greyed violet with strong red-violet rims whereas 'Craola Solstice' (Walker '12) is a more pastel cream lined and banded red-violet. A non-Craola but still a very bright flower is 'Oregon Marmalade' (Walker '03), a bicolor with small purple standards and cream falls strongly veined pastel blue-violet. It has an almost luminescent quality. Walker is one of the few hybridizers that have had good luck crossing tetraploid Japanese irises and raised thousands

'Red Tessa'

of seedlings and he has introduced 'Twilight Marble' (Walker '08), a marbled violet on a greyed lavender background and with a bright violet halo.

Don Delmez grows and hybridizes Japanese irises in suburban St. Louis Missouri and has produced a number of beautiful cultivars. Delmez's first big break was the wide light blue veined darker with darker styles 'Blue Spritz' (Delmez '96), a seedling of and improvement upon Payne Medal winner 'Caprician Butterfly'. 'Blue Spritz' would win the Payne Medal in 2005. Using 'Blue Spritz' as a parent gave what I consider to be Delmez's finest introduction, 'Sue Jo' (Delmez '03) in white vein blue-violet with a cluster of very dark and prominent style arms forming a crown-like center; a real stunner and winner of the Payne Medal in 2010. Delmez's other Payne Medal winner 'Little Bow Pink' (Delmez '98) is a very clear pink single with very broad falls. Other Delmez Japanese irises include the true miniature 'Little Spritzer' (Delmez '98), a true reverse bicolor with small standards of blue violet over white falls veined violet and the tetraploid 'Wonderful Delight' (Delmez '03) that is an improvement upon its grandparent 'Japanese Pinwheel' done in more blue-violet shades.

Steve Smith grows his irises just a few miles from where I grew up in Massachusetts and has a lovely garden with a brook that runs through one edge of the property, the moist conditions near the brook providing a perfect spot for Japanese and other moisture-loving iris species. His 'R. Gisgard' (Smith '00) is a 5' tall selection of *I. ensata* in the rich blue-purple typical of the species. 'My Kathleen' (Smith '11), a seedling from 'R. Gisgard', is slightly less tall at 50" in a clear lavender blossom. These selections give a different look at Japanese irises and they are easy garden plants for the back of the border.

The future for Japanese iris breeding seems very bright with a number of hybridizers having very active programs going in many different directions. It seems amazing that a plant that has been bred for over four hundred years could still be making improvements. I'm sure these original hybridizers would be awestruck to see what the current crop of Japanese irises is, all from a rather humble blue-purple flower.

A FEW FAVORITES

Even older introductions of Japanese irises are still surprisingly modern-looking. This is not to say that improvements have not been made. Far from it. The production of clear blues, better branching and bud and increased substance are obvious improvements in the newer hybrids. However, these older hybrids are wonderful flowers and ones I'm sure you will enjoy.

OLDER FAVORITES

'Rose Queen' (Lilley '15) Although quite ancient as cultivars go, this is a great plant and flower. An interesting shade of rose pink, a very bright color, on a simple three-fall blossom. This blooms early and is of the easiest culture of any Japanese iris I have grown. My only complaint is that it has not been an outstanding parent, producing clones of itself or purple versions. Currier McEwen did produce an improved variation of this plant called 'Joan Trevithick' (McEwen '92).

'Wounded Dragon' (Payne '63). The hybridizer of this flower insisted that we should pronounce "wounded" as we do "sounded," arguing that the classical pronunciation of "wounded" was the only word with these letters pronounced that way! Regardless of the pronunciation, this is a very cool flower, a huge mulberry purple flower with little spritzes of white throughout the petal. No petals are exactly alike.

'Craola Solstice'

'Celestial Emperor'

'Star at Midnight' (Rich '64). A very dark blue violet double flower, nicely ruffled and with a spot of white on each petal (that's the star!). A dark flower that has enough substance to hold up on hot sunny days. Easy grower.

'Frilled Enchantment' (Marx '57). This flower was light years ahead of its time. A huge white double flower with each petal neatly edged rose. Sadly, this iris received no major awards. Has proven to be a very good parent.

'Dancing Waves' (Payne '62). Much as 'Frilled Enchantment' is one of Walter Marx's enduring flowers, this is the one of Payne's. A very wide and waved mulberry violet flower with a prominently edged signal and a narrow white edge. Simply wonderful.

'Worley Pink' (Worley '66). Walter Marx sold seed of his hybrids and many growers raised seedlings from these. Violet Worley selected this lovely lavender-pink with a slight turquoise flush by the signal. A very full six petals and a big improvement on the classic 'World's Delight'. A very vigorous grower that has performed well for me in Massachusetts as well as Mississippi.

'Tuptim' (Rich '71). *Wow* is what I said when I first saw this flower. Basically a light blue flower, with a gathering of very prominent much darker blue-violet styles, that makes the flower pop. A clump of this plant is a real garden statement. Although not a vigorous increaser, it is not difficult to grow.

'Trance' (Warburton '79). Bee Warburton introduced many median and dwarf bearded irises as well as many Siberians. 'Trance' was her only JI introduction and it's a good one. Bee loved 'Wounded Dragon' and this iris is in the same basic pattern of white sprits on a darker background but in 'Trance' the color is much more towards blue-lavender.

'Lake Effect'

NEWER FAVORITES

'Sings the Blues' (Reid '99). Most blue JIs have had tints of lavender or purple. This is really blue. Great landscape effect.

'Celestial Emperor' (Harris '12). This one is definitely fit for an emperor! A lavender six-fall type with a broad rim of mulberry and that thinly rimmed nearly white. Dark purple styles add a dramatic note to the inner workings of the flower.

'Kool Craola Ice' (Walker '06). Lee Walker has produced a series of these very intensely colored flower. This one is almost neon. Light blue-grey petals edged and veined dramatically with a neon sort of red-purple. Very kool indeed, Lee!

'Caprician Butterfly' (Marx-Rogers '85). A big husky plant with large flowers of white strongly veined dark blue-purple. Very showy and a very good grower.

'Lake Effect' (Bauer-Coble '04). Another true blue with a broad edge of white. Stunningly beautiful and a nice plant.

'Lion King' (Bauer-Coble '96). This one is the king of the jungle, at least in the beardless iris world. A big blousy flower in white broadly bordered in dark rose rims. Really outrageous and fun.

REFERENCES

Ackerman, W.L. and M. Williams (1982) Japanese iris flowers with multiple parts beyond the normal sequence of threes. *American Iris Society Bulletin* 244: 22–27.

Hager, B.R. (1969) Japanese irises in the west. *American Iris Society Bulletin* 193: 94–95.

Harris, C. (2012) Japanese irises demystified. *American Iris Society Bulletin* 93 (3): 52–54.

McEwen, C. (1990) *The Japanese Iris.* University Press, Hanover, NH.

Swearengen, C.A. (1969) Kaempferi irises in the Midwest. *American Iris Society Bulletin* 193: 92–93.

'Lion King'

4 PACIFIC COAST NATIVE IRISES

Pacific Coast Native (PCN) Irises can be grown, there is really no more charming group of irises. These irises are certainly one of the jewels of the US flora. Most PCNs are short, from 8 to 18" tall, and form dense clumps of low evergreen foliage over which a cloud of flowers are suspended. PCNs occur in virtually every color from white to black and many have interesting stripes, eye spots and combinations of colors, many of which are very intense. Indeed, the PCN iris rival the Japanese irises in the kinds of patterns that are available in the hybrids and surpass that beardless group in the colors in which these patterns can occur. Originally these were called "California irises" although the PCN species occur over a broader range with many of the important species occurring in Oregon and southern Washington. Joe Ghio coined the term "Pacificas" which is a bit easier on the tongue than "PCNs."

Choices among the PCN cultivars are many. Some of the species are still charming garden plants and collectors and breeders have selected superior clones of these species and wild hybrids. These collected irises tend to be of more simple form, with narrower petals and little to no ruffling. Hybrids, especially the more recent ones, have a much fuller form and are often quite ruffled. Some gardeners that are more interested in wild type plantings will want to choose the species and older hybrid clones whereas those that want more modern looks will want to choose the newer hybrids. However, even the hybrids have a tamed "wildflower look" that fits in well in a more "wild type" garden. Each of the species has contributed characteristics to the group of hybrid PCNs that confer specific colors, patterns, size and branching to the hybrids.

John Taylor seedling

GARDEN USE AND CULTURE

PCNs grow best in a climate in which the winters are relatively mild and which summers are dry and with relatively low humidity. In their native habitat, in the coastal areas of the West Coast of the United States, they tend to be plants of forest edges, clearings and tall grass areas. Reproducing this in the garden generally means planting PCNs in areas of high dappled shade, or on the sides of buildings or fences that provide artificial shade. However, in certain areas, such as the Bay Area and Seattle area, they will perform well in full sunshine. In Salem, Oregon, I give the plants a bit of morning sun, but shade during the warmest portions of the day. Plants prefer acid soil that is well drained. I do keep the PCNs mulched with a light coating of fir bark as well. This mulch is more for weed suppression than to retain moisture.

John Taylor seedlings

John Taylor seedling

Although PCNs tolerate copious amounts of water during the growing season, in the summer they require relatively little moisture and can rot if watered too heavily. Consequently, the PCNs should only be planted with other plants that require similar growth conditions. Bulbs that go dormant in the summer such as hardy cyclamen, snowdrops, autumn crocus, and small jonquil type daffodils are useful companions as are the drought tolerant *Rohdea* and various hellebore species. The PCNs may be used in drifts around shrubs such as azaleas and rhododendrons that prefer the same sort of acid humus-rich soil with the shrubs taking up the extra moisture during the summer that would be detrimental to the PCNs. PCNs will take some summer watering, especially if the ground is well drained. I grow many of mine in a mixed shade border that is raised about 3" above the garden path and in dappled shade. In this situation I give the bed some water each week in the driest times of the summer with no repercussions in poor plant growth or rot. Moreover, the addition of forest humus to raise the beds seems to make the plants grow lustily in this situation. Local iris growers are impressed with the growth of the plants under these conditions.

Transplanting PCNs is the most difficult aspect of their culture. However, the plant will give you a clue as to the time that is best for transplanting. Starting in September, start by pulling away a little soil from around a plant. New roots begin to show at about this time. When these roots have expanded to an inch or more, the plant is ready for transplanting. You can trick the plant into this state by withholding water for 3 to 4 weeks and then begin watering moderately. After the new roots appear the clump may be dug and divided into groups of one to three rhizomes and the foliage trimmed to 3 or 4". Many growers treat these divisions with fungicides such as Subdue® in order to suppress fungal growth. Some gardeners plant them back directly into the soil, whereas others pot up the divisions until new growth is observed before returning them to soil. Drenching the soil with fungicide before planting

John Taylor seedling

also helps the survival of the transplants. Although PCNs do not require much moisture as an established planting, this is one time when keeping the soil moist is required.

Divisions received from mail order nurseries are generally shipped in moist toweling or some other wetting agent. If the plants are showing new roots, the divisions may be planted immediately but even if they are it is probably wise to soak the plants in an area of subdued light for a day in order to stimulate root growth and production. If the plants are not showing roots, do the same soaking routine until root break is observed before attempting to plant. Even in moist soils, it is difficult to stimulate root growth without a soaking. Plant these divisions as described above from transplants. PCNs are difficult to transplant even when one follows all these rules. I still lose a number of plants each year probably because the nursery shipping the plants and my climate are sufficiently different that the PCN does not want to continue forming roots under my conditions. Luckily, PCNs are very reasonably priced so that even losing a few plants is not

a financial disaster. It is likely that the differences in climate between the nursery and your garden are key factors in the failure of many cultivars. Generally buying from nurseries from climates as close as possible to yours will spell the most success in transplanting PCNs to your garden. I have also potted some PCN hybrids and grown them in the pots through the first winter, keeping them in a sheltered location, and then moving the plant to a garden situation either in the spring or in the following fall. Potting up the plants does seem to keep a higher percentage of the plants surviving through the initial shock of transplanting.

Some nurseries will ship potted divisions of PCN cultivars. These are almost foolproof and plants may be obtained virtually any time during the growing season, with minimal chances of losing the cultivar. Simply knock the plant from the pot and dig a hole to accommodate the volume of soil, place the contents of the pot in the hole and water well. Very easy. If you have had trouble getting PCN cultivars to survive transplanting, this is the method for you.

John Taylor seedlings

Although generally PCNs grow in areas that are not prone to the more common iris borer, there is a borer that has been known to cause damage to PCN clumps on the West Coast (Hill 1997). The moth responsible for the damage has been identified as *Amphipoea americana* var. *pacifica*. The damage is generally not extensive compared to the more common iris borer and the plant seems to grow out of the damage.

SPECIES INVOLVED IN PCN HYBRIDS

The species that are classified as PCN occur in a narrow belt of land from Southern California to southern Washington, mostly towards the coast (Cohen 1967). Lenz (1959) discovered that hybrids between the species produced almost 100 percent viable pollen, indicating that these species are very closely related and probably recently evolved based upon their close

relationships in phylogenetic studies as well (Wilson 2004). Lenz (1958) performed an extensive analysis of the PCN group and grouped the eleven species into three groups based on the length of the perianth tube: "long tubes," "short tubes" and the "remaining species."

Species in the "short tube" group are *I. hartwegii*, *I. munzii* and *I. tenax*. *I. hartwegii* is generally pale yellow or cream, although lavender forms are known. This species is particularly difficult to transplant and has had little impact upon hybridization for the garden hybrids. *I. munzii* has the most restricted range of any of the species, occupying just a few localities in foothills of the Sierra Nevadas. This species is more tender than many but it also confers the brilliant blue colors to the hybrids. *I. tenax* is the most northern of the PCN species, venturing into central Washington. It is extremely variable in nature with white, yellow, lavender and purple

John Taylor seedling

forms all known. Plants are single-flowered and have longish, very narrow leaves that are distinctive from the wider leaves typical of many other species.

The "long tube" group is comprised of the following species: *I. chrysophylla, I. fernaldii, I. macrosiphon, I. purdyi,* and *I. tenuissima. I. chrysophylla* is principally a species of Oregon and has slender two-flowered stems with narrow cream-white to pale yellow flowers with veins of lavender. Other than its natural hybrid 'Valley Banner', *I. chrysophylla* has been little used in hybridization. *I. fernaldii,* a species from California, is a soft cream tallow often veined deeper. The flowering stems are shorter than the foliage. Almost no hybrids are derived from this species. *I. macrosiphon* is a California species with a tremendous variability of colors from cream to gold and lavender. Many of these have fragrance that are lacking in the other species. However, *I. macrosiphon*

is a difficult plant to transplant and not vigorous in cultivation, so that virtually no hybrids (and hence fragrance) have been passed on to PCN hybrids. *I. purdyi,* named for famous California plantsman Carl Purdy, is a plant of the coastal redwood forests. The flowers are white to cream and often with a wash of lavender in the falls. A number of wild hybrids have been found. Despite this, *I. purdyi* has been relatively little used in hybridization. *I. tenuissima,* a native of northern California has relatively starry flowers, with the standards and falls in relatively the same plane. Despite or maybe because of its charming wildflower-looking flowers, it has not entered the breeding programs.

The remaining species, *I. bracteata, I. douglasiana* and *I. innominata,* have neither large nor short perianth tubes. These three species are some of the most important in terms of hybrids. *I. bracteata,* a native of Oregon and neighboring areas

John Taylor seedling

John Taylor seedling

of California, is quite distinct from other species in its relatively wide leaves and stems with relatively short overlapping bracts that protect the flowers. The flowers are rather large and have broad waved parts. These floral attributes have been utilized by hybridizers, chiefly though the Lenz hybrids of this species. *I douglasiana* is the most well distributed of the PCN species, occupying a long expanse of the West Coast from the middle of Oregon to Santa Barbara County in California, although generally close to the coast. *I. douglasiana* grows in a variety of soil and exposure types, including full sun. The flowers are relatively large and are produced on branched stems. As one might expect, *I. douglasiana* has been the most extensively used species in the PCN hybrids, imparting size, branching

and ability to grow in different climates to its hybrids. *I. innominata* is one of the gems of the Western US flora, a small flower in bright gold to lavender and purple. The golden forms heavily netted with purple are especially choice. The Walter Marx catalog of the 1950s and '60s featured this species and hybrids with *I. tenax* in color pictures in its catalog, greatly popularizing PCNs.

HISTORY OF HYBRIDIZING

The history of hybridizing of the PCNs has some major gaps in what we know about the pedigrees of the plants involved. Some of this lack of knowledge is due to seed of strains being used by many breeders, partly because of the difficulty of transplanting cultivars. The breeding of PCNs has really been an international effort though because of the exchange of seed from promising strains and seed exchanges of various iris societies. As mentioned above, the species did not contribute uniformly to the development of the modern PCN hybrids. Rather, four species (*I. douglasiana, I. innominata, I. tenax* and *I. munzii*) have contributed most of the germplasm.

As for many perennials, the early development of the PCNs did not occur in their homeland of the West Coast of the United States, but rather in England. Dykes started the purposeful hybridization of PCNs, by crossing *I. tenax* with *I. purdyi*, resulting in the hybrid 'Iota' ('14). Amos Perry was more prolific, introducing 13 cultivars, bringing in *I. douglasiana* and *I. bracteata* into the gene pool. Perhaps more importantly, Perry was the first to cross PCNs with the 40-chromosome Siberian irises, resulting in the production of the first three CalSibes: 'Dougbractifor' ('29), 'Dougraphes' ('24), and 'Margot Holmes' ('27). The latter, a red-violet, is still extant and won the very first

English Dykes Medal. H. Senior Fothergill added to this early English domination of PCN hybridization. He introduced 14 cultivars, mostly from crosses of *I. douglasiana* and *I. tenax*. Combinations of these two species make especially good garden plants, with the vigor and branching of *I. douglasiana* and the yellow colors and patterns from *I. innominata*.

Finally the Americans caught on! Little known hybridizer Edith English of Washington had been crossing *I. douglasiana* and *I. innominata* although none were officially registered; her 'Golden Nymph' was grown for years, even winning a High Commendation at the Wisley trials in 1983. Fred DeForest of Canby, Oregon, had a well respected program in bearded irises, winning several Dykes Medals. However, during the 1930s and 1940s, he hybridized PCNs and introduced fourteen to the market. None of these seem to be involved in subsequent hybrids, however.

The next great group of PCN hybridizers occurred in Southern California. Eric Nies, the dean of early spuria hybridizers, also made significant progress in PCN breeding. In 1943 he introduced the very vigorous 'Orchid Sprite' (Nies '43), perhaps a selection from *I. douglasiana*, which would win the first Award of Merit for a PCN cultivar. The most famous and most used Nies cultivar is 'Amiguita' (Nies '47), an *I. douglasiana* selection in shades of blue-violet with a deeper signal. Both of these cultivars imparted good growing qualities, clear colors and wider forms to their progeny. Marion Walker inherited the Nies stock and produced

'Ojai' (Walker '60) and 'Violet Elf' (Walker '60) from the Nies plants. Actually, 'Ojai' represents the first use of the Australian Danks strain with the American hybrids and is sort of like an intensified version of 'Amiguita'. It would win the very first Mitchell Award in 1975. Richard Luhrsen registered a number of hybrids but only the unregistered blue bitone with a deeper fall spot 'Ami-Royale' ('57), a seedling from 'Amiguita', is well distributed. 'Ami-Royale' is a very vigorous and persistent clone that is often carried by nurseries on the West Coast. Similarly, of the eleven cultivars registered by George Stambach, only Mitchell Award winner 'Western Queen' (Stambach '72), yellow with brown signal 'Garden Delight' (Stambach '75), and one of the first good reds 'Pasadena Indian' (Stambach '62) survive to this day.

Oddly, Sydney Mitchell, for whom the top award for Pacific Coast Native Irises is named, never registered or introduced any of his PCN seedlings. However, he was a strong promoter of this type and his book *Irises for Every Garden* (1949) championed the use of PCNs. Moreover, he spread seed of his hybrids around the world. One of his protégés, Jack Craig, did name a few of the cultivars from these lines and sent seed from improvements of the original Mitchell PCNs around the world of this "Mitchell-Craig strain." These would form some of the basis of the Ghio and other lines. Here is an excerpt from Jack Craig's 1959 Blossom Valley Gardens catalog promoting the Pacific Coast Native irises:

WESTERN NATIVES: To encourage interest in Western Native Iris I will send seeds of Mitchell, Danks and other hybrids free with any order, or for 25¢ plus a stamped, self-addressed envelope. These hybrids have blood of Douglasiana, Innominata and Tenax in different amounts and will range in color from white, blue, lavender, rose, pink, buff, yellow, red and purple. Germination occurs in spring from fall planted seeds. Plant in acid soil in part shade.

This excerpt shows that the range of colors available in 1959 was already quite extensive and nearly match the colors we see today.

Lee Lenz had a unique opportunity to hybridize PCNs as he was a member and finally director of the Rancho Santa Botanical Garden. The mission of the garden was to investigate and improve upon the Western US flora and the PCNs were certainly a group worthy of his study. From 1949 until 1983 he introduced over twenty-five hybrids. Perhaps most importantly he brought in several species that had been ignored by other

'Moderator'

'Blushing Dawn'

'Licton Springs'

'Pacific Dome'

Vaughn seedling

Vaughn seedling

Ruth Hardy of Oregon collected many wild clones of PCNs. Although most were not introduced to commerce, her 'Valley Banner' (Hardy '68) was introduced by the famous Siskiyou Nursery, a purveyor of choice rock garden plants and perennials. 'Valley Banner', a *tenax-chrysophylla* natural hybrid, is a white flower that is boldly veined purple and with very prominent purple styles. This pattern, known as the 'Valley Banner' pattern has been taken into all permutations of ground color and extent of the pattern by subsequent hybridizers.

Marjorie Brummitt, best known for her work with Siberian irises, also did seminal work in the PCNs. Although her Siberians and her husband's bearded iris seedlings were grown on another lot, she grew the PCNs in a large bed along paths in the home garden. She used a combination of the Lenz and Nies hybrids along with her own crosses of the species *I. douglasiana* and *I. innominata* to create her lines. Most of the Brummitt PCNs have the prefix "Banbury," for the town in England in which she lived. Although many of these have not reached the United States, her 'Sugar Candy' (Brummitt '74) was introduced by Bay View Gardens in California. The Brummitt hybrids won many awards in the United Kingdom including Wisley Trial awards for 'Banbury Beauty' (Brummitt

breeders, chiefly *I. munzii* and *I. bracteata*. These two species contributed a really clear blue color, and wide form with ruffles, respectively. The yellow with brown-lined fall duo 'Ripple Rock' (Lenz '66) and 'Grubstake' (Lenz '66) involve crosses of *I. bracteata* to other PCN species (P. Edinger, personal communication) and these hybrids have the rounder form and ruffling that this species brings to the hybrids. Both of these have been used by other hybridizers to incorporate these qualities in their hybrids. 'Alma Abell' (Lenz '80) is a direct cross of *I. munzii* and *I. douglasiana* and was the first to show that unique turquoise color that can appear in *munzii* derivatives. From 'Alma Abell' came two more outstanding blues, 'Claremont Bluebird' (Lenz '80) and 'Claremont Blue Jay' (Lenz '83). 'Sierra Sapphire' (Lenz '72), a pure *munzii* seedling, is a brilliant light blue that won the Mitchell Award in 1977. One of the earlier Lenz hybrids, 'Claremont Indian' (Lenz '56), is the first of the red PCNs that result when yellow carotenoids are over-layered with red-purple anthocyanins. 'Claremont Indian' is in the background of many of the red PCNs.

'Night Crossing'

'Caught in the Wind'

'Distant Nebula'

'Pacific Rim'

Hargreaves strains, so he was starting with the best material of the day to build his strain. Perhaps the most exciting of the Ghio hybrids are variations on the 'Valley Banner' pattern in which the styles are conspicuously darker than the remainder of the petal and generally there is strong anthocyanin veining on the falls and sometimes the standards as well. The Ghio hybrids show extremes of this pattern from blooms nearly completely striped and solid to nearly white flowers with blue styles. Among the lighter ones of the 'Valley Banner' pattern are the whites with small bits of blue veining and blue styles such as 'Fresh Eyes' (Ghio '12), the very vigorous large-flowered 'Costanoa' (Ghio '11), white marked finely

'74), 'Banbury Fair' (Brummitt '74), 'Banbury Gem' (Brummitt '72), 'Banbury Gnome' (Brummitt '74), 'Banbury Magic' (Brummitt '71), 'Banbury Moon' (Brummitt '74), and 'Banbury Snowflake' (Brummitt '74). She also won the Hugh Miller Trophy (best beardless iris) for 'Banbury Velvet' (Brummitt '74), and 'No Name' (Brummitt '73) won both the Hugh Miller Trophy and the British Dykes Medal, the only time a PCN was so honored. The name 'No Name' was a nod to the Latin name for *I. innominata*, literally meaning "no name."

Joe Ghio was already an established breeder of tall bearded irises when he turned his attention to the PCNs or as Ghio refers to them, "Pacificas." Ghio's work totally revolutionized our concept of PCNs. What Ghio did was to transform the plant from the glorified wildling into a round and ruffled (called "the Ghio form") flower and in colors and patterns that were unthinkable before he started breeding. Moreover, he sold seed of his strain throughout the world so that growers that had difficulty in transplanting named cultivars might have more luck in growing them from seed. Almost everyone grew some PCNs from Ghio's seed; the quality of the blossoms was quite amazing. Ghio introduced almost 350 PCNs and I'm only able to touch on a few of them here, mostly some of the newer ones that represent the ultimate in his breeding lines in each of the particular colors and patterns. His record of Mitchell Medal winners is untouched by any other hybridizer and Ghio must have a wall of them by this point! His lines started with the best of the Nies-Walker plants plus seedlings from the Mitchell-Craig and

but intensely blue 'Corralitos Creek' (Ghio '13) and more purple-veined 'Spritzer' (Ghio '10). The next darker group, with slightly more extensive veining, include the bold flower 'Bar Code' (Ghio '04), spidery-veined on a blue background 'Foggy Days' (Ghio '11) and blue standards/white falls veined and edged blue 'Caught in the Wind' (Ghio '12). The darkest of the 'Valley Banner' types verge on dark self-colored blossoms with the veining so intense and extensive, little of the white shows through. These include the lovely and vigorous 'Night Crossing' (Ghio '11) and 'Power Center' (Ghio '12) with a near black spot on the falls. There is a group of Ghio hybrids that I describe as "root beer" colors that are the result of violet and blue anthocyanin colors overlaying cream to yellow base colors. Because of the patterns for color distribution of the purple and yellow pigments, there is an almost infinite variety of color combinations that can be obtained with colors ranging from apricot to dark brown and with all sorts of markings. Foremost among these colors are the toasted gold 'Wilder Ranch' (Ghio '13), dinner-plate formed mauve-apricot blend 'Muwekma' (Ghio '11), deep root beer colored 'Point Lobos' (Ghio '12), apricot with violet edges 'Buffed' (Ghio '03), ruffled root beer with mahogany signal 'Bubble Wrap' (Ghio '05), apricot with mahogany highlights 'Star of Wonder' (Ghio '02), and ruffled mauve and henna blend 'Chemeketa' (Ghio '13). Several of these overlay patterns resemble the plicata patterns of bearded irises including yellow base with rose stitching 'Patchen Pass' (Ghio '13), white blue stitching 'Drip Drop' (Ghio '00), and banded and dotted wine purple on a

latter group often contains areas of the petal that contain flashes of ruby red, most of these latter descended from the eye-catching 'Epicure' (Ghio '03). All of these are lovely flowers but some of my favorites are the red-black with ruby heart 'Wandering Eye' (Ghio '11) and 'War Zone' (Ghio '08), cartwheel-formed 'Red Flag Warning' (Ghio '10) and purple-black 'San Ardo' (Ghio '02). Two of my favorite Ghio irises are his two wonderful bright blues the white overlaid blue 'Bay Street' (Ghio '08) and the incredibly intense nearly turquoise blue 'Blue Plate Special' (Ghio '03). Finally one white, the incredibly ruffled and beautifully formed 'Air Waves' (Ghio '10), which is by far the finest of the white PCNs to date.

Bennett Jones, one of the premier breeders of median irises, introduced only one PCN, but it was a really good one. 'Pacific Rim' (Jones '91) has blue standards, bordered white and white falls with a prominent ¼" blue rim. Although the exact pedigree is not published, 'Pacific Rim' comes from seedlings from Lenz, Abell, Cosgrove and Ghio, and does show the influence of many species. 'Pacific Rim' would win the Mitchell Medal in 1998.

Lewis and Adele Lawyer worked for many years in the vegetable crop breeding world and they would bring this knowledge to their PCN hybridizing as well. Their primary hybridizing interest was in pursuit of blue PCNs. Many of the Lawyer hybrids descend from the Ghio hybrid 'Soquel Cove', a hybrid that combines *I. munzii* with the wide-petaled Ghio lines. An *I. munzii* seedling × 'Soquel Cove' gave the cobalt blue 'Sierra Butterflies' (Lawyer '84) and French blue 'Sierra Stars' (Lawyer '84). A cross of another 'Soquel Cove' seedling with 'Sierra Butterflies' gave the ruffled ultimate gentian blue 'Sierra Dell' (Lawyer '88). 'Sierra Dell' won the Mitchell Medal in 1995. Another important Lawyer hybrid is the four-species hybrid 'Foothill Banner' (Lawyer '90), a vastly improved version of 'Valley Banner' that adds *I. munzii* to the complex. Before giving up their hybridizing, they would create a strain of very late flowering plants (Lawyer 1996) that hopefully are being used by other breeders as seeds from this group were shared with the seed exchanges.

yellow ground 'Wino' (Ghio '08). Ghio has created some incredible gold-flowered PCNs, and some of these have brilliant or contrasted signals as well. These include the incredibly vigorous and floriferous 'Going Bananas' (Ghio '10), very wide-petaled 'Cashing In' (Ghio '08), blue signaled 'Vain' (Ghio '07), mango orange with violet spots 'Rodeo Gulch' (Ghio '04), and butterscotch gold with violet signal spots 'Paicines' (Ghio '07). Ghio's dark flowers are some of his best and they approach black from both the purple side and the red side of the spectrum. This

'Valley Banner'

Vernon Wood was famous for his pink tall bearded iris and almost all of his introductions were in the color range of pink to raspberry. He would also tackle these colors in his PCN breeding. 'Pink Cupid' (Wood '93) is a big stride in these colors, a clear pink with red-purple venation on the falls. It is derived from Ghio lines and has the Ghio form. 'Pink Cupid' won the Mitchell Medal in 2000. 'Pinole Princess' (Wood ' 02) is a more pure pink than its mother 'Pink Cupid' and combines the Ghio apricot 'Local Girl' for an even wider more ruffled flower. Wood's 'Distant Nebula' (Wood '95), is raspberry-orchid with a red black signal on the falls and comes from Ghio lines. The 'Distant Nebula' seedling, 'Raspberry Dazzler' (Wood '96) is an even more intense version of its parent and with luscious veins of a deeper raspberry throughout the blossom.

Not all of Wood's PCN breeding would be in the pink-raspberry color range. 'Three Cornered Hat' (Wood '85), a deep gold with deeper fall ray pattern, would give rise to the more intense 'Mimsey' (Wood '88), on which the veins on the falls are a good brown. 'Mimsey' would give the bright gold with copper fall spot 'Aztec Robe' (Wood '89) and the gold with red veins 'Roman Festival' (Wood '96). Another 'Three Cornered Hat' derivative, the bright red-violet with lighter edges and darker veins 'Indian Paintbrush' (Wood '92) would start another line of bright-colored PCNs, leading to the most brilliant of the yellow with red markings 'Devil's Cauldron' (Wood '04). The Wood white with blue veins line started with the cream veined blue 'Different Drummer' (Wood '87), a seedling from Ghio mixed seed. 'Different Drummer' would give rise to the improved version 'Star Symphony' (Wood '91) which would sire 'Sea Admiral' (Wood '95), a white heavily veined violet with the falls rims leaving a clear ¼" edge of white. 'Sea Admiral' won the Mitchell Medal in 2003.

Colin Rigby greatly increased interest in PCNs by his nursery Portable Acres, which featured these irises and introduced hybrids from many West Coast hybridizers. Besides this contribution, Rigby introduced the very popular blue-violet 'Jean Erickson' (Rigby '93), a seedling of the very vigorous 'Canyon Creek'. 'Jean Erickson' won the Mitchell Medal in 2001. He also introduced another 'Canyon Creek' seedling, 'Cache Creek' (Rigby '93), this time in cream.

Lois Belardi lines are based upon the Ghio lines, especially the 'Valley Banner' type 'Idylwild', which is the parent of 'Skylash' (Belardi '94), a variation on the 'Valley Banner' pattern with lovely form. 'Idylwild' also was the base of a line of blue flowers starting with 'Sea Gal' (Belardi '94), which gave rise to 'Marine Magic' (Belardi '95) and the much deeper blue 'Deep Magic' (Belardi '98) and the ruffled blue 'Pacific Miss' (Belardi '99). Combining 'Skylash' seedlings with 'Marine Magic' gave the white with blue borders 'Steamer Line' (Belardi '02). My favorite of the Belardi irises is 'This Is It' (Belardi '10), a yellow ground plicata type with bright blue-violet stitching.

Will Plotner has been involved with the Species Iris Group of North America and his blue violet blend 'Wild Survivor' (Plotner '03) is a second generation hybrid of *I. tenax* and a pale blue *I. douglasiana*. 'Wild Survivor' is a very vigorous grower and won the Mitchell Medal as a testament to its adaptability and garden presence.

While all of this was happening in Britain and the United States, a quiet revolution of the PCNs was being carried out in Australia (Blyth 1997). Fred Danks and Dan Hargrave both started hybridizing PCNs in the late 1940s. Some of this material was from the Craig-Mitchell strain, others from seed houses such as Thompson and Morgan. Hargrave disappeared from the iris scene for many years and Australians propagated descendants of the Danks strain. Some seed of the Danks strain would also reach the United States and was incorporated into the Ghio strain. About 1972, Barry Blyth, who had been growing seedlings from the Danks and Ghio strain, was visited by Dan Hargrave. After viewing Blyth's plantings, he remarked, "Plough them in and come and see mine." After seeing Hargrave's planting, Blyth did plough his under! Blyth began growing the Hargrave strain and also incorporating the recent Ghio hybrids into his introductions. From these crosses, Blyth introduced more than twenty-five PCN hybrids, most named for Australian locations or Aboriginal names. Unfortunately, these seem not to have made it to the United States, except perhaps through seed. Blyth's daughter Heidi took over the strain and produced some outstanding seedlings. Illness has prevented her from working this strain fully. Ivar Schmidt and Alan Glenn also picked up working on these strains and registered a number of new hybrids. The most recent Australian to take up hybridizing is the outstanding Louisiana iris hybridizer John Taylor, who has taken this strain to a new level of perfection and variety. Examples of some of his seedlings are shown here to give the reader an idea as to the exciting developments that will be available in the near future. Hopefully there will be some successful importation of this strain to the United States. These are a new revolution in the Pacific Coast Native irises, with amazing patterns and very intense colors.

A FEW FAVORITES

Because PCNs are in general short-lived and because of the lack of dealers, the selection of PCNs, especially older ones, available in nurseries is often limited. Several of these older clones are especially vigorous and persistent and might be good choices for a beginner.

OLDER FAVORITES

'Amiguita' (Nies '46) This is the first famous PCN. 'Amiguita' is a lovely blue-lavender with a deeper intensification in the signal area. It has wider parts than most species and a well

'Canyon Snow'

branched stalk. This outstanding selection has proven to be a useful parent, siring a number of outstanding hybrids and in the background of many. This PCN survived one season in New England and bloomed once. It was not equipped for Zone 4 winters though!

'Canyon Snow' (Emery '75) Most PCNs have trouble growing in areas outside the coastal Pacific. 'Canyon Snow' grows well in a variety of climates and is exceedingly vigorous. A clean white flower with a small yellow signal and flowers of good width. If you are considering growing PCNs and live in a less than ideal climate, this is the one with which to start.

'Ojai' (Walker '60) This is a seedling of 'Amiguita' but with more intense coloration and a bit wider parts. Marion Walker inherited the Nies breeding stalk and this is an improvement upon its parent.

'Costanoa'

NEWER FAVORITES

'Costanoa' (Ghio '11) Ghio has introduced a number of variations in the 'Valley Banner' pattern of white veined with blue. This is more subtly marked than most with a turquoise blue blot at the signal and whisker veins of the same shade. Flowers have very wide parts. Outstanding vigor.

'Blue Plate Special' (Ghio '03) If I could grow but one PCN, this would be it. Shockingly blue flowers are indicators of *I. munzii* in its pedigree. The flowers are wide and lightly ruffled. The stalk has three to four flowers per stalk, making for a longer bloom season. Very good plant health.

'High Fire Danger' (Ghio '11) Wow what a color. A black strongly infused with red and prominent yellowish style arms. A good grower.

'Air Waves' (Ghio '09) Bright clear white with wide form and ruffles. Small yellow signal does not detract from the effect of whiteness.

'Blue Moment' (Meek '03) A very nice wide navy blue with outstanding growth habits. Probably the finest from this hybridizer.

'Going Bananas' (Ghio '09) A dark gold with a dime-sized spot of white at the signal area. Very wide, round and ruffled. This is the most vigorous of the Ghio gold ones I grow and a very nice garden plant.

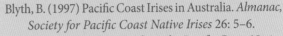

REFERENCES

Blyth, B. (1997) Pacific Coast Irises in Australia. *Almanac, Society for Pacific Coast Native Irises* 26: 5–6.

Cohen, V.A. (1967) *A Guide to the Pacific Coast Native Irises.* British Iris Society Publication, London.

Hill, E. (1997) More borer problems. *Almanac, Society for Pacific Coast Native Irises* 26(1): 6.

Lawyer, L. (1996) Extending the PCI bloom season. *Almanac, Society for Pacific Coast Native Irises* 24 (2): 13–14.

Lenz, L.W. (1958) A revision of the Pacific Coast irises. *Aliso* 4: 1–72.

Lenz, L.W. (1959) Hybridization and speciation in the Pacific Coast irises. *Aliso* 4: 237–309.

Wilson, C.A. (2004) Phylogeny of *Iris* based on chloroplast *matk* gene and *trnK* intron sequence data. *Molecular Phylogenetics and Evolution* 33: 402–412.

'Blue Plate Special'

5 LOUISIANA IRISES

In the bayous of Louisiana and adjacent Southern states, the six species involved in the complex of species known as Louisiana irises, were being extensively intercrossed by bees and hummingbirds, leading to a series of species hybrids that ranged in color from white to nearly black. When these irises were discovered by such workers as Mary Swords DeBaillon, W.B. MacMillan and Dr. John Small, the news of these irises made such a horticultural impact that articles even appeared in the *New York Times*. Literally miles and miles of swampland were covered in various species and hybrids, causing Dr. Small to call Louisiana the "center of the iris universe." These discoveries led to a period when gardeners braved the swamps to collect the more unusual hybrids and species selections so that almost all of the first named varieties were simple selections from the swamp. Tales of these early collecting trips are quite amazing, with certain individuals being particularly adept at keeping the ubiquitous venomous snakes at bay, while a piece from a particularly nice clone was removed from a clump! These collection trips gave a good base to extensive hybridization that would follow. Amazingly, in less than a hundred years since the discovery of these irises in the swamps of Louisiana, they have become one of the most highly sophisticated irises in terms of color and form.

Louisiana irises have some of the brightest flowers of any iris. Blue flowers that are derived from *I. brevicaulis* have an almost electric blue color. Among the Louisiana irises, truer red flowers are found than any other of the iris groups. Stalks will have three to four bud positions, with multiple buds at each position, allowing for several weeks of a bloom from a given cultivar. Because the species have a bloom season that covers a period of 6 to 8 weeks, a judicious choice of cultivars will allow a garden planting to bloom over a similarly extended period. Although the selections from the swamp were mostly tailored flowers, the more modern hybrids are often extensively ruffled. Many Louisiana irises are tall plants and with big foliage that make large clumps in the garden. However, the species *I. fulva* and *I. brevicaulis*, are shorter (10 to 24" tall) and hybrids involving them are of shorter height with smaller flowers.

'All Fired Up'

Flower forms are quite variable in the hybrids ranging from the more drooping pendant forms to the nearly flat Japanese iris-like forms that are most popular today. Marvin Granger produced a series of double Louisiana flowers that result from the conversion of anthers into petaloid-like structures. A few Louisiana iris cultivars have a spidery form, much like the narrow-petal daylilies. 'Black Widow' is the most popular of this spider type and is a true garden conversation piece.

Although Louisiana irises are plants of swamps, they are highly adaptable to garden conditions. Most gardeners grow hybrid daylilies well in the same beds that grow Louisiana irises. They can of course be grown in shallow standing water and continually moist conditions and are one of the few garden perennials that not only tolerate but burgeon under these conditions.

CULTURE AND GARDEN USE

Louisiana irises are generally big plants (exceptions noted in the small and miniature section below) and should be planted so that they can expand to 2 to 3' in three years. The position should be in the sun in the Northern states but in the Southern United States and in desert climates, some shade is beneficial. Louisiana irises are heavy feeders so the soil should be prepared before planting with added compost and composted animal manures, peat moss or other organic matter that will help hold moisture. A clever solution to growing Louisiana irises is to place kiddie wading pools in the flower beds. The pools have slits cut in the bottom to allow some water movement from the pool. A hole in the bed is dug to accommodate the pool, the pool inserted into the hole, and then the pool is filled to the brim with good garden soil supplemented as suggested above. This allows an area with greater water retention in a bed that might not even be suitable for Louisiana irises and can easily be flooded by a garden hose without causing overwatering for nearby plants. Another strategy that works well for growing Louisiana irises is to position Louisiana beds that are just slightly lower than the level of the lawn. Excess water and fertilizer from the lawn flows into the bed of Louisiana irises and growth is exceptional. Here in Oregon, my property has a rather steep hillside and positioning the Louisiana iris beds at the base of the hill allows them to collect the extra moisture. This would be a difficult place to grow many plants but the Louisiana irises thrive in such locations. If you have koi ponds, then Louisiana irises are a great choice for use in these ponds. Because Louisiana irises are such heavy feeders, they absorb much of the nitrogen that might induce algal bloom, thus keeping the pond more pristine. Koi do occasionally uproot newly planted irises, so it is best to pot the irises, let them become established, and insert the potted irises into the pool.

In the Southern United States and the West Coast of the United States, where one grows Louisiana irises in the garden is a matter of choice for the gardener. Louisiana irises look good in flower beds that grow daylilies and other plants that want a bit of extra moisture during the growing season. Louisiana iris rhizomes are long so the clumps tend to wander. In fact a bed planted with daylilies interspersed between the clumps of Louisiana irises will keep the irises from wandering into each other. In the South and other climates through Zone 8, Louisiana irises may be grown in submerged or semi-submerged conditions year-round. In my garden in Oregon, I inherited a rather ugly water feature from the previous owner. By filling in the bowl of the water feature with soil up to about 6" from the brim, the water feature became a large planter for Louisiana irises with the rains adding enough moisture to cover the rhizomes with 2 to 4" of water for most of the year. With the water over the top of the plants, virtually no weeds grow in this bed.

Jim Leonard, in Lafayette, Louisiana, grows many of his Louisianas in barrels that are approximately 2' tall and about 3' in diameter. The barrels are filled up to approximately 4" from the top of the barrel with soil and a constant 2 to 4" of water is maintained by irrigation of the barrels. The rhizomes grow in the soil and are constantly moist, not unlike the native irises growing nearby in the swamps. It should be noted that not all Louisiana irises prefer this sort of culture although ones with a predominance of *I. giganticaerulea* and *I. nelsonii* blood in general perform very well under these conditions.

In the South, one rather unusual plant to include with Louisiana irises is the so-called swamp penstemon, *Penstemon tenuis*. This species prefers moist conditions and produces an abundance of small orchid blossoms that bloom with the irises and complement the bed. They do self-seed but are never invasive. *Penstemon digitalis*, especially the dark-leaved clones such as 'Husker Red' or 'Dark Towers', are useful in bed cultures. The foliage on these adds a note of interest throughout the season.

Other good companion plants include spiderworts (*Tradescantia* cultivars), daylilies, and many other beardless irises described in this book that prefer a little extra moisture. I still prefer Louisiana irises massed with little other companion plant material, much as they look in the swamps of Louisiana in their stands that can stretch for miles.

'Aqua Velva'

or bricks. Winter winds are strong and I have watched many a piece of Remay go somewhere in Oz after coming loose after a 50-mile-per-hour wind!

Compared to other beardless irises, transplanting Louisiana irises is rather simple. Louisiana iris rhizomes are much larger than other beardless irises. Rhizomes are generally obtained from nurseries in the fall, although some nurseries will ship plants early in the spring or right after blooming. Plant the rhizomes around 1" deep in the soil with the long roots spread to each side of the rhizome. Pack the soil and water with a weak fertilizer suitable for transplanting. Keep the soil moist but not sopping wet until new growth is observed. If the irises are growing in a bed, the addition of a mulch of ground

Although Louisiana irises are quite hardy, surviving and even burgeoning in South Dakota and upstate New York, there are areas where they grow less well. Bee Warburton of Westborough, Massachusetts, became interested in Louisiana irises but she lived in a very cold pocket of Worcester County, probably borderline Zone 4. She ordered a number of new hybrids derived from *giganticaerulea – nelsonii* blood from Charles Arny in Louisiana as a trial. Although most were not successful, a seedling of Arny's nicknamed "Bayou Goula" performed very well. Species derived from *I. fulva* and *I. brevicaulis* such as 'Dorothea K. Williamson' and Preston Hale's 'Red Dazzler' also performed well. Warburton did not deep mulch her irises in the winter. At my folks' property we had similarly cold weather but I had more success by putting evergreen boughs, pine straw, and bracken fern fronds around and over the plants as cold weather approached. The bed was placed on the west side of the house so was afforded some protection by the building. Bloom was good using these conditions and no plant losses were noted. Barbara and David Schmeider also had success using a similar strategy in their garden in Concord, Massachusetts. Another solution to the problem of mulching the Louisiana irises for the winter is using products called "Garden Quilt" or "Remay" that can be used to cover whole beds of plants. The fabric can be tied to the ground with landscape pins or weighted down with rocks

pine bark, pine straw or salt marsh hay will improve not only the chance for the survival of the plant but also the moisture retention of the soil.

When someone tells me that they are having problems growing Louisiana irises, I just bluntly say, "You're either not giving them enough fertilizer or enough water." That does solve a majority of cultural problems with these plants! About 6 weeks before bloom, a good fertilizing with a balanced (e.g., 10-10-10) fertilizer and a good inch of water per week until the flowers have bloomed will result in the best bloom and plant health. Another fertilizing early in the fall will help the plants produce increase and set bloomstalks for the following spring. A lot of the growth of Louisiana irises occurs during the winter months in the South and Pacific Northwest.

In Northern climates, culture is slightly different. In these climates the Louisiana irises should not be allowed to go dormant in the summer. Keep the water to the plant during the summer so that growth is sufficient to support bloom. Lessen the water and fertilizer as fall approaches so that the irises are hardened off a bit before really cold weather arrives.

Louisiana irises are relatively trouble free as a group as long as their needs are met. Early cultivars often contracted rust although modern cultivars rarely do. Here in the Pacific Northwest we do see some slug damage in the winter, partly because Louisiana irises are one of the few fresh green leaves in the winter. Either using slug bait or growing the Louisiana irises in standing water are ways to combat the slug problem. The slugs don't do much real damage but they do abrade the leaf surface and small dark brown lesions result. In areas where iris borers are present, Louisiana irises, with their huge rhizomes, are a tasty choice for these pests. Luckily the borer invasion is rarely fatal as the injured rhizome will often make extra increase.

SMALL AND MINIATURE CULTIVARS

Most Louisiana iris cultivars are large plants with broad leaves and produce tall stalks. These are almost all descendants of *I. nelsonii* and *I. giganticaerulea*. Some cultivars, sometimes referred to as "patios," are much shorter, ranging from true dwarfs such as 'Trail of Tears' to intermediate sized plants such as 'Kitchen Music'. Most of these smaller cultivars have a preponderance of *I. fulva* and *I. brevicaulis* blood. The trio of Arkansas hybridizers Henry Rowlan, Frank Chowning, and Richard Morgan all contributed heavily to this hybridizing effort. Although many of the early *fulva-brevicaulis* hybrids had snaky stalks (e.g., 'Dorothea K. Williamson'), these hybridizers produced plants with sturdy stalks. Not all small Louisiana irises are derived from *fulva-brevicaulis* lines, however. Bernard Pryor has introduced a whole series of smaller Louisiana irises derived from *nelsonii-giganticaerulea* lines as is Faggard's small 'Bayou Short Stuff'. Unlike the bigger Louisiana irises, these smaller ones are very useful in the mixed border, making neat clumps.

TETRAPLOID LOUISIANA IRISES

Joseph Mertzweiller became fascinated with the idea of converting diploid Louisiana irises to tetraploids after observing the work of Currier McEwen doing so with Japanese and Siberian irises and many local Louisiana daylily hybridizers doing the same kind of conversions. Because Louisiana irises have much larger rhizomes than Japanese or Siberian irises, Mertzweiller was able to treat individual cultivars rather than just treating seedlings with colchicine. A critical conversion of the sterling parent 'Wheelhorse' was pivotal in producing really high quality tetraploids. The first two fully tetraploid Louisiana irises were named for Claude Davis and Ike Nelson, who were mentors of Mertzweiller during the initial phases of this work. 'Professor Claude' and 'Professor Ike' are both large purple irises that are difficult to distinguish. Ken Durio was one of the first to use these early tets and raised large numbers of seedlings from self-pollinating and intercrossing these cultivars. Besides the purples, he was able to produce 'Welcome Change' and 'Sauterne' that are yellows with infusions of violet in the standards. Joe Mertzweiller continued his

professor series with the rose-pink 'Professor Marta Marie', bright red 'Professor Jim', lavender 'Professor Paul', and a pair of yellows, 'Professor Fritchie' and 'Professor Barbara'. Durio continued his series with the first true white 'Patton Durio', named for his grandson. Other hybridizers would add a few more tetraploids, such as Rusty Osthemier's 'Doctor Ed', Sam Norris's 'Kentucky Cajun', and Bruner's 'Kentucky Thoroughbred'.

Despite these advances, there are problems with the tetraploids. Because of the thicker cells in tetraploid plants, the flowers have such heavy substance that the flowers tend to flip the falls up rather than lying flat. Some cultivars were better than others and some, like 'Professor Fritchie', open beautifully. A more serious problem is their infertility. The percentage of successful crosses is low and the number of seeds per pod is low and the percentage of seeds that germinated is also low. Out of hundreds of crosses I made, I only had four pods that had seeds and only two of them resulted in seedlings! You see why the production of a large number by Ken Durio was such an achievement. Oddly too, the tetraploids seemed to be much more cold-sensitive than the diploids. Even in Louisiana, Joe Mertzweiller suggested that tetraploids be grown near a building so that they would be more protected.

SPECIES INVOLVED IN LOUISIANA IRISES

Six species are involved in the Louisiana hybrids, with each contributing unique qualities to the hybrids. *Iris fulva* has beautiful brick red flowers on relatively short stalks, from 6" to 2' tall. This species is very hardy, growing as far north as the Ohio Valley. The selected cultivars bright red and well-formed 'Devil's Advocate' (McGarvey '72), chocolate-brown 'Bayou Bandit' (Weeks '98), and bright yellow 'Marvell Gold' (Waddick '91) are all variants worth growing. The other shorter species, *I. brevicaulis* (often referred to as *I. foliosa*), has strikingly bright blue flowers on 6- to 18"-tall stalks with a zig-zag pattern of branching. *Iris brevicaulis* grows as far north as southern Canada and is thus very hardy. Cultivars of this species include the pure white 'Trail of Tears' (Chowning '73) and 'Petite and Sweet' (Chowning '78), the white splashed blue 'Finders Keepers' (Chowning '66) and the rose pink 'Pink Joy Roberts' (Roberts '54). *Iris giganticaerulea* is the true giant of this group of irises with plants growing to 4' tall and forming large expanses of bloom in the bayous of Louisiana during the spring. Flowers of this species are a lavender-blue and are relatively large. Cultivars of this species were collected heavily by members of the Society for Louisiana Irises so that some outstanding clones were made available for hybridizers. Some of these cultivars are the pure white 'Barbara Elaine Taylor' (Taylor '54), 'Snow Goose' (Levingston '53) and the very broad-styled and frilly 'Her Highness' (Levingston '57), the large blue 'Ruth Holleyman' (Holleyman '54), and the double blue 'Creole Can-Can' (Granger

'58). *Iris nelsonii*, named for the late Ike Nelson, is found in a very small area around Abbeville, Louisiana, and was formerly called "Giant Fulva," as they appear to be like huge versions of *I. fulva*. Randolph (1966), using morphological criteria, determined that *I. nelsonii* was actually the result of ancient hybridization between *I. fulva*, *I. giganticaerulea* and *I. brevicaulis* and represent a stabilized hybrid that now bred true. These conjectures were supported by the studies of Arnold and colleagues (Arnold et al. 1990; 1991) who used DNA data that showed *I. nelsonii* had sequences unique to each of the proposed parents and chloroplast DNA identical to *I. fulva*. Because chloroplast DNA is maternally inherited, these workers could determine that *I. fulva* was the pod parent for the original cross that gave rise to what is now *I. nelsonii*. Many of the early named cultivars of Louisiana irises were collections of *I. nelsonii* from an area known to the early collectors as "Iris Heaven." Here colors of yellow, brown, plum, purple and red were found on plants 3 to 4' tall and with large flowers of a flat to pendant form. Outstanding among these are the very wide-petaled purple 'Peggy Mac' (MacMillan '43) and red-purple bitone 'Bayou Vermillion' (MacMillan '44). More recently Benny Trahan and Ken Durio have found a number of more interesting selections that we hope will be added to the gene pool of the modern Louisiana irises. *Iris hexagona* is one species that is not found in the swamps of Louisiana although this species is the prevalent species in Florida north to South Carolina. *Iris hexagona* is a big mainly blue flower although white forms are known. The bloom season of *I. hexagona* is much later than the other Louisiana irises and the flowers tend to have very strong substance. Relatively few hybridizers have incorporated *I. hexagona* in their breeding, although 'Lone Star' (Campbell '97) is an outstanding clone from a direct cross of *I. hexagona* and 'Clara Goula'.

HISTORY OF HYBRIDIZING

Recently the Society for Louisiana Irises has published two compendiums of the early (Caillet and Vaughn 2007) and later (Claunch 2012) hybridizers of Louisiana irises. Much was written in the hybridizer's own hand so we have a first-person account of their hybridizing activity, and these may be purchased from the Society for Louisiana Irises. These publications serve as a basis for the narrative here, as do the author's personal experiences with the plants and in some cases with the hybridizer him/herself.

Like many aspects of hybridizing beardless irises, hybridizing started in England with Dykes's cross of *I. fulva* and *I. brevicaulis* resulting in 'Fulvala', a nearly prostrate purple, still grown in Britain as a curiosity. In the United States, Bruce Williamson made the same cross and selected the bigger and showier dark purple 'Dorothea K. Williamson' (Williamson '18). 'Dorothea K. Williamson' is extremely hardy, surviving Zone 3 and 4 winters with no problem, as might be expected as both species grown into the Midwest and southern Canada and Bruce himself residing in Indiana. Oddly, 'Dorothea K. Williamson' did not spur on tremendous interest in these plants, despite its durability and beauty. It was not until many years later that this plant was used in crossing.

The next major push came in the state of Louisiana. Gardeners such as Mary Swords DeBaillon collected irises throughout the swamps in an effort to preserve and promote the local flora. She selected many clones and was one of the

> Many of the early named cultivars of Louisiana irises were collections of *I. nelsonii* from the swamps surrounding Abbeville, Louisiana—an area dubbed "Iris Heaven" by the early collectors. Here colors of yellow, brown, plum, purple and red were found on plants 3 to 4' tall.

ones instrumental for interest in Louisiana irises to this day. Moreover, she was one of the first to make crosses among these cultivars. The top award for Louisiana irises is named for this forward-thinking woman, who recognized the horticultural potential of these plants. Most appropriately the first DeBaillon Medal was awarded in 1948 to the iris named for her posthumously, 'Mary S. DeBaillon' (registered by Dormon '45), a pinkish lavender.

MacMillan (known affectionately as "Mister Mac") is perhaps the most important of the early hybridizers and collectors of Louisiana irises. In the swamps surrounding Abbeville, Louisiana, three species, *I. giganticaerulea*, *I. fulva*, and *I. brevicaulis* grow together and a stabilized natural hybrid, *I. nelsonii*, is found in close proximity. In this one area all of these species came together and would hybridize with each other, resulting in a nearly complete range of colors and types. This area was dubbed "Iris Heaven" and rightly so. Most important of these hybrids found in Iris Heaven were the very large reds, dubbed "Abbeville fulvas," but later recognized as *I. nelsonii*. To this point, the red irises had all been of the low, *I. fulva* type and rather small flowers; the Abbeville fulvas were large flowers on tall plants. MacMillan introduced this area to Mary Swords DeBaillon and it became a hotbed for collectors. I think you will be amused at the *way* MacMillan got to see Mary DeBaillon's garden after a chance meeting earlier in Florida. In his own words (MacMillan 1967):

> Our next encounter was in her own "far more than lovely" fifteen-acre garden located some five miles out of Lafayette, Louisiana, just off the present new Highway 10 as it passes Lafayette. Of course, I found that it was then, as now, enclosed in a netting wire fence that to me looked twelve feet tall, with the gates all locked; but I had to see Mary again, and having been brought up in West Texas and being naturally a friendly type, I took advantage of a strong-looking limb reaching from a sturdy inside oak to my side of the fence, and I soon found myself on the inside; and with the trespassing sign completely out of sight giving me a relatively clean conscience, I soon found Mary DeBaillon on her knees caressing a newly emerging camellia graft. If you could have seen her expression of mingled surprise and disbelief as she looked up and saw me, I am sure you would have agreed that we were by that time irrevocably introduced; and the smile that followed, though perhaps grudgingly given, told me that we were also friends forever.

The lengths to which MacMillan went to visit this horticultural giant certainly speak volumes for his enthusiasm for all things horticultural. It was a good thing because this "introduction" took Mary DeBaillon to the Abbeville swamps and all the tremendous variety of colors and forms that were there.

Many of MacMillan's early introductions such as the dark 'Haile Selassie' (MacMillan '43), dark red 'Bayou Vermillion' (MacMillan '43), and very wide-petaled 'Peggy Mac' (named for his wife; MacMillan '43) were collected from the Abbeville swamps. Ike Nelson commented that 'Haile Selassie' was discovered where the "upland foliosa (= *I. brevicaulis*) meets the Abbeville reds." These show the big plant habits of the Abbeville reds but with darker coloration and the more widely spaced branching habits of *I. brevicaulis*. All of these collected natural hybrids would become important parents for further hybrids. Later

MacMillan began to grow seedlings from collected seeds and later to hybridize. Mary Swords DeBaillon gave MacMillan the seed from her last crosses and the monumental 'Bayou Sunset' (MacMillan '45) arose from these seeds, which became the winner of the DeBaillon Medal in 1949. 'Bayou Sunset' was a blend of sunset colors and has a very distinctive sort of sprayed signal pattern that it passed to its offspring. One of my favorite Louisiana irises is the very spidery-formed 'Black Widow' (MacMillan '53). The petals are nearly black and are dispersed nicely along the stalk, looking much like a sea of spiders. It won the DeBaillon Award in 1968 after it was one of the stars at the American Iris Society convention in California. Later greats from Mr. Mac include magenta 'Olivier Monette' (MacMillan '70), the large blue with white styles 'Mac's Blue Heaven' (MacMillan '70), one of the first purple overlaid yellow creating a brown color 'Harland K. Riley' (MacMillan '70), and the first of the dark-edged/light petal Louisiana irises 'Margaret Hunter' (MacMillan '70). Mr. Mac also hybridized daylilies and produced some of the most amazing cultivars of the day. When bed space became tight he sold off his Louisiana irises to Ken Durio. His logic was that he could sell a daylily for $25 but an iris only for $5!

The next center of Louisiana iris hybridizing occurred in the northwest corner of Louisiana, near Shreveport. All of these hybridizers had large gardens (sometimes many acres of gardens) that featured all the new Louisiana irises plus many seedlings from their own hybridizing. Lillian Trichel started early in making hand crosses of Louisiana irises, being the first to cross red flowers with the white variants of *I. giganticaerulea,* resulting in the first approaches to pink flowers, a hybrid named 'Lilyana'. Her 'Haile Selaissie II' (Trichel '50) was one of the darkest red-violets of the early era of hybridizing and her 'Caddo' (Trichel '50) was one of the broader bronze reds and won the DeBaillon Award in 1950. It is a cross of the pink 'Lilyana' with red 'Bayou Vermillion'. Trichel's hybrids were introduced by Fairmount Gardens in Massachusetts and also grown by a number of California nurseries, ensuring a wide distribution. Lenora Matthews introduced a number of irises in the 1950s and her 'Dixie Dusk' (Matthews '50), one of the darkest purples of the day, won the DeBaillon Award in 1962. Sally Smith has the distinction of being the only hybridizer for winning a President's Cup (favorite iris seen at a national convention of the American Iris Society) awarded to a Louisiana iris for her wide-petaled maroon 'Royal Gem' (Smith '47). Smith's other major introduction is 'Blue Chip' (Smith '50), a clear blue with very wide petals. 'Blue Chip' won the DeBaillon Award in 1957. All of these yards were toured during the American Iris Society convention in 1951 and did much to promote interest in Louisiana irises with the larger membership, whose main interest was centered on tall bearded irises.

Mr. Mac also produced some of the most amazing daylily cultivars of the day. When bed space became tight, he sold off his Louisiana irises to Ken Durio. His logic: he could sell a daylily for $25 but an iris only for $5.

Caroline Dorman was a woman of many talents: artist, naturalist and horticulturist supreme. The nature preserve Briarwood in Saline, Louisiana, was established by her to preserve the best of the wild Louisiana flora and much of her Louisiana iris plantings still exist on the grounds of this preserve. I was privileged to visit her lovely place that was so lovingly cared for by her long-time friend Richard Johnson. It truly is a shrine to American wildflowers with Louisiana irises as its star. Dorman was introduced to Louisiana irises in the 1920s after seeing them growing wild in south Louisiana. Mary Swords DeBaillon willed her collection of irises to Dorman and Dorman quickly used these plants to develop a series of very lovely hybrids. Dorman's legacy is in taking the best of the recently discovered Abbeville reds, purples and yellows and combining them to bring out new colors and shades. Her dark violet 'Violet Ray' (Dormon '49), brilliant coral red 'Saucy Minx' (Dormon '49) and rose-pink 'Wheelhorse' (Dormon '52) are the best of these, each winning the DeBaillon Award and all proving to be exceptional parents as well. Indeed, Bill Levingston once said hybridizers were told to "'Wheelhorse' everything," meaning that they should cross 'Wheelhorse' with every other cultivar. This was generally good advice! 'Wheelhorse' did contain many genetic goodies, giving wide form and in many cases the first good quality yellows. Dorman's sister-in-law, Ruth Dormon, also grew and raised iris seedlings, most likely from bee pods. Her 'Wood Violet' (Dormon '43) is a very nice shorter dark blue violet that went on to win the DeBaillon Award in 1956.

Ike Nelson was a new professor at what is now the University of Louisiana Lafayette in the 1940s when MacMillan discovered the population of what is now *I. nelsonii*. He immediately recognized the significance of this population and recognized that not only were there huge reds but also purples that were the result of crosses to *I. giganticaerulea*. Nelson worked with Fitz Randolph to define the new species and the roles of the other species in this stabilized complex. Besides his role in defining this species, he also produced a number of outstanding hybrids. 'Cherry Bounce' (Nelson '46) came from crosses of selected wild irises and is a brilliant shade of red with an almost metallic sheen. It won the DeBaillon Award in 1951. 'Plum Good' (Nelson '51) is one of my favorites of Nelson's introductions, a very wide-petaled plum purple with a bright orange yellow signal. Although this iris is over sixty years old, it still fits in well with modern cultivars and is a unique color.

The next hotbed of Louisiana iris activity occurred in the Lake Charles area of Louisiana, with Bill Levingston, G.W. Holleyman, Bill Neugebauer, Sam Redburn, and Marvin Granger. All of these hybridizers were collectors first and they had the Cameron Swamps that contained large populations of *I. giganticaerulea* from which they could select the most unusual clones. The most important of these collected irises

from the Lake Charles swamps are the whites 'Snow Goose' (Levingston '53) and 'Her Highness' (Levingston '57), the huge blue 'Ruth Holleyman' (Holleyman '54) and the first double Louisiana iris 'Creole Can-Can' (Granger '56). 'Her Highness', with its huge prominent style arms and frilly petals, won the DeBaillon Award in 1957 and all of these irises would find their way into pedigrees of both theirs and others' irises.

G.W. Holleyman became a private oil lease broker, which enabled him to spend time on his hobbies, chief among them growing and hybridizing Louisiana irises. Three of the Holleyman irises have stood the test of time as cultivars and/or important parents. 'Pegalleta' (Holleyman '63) inherited its wide petals and dark purple color from its parent 'Peggy Mac' and 'Holleta' (Holleyman '52) contributed vigor to this hybrid. Indeed, 'Pegalleta' is a perfect iris for naturalizing as it will rapidly form clumps and is extremely floriferous. 'G.W. Holleyman' (Holleyman '60) was the first really high quality yellow Louisiana iris, which combines 'Wheelhorse', 'Peggy Mac', the Chowning yellows, and collected yellow irises. Aside from the flower color, 'G.W. Holleyman' had a marvelous stalk, often displaying three flowers out at time, making it an outstanding show flower. It is behind many of the best yellows to come subsequently. 'Queen o' Queens' (Holleyman '66) was the beginning of the very compact wide and ruffled form that is so much the norm now in Louisiana iris hybrids. The flowers are white, opening from cream buds and are delightfully ruffled.

Marvin Granger had the longest stint as a Louisiana iris hybridizer and many of his introductions stem either from his collected iris 'Creole Can-Can' (Granger '56) or from hybrids raised by his Lake Charles area colleagues. The double flowers of 'Creole Can-Can' proved quite a challenge for Granger to transmit into other colors. 'Creole Can-Can' has no pollen because the anthers have been converted into petals, the double trait is a recessive so that crosses to non-double flowers resulted in no doubles, and the blue-violet coloration of 'Creole Can-Can' is dominant to whites and other colors. However, these first generation crosses often resulted in cartwheel types in which the flowers were not double but the flowers had signals, generally only found on the falls, on all of the petals and are quite lovely themselves. 'Wheelhorse' proved to be a very useful parent, imparting wider petals, rose-red and yellow shades, and better plant habits when crossed into the doubles. Granger persisted in his breeding for doubles and after several generations of breeding he was able to produce an amazing array of doubles: the deep purple 'Double Talk' (Granger '71), the unruly yellow 'Creole Canary' (Granger '76), the rose-red 'Rose Cartwheel' (Granger '80), blue-purple 'Instant Replay' (Granger '81), light blue 'Flareout' (Granger '88) and the cream-white 'Starlite Starbrite' (Granger '85). Granger was also known for his line of orchid-pinks that started with his introduction of 'Bramble Queen' (Granger

'62), that combines white *giganticaerulea* and the Abbeville reds, much as did Lillian Trichel's pinks. Later developments in this line include one of the truest pinks 'Medora Wilson' (Granger '70), rose-pink 'Danielle' (Granger '88), and orchid-pink 'Oklahoma Kitty' (Granger '90), named for irrepressible Kitty Dyer. However, my favorite of the Granger pinks is the very lovely ruffled orchid-pink 'Kay Nelson' (Granger '86). It honors the departed American Iris Society registrar, a classy iris for a classy lady, and it won the DeBaillon Medal.

Frank Chowning broke the stranglehold of the state of Louisiana on the development of new Louisiana iris hybrids in his Little Rock, Arkansas, garden. His long career as a hybridizer was based upon *I. fulva* and *I. brevicaulis* that were not as widely used by the Louisiana hybridizers, but which conferred greater hardiness to his hybrids. 'Dixie Deb' (Chowning '50) was the first of Chowning's hybrids to receive national recognition, the flowers are yellow and of more pendant form but are born abundantly. The plant habit of 'Dixie Deb' is superb; Joe Mertzweiller once told me of a swamp that had completely filled with this cultivar. Now that's vigor! Seventeen years after it was introduced 'Dixie Deb' won the DeBaillon Award in 1967. It is still winning shows as it has copious buds and perfect branching so that three open flowers on a stalk are not rare. Three chiefly or totally *I. brevicaulis* hybrids include the small white 'Trail of Tears' (Chowning '73), sparkling blue 'Pristine Beauty' (Chowning '59) and tiny white 'Petite and Sweet' (Chowning '78) that kept the shorter and zigzag stems of the species, but added new colors and/or superior forms. Chowning had two very interesting smallish lines that are very distinct from those of his Southern Louisiana hybridizers, in no small part due to the use of *I. fulva*. A series of small brightly-colored irises, some with darker petal edges, are all on the short side, belying their strong *I. fulva* ancestry, are an important part of the Chowning legacy. This line has flowers that are bright golds variously infused, edged or lined with some shade of red. All are short and relatively small-flowered but have wider petals and more modern form than *I. fulva*. These hybrids include the gold-infused red 'Gold Reserve' (Chowning '73), cantaloupe-colored 'Melon Party' (Chowning '78), bright rose-red 'Miss Arkansas' (Chowning '73) and orange-red 'Shines Brightly' (Chowning '81). The most famous of the Chowning introductions are his DeBaillon Award and Medal winners: rose-pink 'This I Love' (Chowning '73), huge brick-red 'Ann Chowning' (Chowning '76) and black-purple 'Black Gamecock' (Chowning '78). The appearance of 'Ann Chowning' on the cover of the Melrose Gardens catalog, a beautiful color photo, assured its quick rise through the award system. 'Ann Chowning' proved to be an exceptional parent for red color and is involved in the pedigree of many subsequent award-wining irises. 'Black Gamecock' is not the most sophisticated form nor is it the darkest color but it had two very important attributes that ensured its success: it grew very vigorously, sometimes with 15 to 20 increases on each fan, and it grew equally well in very cold climates. If you live in a marginal climate for Louisiana irises, this is the iris for you. The Chowning iris also served as the basis for the breeding work of fellow Arkansas hybridizers Henry Rowlan, Dick Butler, Richard Morgan and MD Faith.

Perhaps the giant of the last century in terms of Louisiana iris hybridizing was Charles (know affectionately as "Charlie") Arny. From his small property in

Blue cartwheel seedling

Lafayette, Louisiana, he produced an outstanding array of hybrids in virtually all colors. Moreover, he was the first to produce what is considered "the modern form" in Louisiana irises. Many of these bore the stable name of "Charjoy," a combination of the first part of his name and his wife Joyce. Others had the stable name "Charlie's," meaning it was one of Arny's seedlings. It seems that everyone of importance in the Arny family and in the early days of the Society for Louisiana Irises was honored with having an iris named for them. Arny's first success was the nearly cup-formed and heavily substanced pinkish lavender 'Louise Arny' (Arny '56). It was his first DeBaillon Award winner and it proved to be a prodigious parent, siring or being in the background of virtually all of the subsequent hybrids from this hybridizer. The other important early Arny iris is 'Dora Dey' (Arny '57), which combines the DeBaillon Medal winner, primarily *I. nelsonii* 'Bayou Sunset' with a blue *I. giganticaerulea*. 'Dora Dey' would lead directly to clear blue 'Puttytat' (Arny '58). Another phase of the Arny blue line came through 'Louise Arny', a cross of 'Louise Arny' × Davis's navy blue 'New Offering' gave what I consider the first "modern-looking" blue iris, 'Eolian' (Arny '67). 'Eolian' not only had a clear blue color but also very wide parts; it won the DeBaillon Award in 1976. Another 'Puttytat' seedling gave the very blue and VERY vigorous 'Clyde Redmond'. This proved to be an outstanding garden plant as well as a breeder. Combining 'Louise Arny' and a seedling from 'Puttytat' gave the very tall and well-branched white 'Ila Nunn' (Arny '67). Here we had a white iris with outstanding vigor and a source of white genes through the *I. giganticaerulea* side but in a much better form than the collected clones. Arny also used 'Wheelhorse' in his breeding and his most important 'Wheelhorse' seedling was the ruffled and round 'Charlie's Michelle' (Arny '69). 'Charlie's Michelle' was not a good grower but it had so many outstanding characteristics it was used in breeding right away to confer ruffling to the hybrids. For Arny, the most outstanding of these was the white 'Clara Goula' (Arny '75), named for his neighbor and mother of hybridizer Richard Goula. 'Clara Goula' has much more ruffling than 'Charlie's Michelle' and the wide overlapping petals from its grandparent 'Queen o' Queens'. This melding was magic and it did what 'White Swirl' did for Siberian iris breeding in imparting the wide ruffled form to its progeny. Perhaps Arny's finest iris is 'Acadian Miss' (Arny '80) that combines 'Clara Goula' with the vigorous 'Clyde Redmond' resulting in a shorter plant with abundant ruffles and great vigor. 'Acadian Miss' is an excellent garden iris, performing well under normal perennial bed conditions and with shorter rhizomes that make neat clumps.

The late Joe Mertzweiller had a very active hybridizing career and accomplished amazing things in a very small backyard garden, including several DeBaillon Medals and the Hybridizer's Medal from the American Iris Society. Of course he is most famous for creating the tetraploid Louisiana irises but he also produced a string of very fine diploid irises as well. His first real break in the diploid irises was the fine yellow 'President Headley' (Mertzweiller '79). This iris had one of the most amazing stalks, with often three open blossoms for a perfect "Queen of the Iris Show" stalk and with more ruffles and width than had been seen previously. It also proved to be a very useful parent, imparting not only its form and branching but also a number of progeny with prominent halos

'Edna Grace'

of lighter colors. 'Cajun Sunrise' (Mertzweiller '92) is probably the most popular of the Mertzweiller diploids and was featured on the cover of our book on Louisiana irises (Caillet, Campbell, Vaughn and Vercher, 2000). It is a rusty red iris with prominent gold halos on all the flower parts, really the first one to have such a coloration in a consistent manner. It rose to stardom quickly, winning the DeBaillon Medal in 2000. Other diploid Louisiana hybrids from Mertzweiller include the first really good amoena 'Colorific' ('78), reverse bicolor 'Just Helene' ('90), the huge pink 'Aunt Shirley' ('90), and the navy banded cream 'Bera' ('96).

Mertzweiller started his work with tetraploid Louisiana irises, being inspired by the success of daylily breeders at creating tetraploids and spurred on with this project by his mentors Ike Nelson and Claude Davis. The first two tetraploid Louisiana irises to be introduced, 'Professor Ike' (Mertzweiller '73) and 'Professor Claude' (Mertzweiller '73), honored these two mentors on his project. 'Professor Ike' and 'Professor Claude' were both similar large purples of very heavy substance and they were immediately recognized as a great break. Unfortunately, both were purple but luckily both had genes for yellow and white coloration in their genetics. The conversion of the great Louisiana breeder 'Wheelhorse' to a tetraploid form was critical in producing the next generation of tetraploids,

of the seed, Durio had his children peel the corky seed coats off before planting to obtain higher levels of germination. This first group of seedlings resulted in not only purples but also the clean red 'Bayou Rouge' (Durio '80), lavender 'Decoy' (Durio '81), and the lavender/yellow bicolors 'Sauterne' (Durio '81) and 'Welcome Change' (Durio '83). Other fine tetraploids from Durio include the enormous 'Godzilla' (Durio '87) and 'Swamp Monster' (Durio '92) that show the possibilities for increased size in the tetraploid Louisianas, and the more blue violet 'Blue Wyble' (Durio '87). Besides these tetraploids, he has produced a nice series of diploid reds as well with 'Carmen' (Durio '72), 'Daniel' (Durio '87) and 'Lizoo' (Durio '92) being the most outstanding.

'Our Dorothy'

'Park Ave Princess'

leading directly to the production of the clear red 'Professor Jim' (Mertzweiller '85), the wide-petaled rose pink 'Professor Marta Marie' (Mertzweiller '90) and the lavender 'Professor Paul' (Mertzweiller '80). Mertzweiller produced two fine yellows, the clean lemon 'Professor Barbara' (Mertzweiller '90) and the slightly lavender-flushed 'Professor Fritchie' (Mertzweiller '93). Crosses of diploids to tetraploids resulted in the impressive 'Creole Rhapsody' (Mertzweiller '98), a strong bicolor with much better substance than other bicolors.

Ken Durio had worked extensively with tetraploid daylilies so he knew the impact that tetraploidy had on that genus. He acquired the first Mertzweiller tetraploids and proceeded to self- and cross-pollinate them to obtain large quantities of seed that would be critical for obtaining the recessives that were buried in the first red purples. To promote germination

If you've seen Ben Hager's name in several of the chapters in this book, this is no surprise. Hager and I share the problem that no plant with pollen is safe in our yards! Hager has produced award-winning irises in not only the beardless classes but in all the bearded ones as well. He might have accomplished more with Louisiana irises but he had problems germinating seeds of Louisiana irises. The reds fascinated him and he used some of the brightest reds to use in his crosses, resulting in the strong red 'Delta King' (Hager '67), red-brown 'Cajun Country' (Hager '85) and the brilliant red 'Cajun Cookery' (Hager '89). The last is my favorite of the Hager irises and was one I used directly in my own crosses. An interesting side product of this line was the bright pink 'Shrimp Louis' (Hager '78) that has the colors of the famous salad from New Orleans. Hager's pair of dark purples 'Full Eclipse' (Hager '77) and 'Dark Tide' (Hager '81) are descendants of 'Black Widow' and are in the pedigree of virtually every dark Louisiana irises introduced subsequently. Both have nearly perfect stalks with lots of buds and excellent growth habits, both traits being passed on to the seedlings. 'Mary Dunn' (Hager '74) is one of the finest of the pale orchid approaches to pink and was named for one of the most productive of the American hybridizers.

Mary Dunn had a very small yard and it was even joked that Dunn's garden was so clean because "she had no room for weeds." Despite these small spaces she made significant progress in many different colors. One of Dunn's early successes was the warm white 'Monument' (Dunn '77), which brought the ruffles and wide parts from 'Charlie's Michelle' but in a more vigorous plant and a more neutral color in hybridizing. Dunn took 'Monument' to all colors to impart these qualities to its seedlings. Some of the more special 'Monument' seedlings include rosy-pink 'Fait Accompli', lavender 'Vive La Difference' (Dunn '89), and rose 'Coup de Ville' (Dunn '90). Another key plant in Dunn's breeding is the bright orchid-lavender 'Plantation Beau' (Dunn '85), which combines Holleyman's wide cream 'Queen o' Queens', Arny's wide lavender 'Mrs. Ira Nelson' and Hager's near black 'Dark Tide' in one flower. 'Plantation Beau' inherited all the best aspects of these parents as well as proving to be an incredible parent in its own right. This must have been an incredible cross as the near black 'Bout Midnight' (Dunn '89) and iridescent magenta-plum 'Concours d'Elegance' (Dunn '89) were sister seedlings. If all crosses were that good! Dunn made what many of us would call "unorthodox" crosses, which combined diversely colored parental plants. These wide crosses produced the very unusual blended colors such as sunrise-colored 'Delta Dawn' (Dunn '82), grey blended 'Delta Dove' (Dunn '84), and lilac with hints of other colors 'Delta Twilight' (Dunn '95). 'Bayou Mystique' (Dunn '88) is a Louisiana iris version of the Dykes Medal-winning neglecta tall bearded iris 'Mystique' and is still one of the best of this color type in Louisiana irises. Besides these fine hybrids other Dunn hybrids of note include the huge dark blue-violets 'Extraordinaire' (Dunn '90) and 'Far and Away' (Dunn '91), lavenders 'Image' (Dunn '98) and 'Arrows' (Dunn '98), yellows 'Sorbet' (Dunn '91) and 'Gourmet' (Dunn '89), and reds 'C'est Fantastique' (Dunn '90) and 'Hail Mary' (Dunn '99).

Three of our prominent American hybridizers were definitely inspired by the stellar work of Charles Arny: Richard Goula, Dorman Haymon, and Neil Bertinot. All three lived in close proximity to the master and in Goula's instance *very* close, as in next door! They were inspired to try crossing themselves and each had an impact upon American hybrids.

Goula was the first to take advantage of the ruffling that was appearing in the Arny patch and his 'Lavender Ruffles' (Goula '79) was for many years the most ruffled Louisiana iris and a pretty shade of lavender. Other important hybrids from Goula are the clean and vigorous white 'Blanchette' (Goula '84), ruffled and broadly formed 'Vermillion Queen' (Goula '92) and darker-edged blend 'Lynn Hantel' (Goula, not registered). These three are all excellent parents and are in many of the author's breeding programs.

Neil Bertinot used many of the outstanding Louisiana cultivars in crosses, including the Arny cultivars 'Ila Nunn' and 'Clara Goula', the MacMillan cultivar 'Olivier Monette' and the Chowning cultivar 'Ann Chowning' and raised large numbers of progeny from these crosses. Many of these carry the stable name "Bellevue." 'Bellevue's Mike' (Bertinot '84), from a cross of 'Olivier Monette' × 'Ann Chowning', is an intense purple and one of my favorites, the intense magenta 'Bellevue's Native Charmer' (Bertinot '83). A cross of 'Bellevue's Mike' with Hager's 'Full Eclipse' gave the much improved version of the pollen parent called 'Jeri' (Bertinot '85). 'Jeri' is a very good grower and is one of the first Louisiana irises to bloom; it won the DeBaillon Medal in 1994. A cross of 'Ila Nunn' × 'Clara Goula' gave the very large and ruffled lavender blue 'Bellevue Coquette' (Bertinot '84).

Dormon Haymon produced a number of wonderful Louisiana iris hybrids. Besides being wonderful flowers Haymon insisted on wonderful stalks and plants that grew easily. They are an outstanding group and Haymon won the best seedling prize at the Society for Louisiana Iris show many times for his creations. Haymon selected different cultivars as the basis of his line, but most of them were Arny cultivars. My favorites of the earlier hybrids of Haymon include the very vigorous white with orange signal 'Marie Dolores' (Haymon '88), greenish yellow 'Teresa Margaret' (Haymon '88), huge and husky purple 'Hurricane Party' (Haymon '88), and the incredibly rich black purple 'Empress Josephine' (Haymon '89). A cross of 'Valera' × 'President Hedley', which combines the blended yellows from Arny and Mertzweiller lines, gave two extraordinary sister seedlings, the caramel-colored 'Praline Festival' (Haymon '92) and the clear yellow 'Rokki Rockwell' (Haymon '92). Both of these plants have perfect branching and are great garden plants. 'Praline Festival' would win the DeBaillon Medal in 2001 and deservedly so. Other great plants from Haymon include the white with pale lavender flushes 'Longue Vue' (Haymon '00), the huge dark purple 'Great White Hope' (Haymon '00), flesh pink 'Cajun Love Story' (Haymon ' 00), rose red with white halos 'Chuck Begnaud' (Haymon '00), the exquisite cream edged pink 'Elaine Bourque' (Haymon '08) and the navy edged white 'Hector Duhon' (Haymon '14).

A similar triumvirate of hybridizers to the one that spurred activity in Louisiana also occurred in Arkansas. Their work was influenced strongly by the work of Frank Chowning: Henry Rowlan, Richard Morgan, and MD Faith all made significant contributions to the production of new Louisiana irises.

Henry Rowlan's breeding program was almost all Chowning in origin. These flowers lacked the ruffles and wider parts that were occurring in the Louisiana- and California-bred irises of the same era but were very hardy plants that would grow easily in the Northeast. Significant plants from Rowlan include red 'Frank Chowning' (Rowlan '84), the bright blends 'Spanish Sunset' (Rowlan '86) and 'Spanish Sunrise' (Rowlan '90),

'Hector Duhan'

than other Louisiana irises, making them perfect for the front of the border or to face down larger varieties. Morgan used a white *I. brevicaulis* selection of Frank Chowning named 'Trail of Tears' (Chowning '73) in many of these crosses and this imparted both smaller size and blues with the intensity of the *I. brevicaulis*. The outstanding blues from the Morgan work include the blue violet 'Territorial Rights' (Morgan '84) and the very clear blue pair of 'Lake Sylvia' (Morgan '91) and 'Lake Ouchita' (Morgan '92). 'Meadow Frost' (Morgan '91) is a white companion to these three blues that match them in size and form. 'Sea Knight' (Morgan '89) is from other lines and remains one of my favorite irises, a brilliant navy blue. It is still shorter but not as short as the other blue irises he introduced. Morgan's progress in reds and tawny shades were descended from the reds and blends of Chowning. Outstanding among these are the red-brown 'Parade Music' (Morgan '83), bright cherry red 'Cherry Cup' (Morgan '88), and the brown blend with prominent green styles 'Heavenly Glow' (Morgan '88). In the Chowning lines with lots of *I. fulva* influence, a number of small blends with darker edges appeared such as 'Dream Wish' (Morgan '97), 'Clown About' (Morgan '91), and 'Kelly's Choice' (Morgan '91). Although of unknown parentage, Morgan's 'Night Thunder' (Morgan '00) is an outstanding very dark purple with a strong orange-yellow signal. It went on to win the DeBaillon Medal, a fitting tribute to a fine hybridizing career.

lemon yellow 'Sunny Episode' (Rowlan '83), and pink-toned 'Twirling Ballerina' (Rowlan '86). My favorite of the Rowlan cultivars is 'Voodoo Queen' (Rowlan '92), a clear dark navy, that descends from non-Chowning lines.

Richard Morgan's irises are a unique set of plants that descend more from *I. brevicaulis* than most other breeders. Because of this, many of the Morgan cultivars are much smaller

MD Faith was the most recent of the Arkansas hybridizers but quickly produced an outstanding series of hybrids. One of his accomplishments was rescuing an outstanding red seedling of the late Dick Butler, which he named 'My Friend Dick' (Butler by Faith '00). This was a big improvement over its parent 'Ann Chowning' and went on to win the DeBaillon Medal. 'Henry Rowlan' (Butler '00), named for Faith's mentor in the Louisiana iris projects, is a very deep purple, as is 'James Faith' (Faith '00). Both of these outstanding irises went on to win the DeBaillon Medal. My favorite of the Faith irises is the light blue standards over light yellow falls

'Enviable' seedling

named 'Enviable' (Faith '02). Unlike many irises of this color combination, the stalks of 'Enviable' are tall and well-branched and the flowers have great form and substance. It has proven to be a most interesting parent. Other fine irises from Faith include the whites 'Ann Faith' (Faith '98) and 'Lulu E' (Faith '05), violets 'Sam W' (Faith '05) and 'Circe Queen' (Faith '06), and yellow 'June's Pick' (Faith '02). I find that all of the Faith irises are easy growers and very good garden plants.

Patrick O'Connor's breeding program involves a unique blend of the work of the Arkansas hybridizers (O'Connor lived in Little Rock prior to moving to Louisiana and had contact with the hybridizers there) and those from Louisiana. Because of this, his hybrids often have unique combinations of colors and patterns that are not seen in irises derived solely from either Arkansas or Louisiana lines. O'Connor's names are very much Louisiana inspired, and feature festivals, customs, foods and locations of the area. O'Connor works in the very difficult ice blue colors and his first, 'Southdowns' (O'Connor '92), gave rise to the much improved 'Bywater' (O'Connor '02). The Chowning influence is clearly felt in O'Connor's red lines, as almost all are descended from the Chowning irises. These reds include the rich red 'False River' (O'Connor '92), bright red with prominent signals 'Tickfaw' (O'Connor '92), white-edged red 'Andouille' (O'Connor '99), bright red 'Red Beans' (O'Connor '07) and my favorite the intense red 'Gris Gris' (O'Connor '11). His 'Zydeco' (O'Connor '99) is one of my favorites and is difficult to classify, a red but so heavily infused bronze that it appears more as a blend than a red. 'Frenchmen Street' (O'Connor '04) is another that is in that "difficult to classify" colors it has tones of peach, amber, brown, and almost orange. Among the pink irises O'Connor's are among the pinkest: his very broad-petaled 'Feliciana Hills' (O'Connor '87) and the very broad and huge-flowered 'Big Charity' (O'Connor '05). O'Connor has done some work with shorter irises and his 'Mudbug' (O'Connor '99) is a real cutie in a bright violet blue with a spray pattern signal.

Richard Sloan managed to have a hybridizing career despite moving from Illinois to California, Arkansas and finally Louisiana. From his California hybridizing days he introduced 'Ruth Sloan' (Sloan '84), a bright gold, one of the few irises with the pendant form that harkens back to the *I. nelsonii* forms but in a much larger and fuller version. 'Maroon Monarch' (Sloan '84) is one of my favorites in bright maroon with a very distinctive spray pattern on the falls. More recently, Sloan introduced an interesting cream overlaid with lavender veins giving a pink effect 'Edmond Riggs' (Sloan '05) for an African-American pioneer Louisiana iris hybridizer. A similar patterned flower over a yellow base creates a green effect in his 'Lineage' (Sloan '05).

Farron Campbell became involved with Louisiana thanks to the influence of Marie Caillet and he introduced a number of very nice plants in his short hybridizing career. His first hybrid, 'Lone Star' (Campbell '97), is a large cartwheel blue that descends from *I. hexagona*, and is one of the last Louisiana iris to bloom. 'Atchafalaya' (Campbell '98) is my favorite of Campbell's introductions, a huge dark purple with a ruffled cartwheel form. It has the marvelous plant habits of its parent 'Jeri', with nearly perfect branching and vigorous growth. 'Rilla Hickerson' (Campbell by Wilhoit '07) is a light lavender veined darker. The vigor of this iris is outstanding.

The author lived in Mississippi for thirty years and in that time developed a program in Louisiana irises. My first cross, 'Jeri' × 'Cajun Cookery', resulted in the red-black that was christened 'Red Velvet Elvis' (Vaughn '97) upon its first bloom. 'Red Velvet Elvis' combines the best qualities of each of its parents and has been very popular, earning the Marie Caillet Cup, the DeBaillon Medal and the Charles Arny Award for the most popular Louisiana iris. 'Beale Street' (Vaughn '97) is a strong navy blue with wide ruffled flowers and nearly perfect plant habits. Both 'Beale Street' and 'Elvis' have proven to be fine parents and they pass on their vigor and perfect stalks to their progeny, such as the 'Beale Street' seedling 'Jaws' (Vaughn '09), with laciniated petal edges. Besides these, other fine plants from the author include the very vigorous white 'Cajun White Lightning' (Vaughn '00), and the two ruffled yellows 'Lemon Zest' (Vaughn '09) and 'Candlelight Supper' (Vaughn '08). 'Lemon Zest' has very prominent green style arms and in an effort to push the green colors into the petals, I was able to produce 'Lime Zest' (Vaughn '08), in which the petal color is infused and veined in green. Several irises are in the pipelines to be introduced shortly including the brilliant navy blue 'In the Navy' (Vaughn '09), crystal blue 'Ina Garten'

'Beale Street'

'Jaws'

'Jaws', detail

'In the Navy'

bearded irises that he had so enjoyed in Ohio. Although the bearded iris would not persist in Florida, Louisiana irises provided Wolford a new outlet for growing irises and he quickly started breeding Louisiana irises. Success came quickly with the production of bright red narrowly edged gold 'Seminole Sunrise' (Wolford '06) and gold-flushed caramel brown 'Seminole Autumn' (Wolford '06). Wolford's biggest triumph to date is his bright lemon yellow with greenish styles 'Edna Claunch' (Wolford '07), named for a lifelong friend of Wolford and his wife Donna. Many Louisiana irises don't make good tight clumps with lots of bloom; 'Edna Claunch' certainly does and it has up to 12 buds on well spaced branches that ensure it blooms for a long time. It captures the best habits of its parents 'Atchafalaya' and 'Dural White Butterfly'. It is also proving to be a useful parent. Wolford has found several stands of native irises in Florida that have not entered the gene pool of our Louisiana iris hybrids. Crosses of these are giving interesting flowers already and may make Louisiana irises adapted to very tropical areas of the world.

Ron Betzer became interested in Louisiana irises while living in California and became associated with both Mary Dunn and Joe Ghio. He later retired to Lafayette, Louisiana, and became a big part of the Society for Louisiana irises. His first parlay into hybridizing, a cross of 'Louisiana Teddy Bear' and 'Gladiator's Gift' resulted in the very bright and vigorous caramel-brown 'Honey Galore' (Betzer '00). His 'Cala' (which is an abbreviation for <u>Ca</u>lifornia bred <u>L</u>ouisian<u>a</u> iris; Betzer '06) and 'Rooster' (Betzer '14) are both pastel creams with prominent dark edges to the petal. My favorite of the Betzer hybrids is the very dark purple 'Dark Dude' (Betzer '06). Unlike many very dark irises, this one has very wide petals and grows very well.

Hooker Nichols has hybridized irises since he was a child living in Oklahoma and has produced many award-winning bearded irises. A move to Texas and an association with Marie Caillet spurred him on to try his hand at hybridizing Louisiana irises as well. His first hybrids include the dark amethyst 'Cajun Serenade' (Nichols '08), bright purple 'Festival Banner' (Nichols '08), and clear blue with cartwheel form 'Orlean's Blues' (Nichols '08). His most recent hybrids include the very showy bright rose reds that are descended from 'Chuck

(Vaughn '08), lemon edged raspberry 'Crisp and Clear' (Vaughn '09), bright magenta with a spray pattern 'Dick Sloan' (Vaughn '08), brilliant magenta-orchid 'Magenta Madness' (Vaughn '09), and bright red 'Cajun Hot Sauce' (Vaughn '09). I have worked extensively with the doubles and cartwheels from the Granger doubles and the purple and gold cartwheel 'Geaux Tigers' (Vaughn '09), which has the school colors of the Louisiana State University Tigers. The "geaux" is the Cajun spelling for "go."

Wayland Rudkin, a California native, had been growing Louisiana irises and tried his hand at hybridizing, by crossing some of his favorite cultivars. A cross of Mary Dunn's fine cultivars 'Cotton Plantation' and 'Bayou Mystique' resulted in the cartwheel-formed blue violet 'Ginny's Choice' (Rudkin '05). Another cross with 'Bayou Mystique', this time with a seedling, resulted in the nearly self-colored maroon blossoms with a slit-like gold signal.

Harry Wolford, like many retirees, moved from the cold Midwest to Florida upon retirement but missed growing the

'Crisp and Clear'

LOUISIANA IRISES

'Magenta Madness'

CHAPTER 5

Begnaud': 'Heartbreak Warfare' (Nichols '13) and 'Valentine Passion' (Nichols '13), and the clear white 'Reverchon Snowfall' (Nichols '13). My pick of these newer hybrids is the very wide-petaled bright lemon yellow (and sunfast) 'Melody Wilhoit' (Nichols '13), named in honor of the recently deceased Louisiana iris promoter.

Although much of the work on Louisiana irises was done in the United States, Louisiana irises grow extremely well in the warmer, moister areas of Australia and even in the drier areas of Western and South Australia if supplemented with extra water. Hybridizers from Australia include Bob Raabe, John Taylor, Heather and Bernard Pryor, Peter Jackson, Janet Hutchinson and Don Grieves.

Bob Raabe was the first Australian hybridizer of Louisiana irises to achieve acclaim here in the United States and several of his irises were actually introduced in the United States. 'La Perouse' (Raabe '75) is a very clear blue but of poor substance. Much better is the wonderful clear blue 'Sinfonietta' (Raabe '87). Besides being a wonderful color, 'Sinfonietta' is a strong grower and the flowers open well at all positions on the stalk. My favorite of the Raabe irises is the unusual orchid with halos of cream 'Gerry Marstellar' (Raabe '88) and the petals are exceptionally wide, making for a very lovely flower. Raabe also participated in the tetraploid breeding, introducing two purples, 'Magistral' (Raabe '83) from 'Professor Ike' self pollinated and 'Coorabell' (Raabe '88), from crossing 'Magistral' back to 'Professor Ike'.

John Taylor is the most prolific of the Australian Louisiana iris hybridizers and he was awarded seven Australasian Dykes Medals and the Hybridizer's Medal from the American Iris Society. His plants have been used by hybridizers all over the world and with outstanding results. Taylor's lines started primarily from Charles Arny's lines and amongst them 'Clara Goula' was the most important of these plants. Taylor's lines should serve as blueprint for all of us breeding beardless irises as he very effectively used the recessive whites to confer their ruffling and other good plant qualities to their progeny. He also quickly capitalized on his breaks and by doing so advanced Louisiana irises more quickly than we had seen previously. 'Helen Naish' (Taylor '79) was the most important of the early Taylor plants a clear and very ruffled white from 'Clara Goula' × 'Charlie's Ginny'. 'Helen Naish' proved to be an incredible breeder,

'Dick Sloan'

conferring wonderful forms, clear colors and sterling plant habits to its progeny. One of Taylor's crosses for pink Louisianas, Arny's wide pink 'Screen Gem' crossed with 'Helen Naish', produced one of the premier Taylor irises, the crystalline white 'Dural White Butterfly' (Taylor '89). 'Dural White Butterfly' is a difficult pod parent but has very fertile pollen and has produced many outstanding progeny. It is also an excellent garden plant, much improved over the performance of 'Clara Goula', its grandparent. A cross of 'Dazzling Star' × 'Helen Naish' gave three outstanding progeny, the very wide and extremely heavily substanced rose red 'Margaret Lee' (Taylor '89), the clearest pink 'Dancing Vogue' (Taylor '91), and the tall, variably double brick red with light splashes 'Gate Crasher' (Taylor '91). Each of these has proven to be exceptional parents as well with 'Dancing Vogue' siring the ultimate lavender with ruffles 'Italian Affair' (Taylor '98) whereas 'Margaret Lee' produced all sorts of incredible offspring, including the *huge* 'Betty Blockbuster' (Taylor '94), very wide and clean pink/red bicolor 'Better Watch Out' (Taylor '94), bicolor pink 'Never Say' (Taylor '93) and creamy lemon boldly edged red purple 'Better Believe It' (Taylor '96). Taylor's yellow lines also descend from the Arny irises, with the magnificently ruffled bright yellow 'Koorawatha' (Taylor '84) descended directly from 'Clara Goula' has probably the most incredible branching of any Louisiana iris, with as many as fourteen buds. Three others of Taylor's yellows that are special are the deep

'Geaux Tigers'

and sunfast 'Alluvial Gold' (Taylor '91), heavily ruffled cream yellow 'Spanish Ballet' (Taylor '91) and the ruffled lemon yellow 'Classical Note' (Taylor '90). 'Alluvial Gold' has proven to be a very good parent for several hybridizers. Taylor used his whites to improve the form and color of his blue irises too. 'Malibu Magic' (Taylor '90) is a violet blue with darker veins and one of my favorite of Taylor's irises. 'Dural Bluebird' (Taylor '93) combines the two great Taylor breeders, 'Margaret Lee' and 'Dural White Butterfly', and is a ruffled blue violet self. Two of the last Taylor blues, 'Seriously Blue' (Taylor '00) and 'Ocean Going' (Taylor '98) are among the bluest of the taller Louisiana irises and are both very good garden plants as well.

Heather and Bernard Pryor started their hybridizing using the latest of the Taylor cultivars although they took their lines in different directions, with Heather concentrating on warm colors, with a goal of orange, and Bernard concentrating on the shorter and smaller cultivars. Both programs have yielded lots of very nice flowers including several DeBaillon Medals. One of Heather's first winners is still one of my favorites, 'Garnet Storm Dancer' (Pryor '94), an unusual shade of dark maroon with slit-like signals of gold on all the nicely ruffled petals. Another favorite of Heather's is the appropriately named 'Peaches in Wine' (Pryor '97), with peach standards and rich wine-colored falls with incredible petal width. 'Peaches in Wine' won the DeBaillon Medal. Heather's initial plan was to produce orange irises but the side products of these crossings in yellows and

bright blends were outstanding in their own right. Orange-yellow 'Bound for Glory' (Pryor '99), bright lemon rebloomer 'For Dad' (Pryor '96), red-orange blend 'Hot and Spicy' (Pryor '95), and bright orange and yellow blend 'Bushfire Moon' (Pryor '94) are the most outstanding ones of the earlier quests towards orange. The ultimate goal of a glowing orange was reached in

'Rooster'

CHAPTER 5

'Dark Dude'

The blue breeding seems to be more of a joint effort between Bernard and Heather. Heather has introduced the strong navy blue 'Donna Wolford' (Pryor '10), the wide blue-lavender 'Queen Jean' (Pryor '03), the cobalt blue 'Sydney Harbour' (Pryor '04), and the more lavender blue 'Swirling Waters' (Pryor '10). Bernard's premier blue is his 'Blue Mountain Mist' (B. Pryor '07), a fine-growing pastel blue that has a misty quality to the flower.

Bernard's program has centered on the smaller-flowered, shorter clones from a fortuitous cross that produced numerous small flowers from a self pollination of 'Gladiator's Gift', which gave Heather 'Little Nutkin' (Pryor '94). Small flowers from Bernard's hybridizing include the apricot 'Hey Little Devil' (B. Pryor '00), bright ruffled ruby red 'Little Ruby Slippers' (B. Pryor '00), and ruffled lavender flushed white 'Elaine's Wedding' (B. Pryor '96).

Peter Jackson is from South Australia where conditions for growing Louisiana irises, low rainfall and high soil alkalinity, are hardy ideal for growth. Despite these conditions, Jackson has produced a series of wonderful hybrids. Most of these are descended from Taylor irises. Jackson's irises are typified as having abundant ruffles and wide overlapping petals. Outstanding among his irises are wine red 'Coonawarra Claret' (Jackson '99), frothy lilac 'Going Baroque' (Jackson '99), and the blue-violet with frosted lighter edges 'We Are Sailing' (Jackson '05).

Other Australian breeders include Janet Hutchinson, who produced the lovely creams 'Soft Laughter' (Hutchinson '87), soft yellow 'Daisy Jane' (Hutchinson '98), and clear pink near amoena 'Sweet Miriam' (Hutchinson '98). Peter Grieves introduced the truly unusual 'Splitter Splatter' (Grieves '02), a near white bold splashed and striped red violet, much

the appropriately named 'Tandoori Sizzler' (Pryor '08), with wide petals and small art-like signals of gold on each petal. Veined irises have been rather rare in Louisiana irises but Heather has pursued this line with the yellow with strong purple veined 'Wow Factor' (Pryor '02), rose red veins on cream 'Creative Artistry' (Pryor '04), and lavender on cream 'Cobweb Concerto' (Pryor '06). Many of the Taylor irises on which Heather's lines are based show broken color, with swirls of lighter colors that are variably expressed in the blossom. Not surprisingly Heather has named two outstanding ones, 'Wizard of Aussie' (Pryor '97), with lemon sectors on red-brown, and 'Kakadu Sunset' (Pryor '10), a brilliant red with streaks of gold. Cultivars with cream to lemon petals and rims of pink-violet to brown darker edges have been a trademark of the Pryor breeding program and there are several outstanding ones. 'Ann Hordern' (Pryor '97) started this trend and was followed by 'Sugarplum Treat' (Pryor '04) and ruffled and more pastel 'Amanda Grainger' (Pryor '10).

'Peaches In Wine'

'For Dad'

'Tandoori Sizzler'

like what is seen in the broken color bearded irises. T. John Betts hybridized in the harsh climate of Western Australia and has produced a number of interesting hybrids including the lime with deeper green styles 'Green-Eyed Surfie' (Betts '97), cream with green veins 'First Lime' (Betts '00) and miniature blue-violet 'Crayfish' (Betts '80). Many of these have not reached the United States but those that have are strong-growing plants as might be expected from plants selected in the extreme climate of Western Australia.

Although all beardless irises could use more hybridizers there is a group of new active hybridizers in the Louisiana iris, including the very enthusiastic Joe Musacchia, the cutting edge grower and hybridizer Robert Treadway, and Jeff Weeks, who is trying to meld the best of the older cultivars with the newer hybrids.

A FEW FAVORITES

OLDER FAVORITES

'Black Widow' (MacMillan '53) A perfect name for this near black with long velvety petals that very much resemble a spider. Despite the popularity of this plant, there was no concerted effort of breeders to produce spidery type as there have been in daylilies. Rather, there was a push towards wider and ruffled petals. Luckily, 'Black Widow' is still available to keep this lovely and graceful spider form type bloom in our gardens.

'Plum Good' (Nelson, introduced in '51 but not officially registered until 2000) Another great name. A very clear plum purple with a striking orange signal. Surprisingly wide petals for its day and a good sturdy garden plant. No one that visits your garden will believe this plant is over 60 years old.

'Finders Keepers' (Chowning '61) and no losers weepers either! This is a pure *I. brevicaulis* selection in white with bold splashes of blue-violet. No two flowers are alike. A short grower with the zig-zag placement of blooms typical of the species. Blooms late in the season.

'Red Dazzler' (Hale '69) This flower is sometimes listed as an *I. fulva* but it really has *I. brevicaulis* blood as well. Preston Hale was concerned with producing really hardy Louisiana irises and 'Red Dazzler' certainly achieves that in an amazing bright brick red flower. Short plants are perfect for the front of the border. If you live in colder climates, this is the Louisiana iris for you. When I lived in Massachusetts, this was a Louisiana that would grow with no extra care and still bloom every year.

'Olivier Monette' (MacMillan '70) I almost didn't list this plant as it's such a frustrating parent but it is a gorgeous color. Sort of a silvery-orchid shot all over with magenta that is very unique. The substance of the flowers is a little weak but the stalks are very well branched, allowing for a good bloom season.

'Starlite Starbrite' (Granger '70) Marvin Granger worked with the double and cartwheel Louisiana irises for much of his hybridizing career. Some of them are messy/ asymmetrical but this one is not. A soft cream white with darker signals. This one also has a much better stalk than many of the other double Louisianas.

NEWER FAVORITES

'Edna Claunch' (Wolford '09) Named for an equally classy lady this lovely ruffled yellow with more buds and branches than I care to count and precisely formed flowers in lemon. Unlike many yellows, this one makes an outstanding clump effect as the flowers sit mostly above the foliage mass.

'Lemon Zest' (Vaughn '09) Sometimes your crosses come out just as you wanted. One parent, 'Heavenly Glow', has lovely green style arms but the flower is a brown. Crossing it to yellows gave the pretty ruffled yellow flowers and the electric green style arms in one flower. Shorter and with very restrained foliage.

'Italian Affair' (Taylor '01) John Taylor has introduced many outstanding Louisiana irises. This is one of his last introductions in a lovely shade of lavender with heavy ruffling and wide, overlapping petals. The buds are much lighter and this bud back color show through in the edges of the ruffles.

'Better Believe It' (Taylor '99) Actually this was so lovely that it was hard to believe when you first saw it. I feel this is

'Garnet Storm Dancer'

John's best flower. A bright and odd shade of rose red with prominent signals and lighter area on all petals as well as a lighter edge to all petals.

'Garnet Storm Dancer' (H. Pryor '94) This was one of Heather's first hybrids but to my mind one of her prettiest and most unique. The flowers are an unusual shade of a very dark maroon with slit like gold signals. The flowers are ruffled to the extreme but the flowers open well on the stalk, which many heavily ruffled ones don't.

'Southern Star'

'Southern Star' (H. Pryor '10) A bright red cartwheel with bold gold signals on all petals. Very wide and ruffled and a plant that grows very well. A real winner.

'Red Velvet Elvis' (Vaughn '97) When I moved to Mississippi I saw a great many velvet Elvis paintings that I had never seen in Massachusetts! When this red-black flower with velvety falls first bloomed for me it was immediately dubbed 'Red Velvet Elvis' as it so reminded me of those ubiquitous Elvis paintings. The further north one goes, the more magenta the flower becomes.

'Elaine Bourque' (Haymon '10) *Wow,* what a flower. I first saw this in Dorman Haymon's garden as a seedling and couldn't believe how lovely it was and that it came out of a very dark purple parent. A big flower of a clean white with all the petals edged in a bright rose pink band. Exemplary plant habits. Named for an equally lovely lady, who served as secretary for the Society for Louisiana Irises more years than she would like to admit.

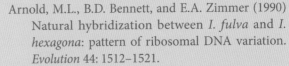

REFERENCES

Arnold, M.L., B.D. Bennett, and E.A. Zimmer (1990) Natural hybridization between *I. fulva* and *I. hexagona*: pattern of ribosomal DNA variation. *Evolution* 44: 1512–1521.

Arnold, M.L., C.M. Buckner, and J.J. Robinson (1991) Pollen mediated introgression and hybrid speciation in Louisiana irises. Proceedings, National Academy of Sciences USA. 88:1398–1402.

Caillet, M. and K.C. Vaughn (2007) *History of Hybridizing.* Special publication, Society for Louisiana Irises, Shreveport, LA.

Caillet, M., J.F. Campbell, K.C. Vaughn, and D. Vercher (2000). *The Louisiana Iris: Taming of a Native American Wildflower.* Timber Press, Portland, OR.

Claunch, E. (2012) *Louisiana Iris Hybridizers 1985–2010.* Special publication, Society for Louisiana Irises, Shreveport, LA.

MacMillan, W.B. (1967) Mary DeBaillon, as we knew her. *American Iris Society Bulletin* 186: 30–32.

Randolph, L.F. (1966). A new species of Louisiana iris of hybrid origin. *Baileya* 14: 143–169.

'Red Velvet Elvis'

6 SPURIA IRISES

Spuria irises have suffered an image problem ever since Linnaeus classified them as spurias (for false or "bastards"; Mitchell 1949). The reason for this designation was Linnaeus's contention that spurias were somehow odd hybrids of bearded and bulbous irises. Phillip Corliss suggested the spurias be called "butterfly irises," which would be a better and more positive descriptor, but it never caught on with the gardening public or the prominent spuria hybridizers of the time. Regardless of what they are called, spuria irises are superb garden plants. One of the few flowers you can plant and forget; they just get better each year. Most spurias are tall plants (3 to 5' tall) that have large dramatic flowers above a tall mound of sword shaped leaves. These are plants for the back of the border or for dramatic accents.

Spuria flowers range in color from white, yellow, lavenders, browns and purples, the latter including some near black flowers. Many spuria flowers have a prominent signal, generally of yellow, but sometimes verging on orange. Although the earlier spuria hybrids had rather tailored flowers and a rather open form, the present trends are to shorter-shanked rounder falls and broader standards, all with ruffling (McCown 1969). Most of the newly introduced spurias are still large plants that produce tall stalks. However, there are a growing number of smaller cultivars, suitable for at least the middle of the border. Branching on the spuria talk has been referred to as "serpentine" as the branches are covered by elaborate sheaths, so that the flowers open up in a line, almost like flowers in a corsage. Most new spurias have at least four buds per stalk, but six to eight buds on a stalk are not uncommon.

Most of the available spuria hybrids are called "summer dormant." That is, in some climates, the plants will go dormant and lose their leaves during the summer. This may because the majority of spuria hybridizers were from the dry southwestern part of the United States and this summer dormancy was selected as a positive trait. In cooler climates, such as here in Oregon, this never really happens, or occurs just as a new set of leaves are being produced in the fall. Some species, and especially the smaller species, do not become dormant in the summer and rather have less leaves in the winter months. Many of these are more successful in northern climates.

'Adriatic Memories'

Spuria flowers superficially resemble the bulbous Dutch iris, and it is now known that in fact the spurias and the Dutch iris are related genetically as well (Tillie et al. 2000). Like their Dutch iris cousins, spuria irises are superb cut flowers. The individual flowers last for a long time and other buds not yet expanded will continue to open. The large flowers are also appropriate as corsages.

Another distinctive feature of the spurias are the seeds and seed pods. Spurias produce pods (botanically they are capsules, not pods, but are frequently described as such in the iris literature) from almost every flower, and the pods are strikingly ribbed with tops of each portion of the pod distinctly spined. The stalks with pods are a favorite material in dried arrangements because of their exotic appearance.

Spuria seeds are surprisingly lightweight and they have a papery covering that probably aids in wind dispersal of the seed.

'Missouri
Boon'

Spurias tend to be big plants and unless you buy one that is described as "dwarf" or "small" most of them want to be planted in a position towards the rear of a border or where a large specimen clump can be appreciated. Shorter spurias fit in well more towards the middle or front of the border, much as do Siberian irises. Spurias do not like to be moved frequently and can form rather large clumps so you should plan on several feet of bed space when you decide where to plant your spuria plants. Although spurias want sun, I have found that they not only tolerate a half day of shade but actually perform nearly equally to my plantings in full sun. In my garden in Oregon, I use them in a massed planting of primarily spurias, with hardy geraniums and the taller large-flowered penstemons planted between the spuria clumps. With the addition of these two other perennials, these beds have color through much of the season, with the spurias overlapping into the seasons of both. One other use came about quite by accident. When I arrived in Oregon, one of the large Douglas firs on my property was rotten and needed to be taken down, leaving a stump that blighted the landscape. I constructed a raised bed encircling the stump and then planted spuria rhizomes in the bed. In a year's time the spurias had made nice clumps and by two years had completely obscured the ugly stump. Many visitors have been impressed with the way that spurias can be used in this fashion.

Although what I have said about the conditions that favor growth of spurias is accurate, they are much more accommodating than you might expect. In my haste one season, I was planting a large number of Louisiana irises from a nursery in my pool garden on my patio. There was a spuria rhizome in that group and I inadvertently planted the spuria in the pool. Not only did it survive but it bloomed and increased! I don't recommend such a strategy but it does point to the adaptability of spurias

Spuria irises are heavy feeders and I use a balanced fertilizer (10-10-10 or 5-10-10) on them in the spring, about 6 weeks to a month before peak bloom. I have also used the slow-release fertilizer pellets with good effect in both Oregon and Mississippi. Although there is some growth of the spuria foliage during the fall and winter months, most of the growth occurs in spring as they produce their massive leaves and stalks. During this time, adequate soil moisture is necessary for the production of stalks and leaves. If spring rains are inadequate make sure the plantings have ½ to 1" per week until blooms start.

In some areas of the country, spurias go dormant in the summer months. However, in

'Missouri Morning'

more northern areas, spurias retain their foliage during the summer, with the leaves only senescing in the fall and quickly being replaced by new foliage. If the plants in your climate do go dormant and your summers are hot, refrain from watering until new growth appears in the fall as excessive watering of the dormant rhizomes can cause the growing points to rot. However, even in Mississippi, the spurias would retain foliage and I could keep watering them throughout the growing season. Keeping the plants growing throughout the season seems to produce better plants and more abundant bloom.

Transplanting spurias is one of the more difficult aspects of their culture. Generally plants arrive in August-October from nurseries, with the plants in a near dormant state with the rhizomes wrapped in moist towels or other substances that will keep the rhizomes moist. Dig a hole deep enough so that the rhizomes will be covered by about 1 to 2" of soil. Cover the rhizome with soil, pat down lightly, and water the plant thoroughly with the addition of a little weak fertilizer such as in those designed for transplanting. I mulch my spuria irises to keep the soil uniformly moist and to suppress weed growth. Pine or fir bark, cotton or buckwheat hulls all make fine mulching material for spurias. Keep the new planting moist but not soggy until new growth is observed. If you live in a colder climate, mulching the newly transplanted spurias with evergreen boughs or salt marsh hay in the winter is recommended. Use this mulching *after* the ground has frozen. The goal is to keep them cold so that they don't suffer from repeated freezing and thawing.

Growers in the Southwest often dig their spuria rhizomes just when they became dormant. The rhizomes are then wrapped in moist toweling and stored in a cooler at approximately 40° F. Interestingly, plants that have been treated in this manner seem to come back from dormancy more quickly than rhizomes otherwise not so treated. I have left rhizomes in the crisper areas of my refrigerator for several weeks and planted them with the same good results. Chances for fungal attack under these conditions are great. Pre-treatment of the plants with a 5 percent household bleach solution prior to storage seems to help in keeping the plants fungus-free during their refrigerator nap.

If you do need to move or want to start a new clump of a favorite cultivar elsewhere in your yard, simply cut away a portion of the clump and follow the transplanting methods described above. Do not allow the rhizomes or roots to dry at any point during the process.

Spurias in general are very healthy garden plants but there are two diseases that are of concern. Mustard seed fungus can be devastating to spuria plantings, especially in the South. It can be recognized by a soft slimy rot around the leaves, accompanied by a web-like mycelium and mustard seed-shaped bodies that are the fruiting bodies of the fungus. In Mississippi, I made a habit of treating all planting areas containing spurias with Terraclor*, although the availability of this product at the time of this writing is somewhat in question. Other products may prove to be a useful substitute and you should contact your county agent for any good substitute.

Viruses often mar spuria flowers and less often leaves. These take two forms, slits of lighter, off color in both leaves and flowers, and in other cultivars more extensive purple splashes on a paler background. Some cultivars are more affected than others and cool and moist conditions seem to cause more symptoms than warm and dry conditions. Because there is no cure for the virus, it is best to destroy the offending cultivars and the discarded plants should not be used in any compost. Aphids are the agent of viral spread, so protocols to control both aphids and ants are effective in controlling the spread of the virus. 'Wadi Zem Zem' is one parent that imports resistance to its progeny and most of the resistant plants contain blood of this cultivar.

Spurias have nectaries at the base of the flower and this nectar proves irresistible to ants as well as pollinating insects. Use of ant baits around the plants will prevent the stalks from becoming covered with aphids and ants around the nectaries. If you are using the flowers in arrangements or if you are using them in crosses, this treatment is more necessary.

In the Pacific Northwest, both slugs and snails can be a problem in the winter and spring, when there are few other choices of fresh green material. By baiting in the fall around the clumps, this damage should be minimized. Because spurias tend to be tall plants, neither snails nor slugs are much problem with the bloomstalks, even here in the slug-ridden Pacific Northwest.

What I have written above pertains more to the cultivars that have been developed in warm climates and which have a tendency towards summer dormancy. Cultivars derived

'Steely Don'

from 'Belise' and some of the shorter spuria species such as *I. graminea* will not have any tendency towards summer dormancy. These may be incorporated into normal herbaceous borders and receive watering that are typical of Siberian irises.

Almost all of the beardless irises may be used as cut flowers with success. The spurias are some of the best for this purpose. Australian Barry Blyth actually made a commercial success of selling spuria stalks to the cut flower industry. Spurias last very well in a vase, can be stored at 40° F to keep them fresh and are very resistant to being bruised in handling. The late Ben Hager would famously go into a class of judges training on exhibiting spuria irises with an armload of spuria iris stalks and promptly (and purposively) throw them on the floor! After the gasps of the audience subsided, he would pick them up and show that they were unharmed even by the rough treatment. Spuria stalks tend to be tall. Cutting off the bottom third of the stalk of the taller cultivars makes stalks that are better for most arrangements. Stalks of shorter cultivars may be used as is.

SPECIES INVOLVED

There are two major groups of spuria iris species: a group of tallish, mostly tetraploid species and a much smaller group of probably diploid plants. Spuria irises are one of the exceptional groups of beardless irises in which tetraploidy occurred as a natural event.

TALL SPECIES

I. spuria, for whom the group is named, exists as varieties that differ significantly in chromosome number, plant habit, habitat and behavior in breeding so it is more likely that many of these subspecies or varieties are real species. Certainly they behave very differently in crosses (Niswonger 2009). Hopefully DNA studies of this complex will resolve these issues. Herein I follow the Matthews classification of this species complex as described in detail by Bowley (1997). *I. spuria* ssp. *maritima* is a very distinct plant from others in this complex. It is only 12 to 15" tall and a dark blue-purple with a pattern of blue veins on white and occurs in France and Spain. This subspecies has 38 chromosomes (Lenz 1963). *I. spuria* ssp. *demetrii* is a tall plant (approximately 36" tall) and a lovely shade of blue and grows wild on dry hillsides in the Caucasus. This species also has 38 chromosomes. *I. spuria* ssp. *notha* is a very robust plant that grows approximately 3' tall with flowers of a navy blue with a small white signal (The hybrid 'Whitewater River' approximates the color of the species.) This species grows from the Caucasus to Kashmir and has 44 chromosomes. In contrast to the other subspecies of *I. spuria*, *I. spuria* var. *carthalinae* is a much lighter shade of blue, with nearly sky blue flowers. The selected clone 'Georgian Delicacy' (Schafer-Sacks '98) is a good example of the color with a more quilled form typical of the species. *I. spuria* var. *carthalinae* is found in areas of the former Soviet Union and has 44 chromosomes. The most widespread and vigorous subspecies of the complex is *I. spuria* var. *halophila* and is distinctive in color from the other species in having white through pale yellow flowers. *I. spuria* var. *halophila* is found throughout European Russia, the Caucasus, and extends further east into Mongolia, Afghanistan and China, growing in marshy areas, as one might suspect from its species name. The subspecies *musulmanica* and *klatii* are often considered the same species

although the breeding behavior of the two species observed by Niswonger (2009) indicates that they may be different. Both have 44 chromosomes and are large blue-violet flowers on 3' stalks. Both species are natives of the Caucasus extending eastward into Kashmir and Azerbaijan. *I. spuria* var. *spuria* is a moderately-sized plant with blue violet flowers. It is native of many parts of Western Europe but everywhere is extinct or endangered. Unlike the other subspecies of this species, *I. spuria* var. *spuria* is a diploid with 22 chromosomes. Because many irises with 40+ chromosomes are tetraploid, it can be assumed that the subspecies with 44 and probably those with 38 chromosomes are tetraploid. Hadley (1958) observed chromosomal arrangements in meiosis such as quadrivalent chromosome associations that are noted in tetraploids in 40-chromosome garden hybrids. Thus, one can explain the 44-chromosome forms as tetraploids and the *I. spuria* var. *spuria* subspecies as a diploid. The subspecies with 38 chromosomes may also be tetraploids but of different species with lower base chromosome numbers or ancient amphidiploid hybrids. Most of the blue-flowered spuria species do not make good garden plants as they will grow fine and then suddenly rot and die for no apparent reason. Luckily, hybridizers have been able to incorporate the desirable characters of these species into the persistent garden hybrids.

Perhaps the most important species is *I. orientalis,* a native of Turkey and some of the Greek islands. This plant was known for years as *I. ochraleuca* and you will often see the plant listed under this name. *I. orientalis* is a tall white flowered plant with a large golden signal; many clones of this species have falls that tuck under giving an odd shape to the flower. This species is very persistent. Around the Salem, Oregon, area, I have observed huge clumps in long-deserted lots. Several clones of this species have been registered with 'Shelford Giant' stretching to 6' tall. *I. orientalis* has 40 chromosomes and is most likely a tetraploid and is involved in the pedigree of virtually every spuria iris hybrid.

I. crocea is a beautiful plant, a huge clear yellow with a slightly darker signal and very good form. This species contributed its yellow color to many of the early hybrids. Although *I. crocea* was collected in Kashmir, it was found only around cemeteries, suggestive of some influence of man on its distribution. *I. crocea* is a very persistent plant and makes large clumps that last for years. This species has 40 chromosomes.

"*I. monnieri*", a clear light yellow flower of fine form, is no longer considered a species. It was originally described as coming from the island of Rhodes but has not been found again in the wild. Self-pollinated progeny of this plant are very similar to *I. orientalis*. These data led Lenz (1963) to suggest that "*I. monnieri*" is a hybrid between *I. orientalis* and one of the yellow-flowered species, either *I. crocea* or *I. xanthospuria* as "*I. monnieri*" is also a 40-chromosome plant.

"*I. monnieri*" was used extensively in hybridization and is responsible for the Foster series with the prefix "Monspur."

The most recent addition to the tall spuria species is *I. xanthospuria*, formerly called "Turkey Yellow." Lee Lenz grew this species from seed collected near Ankara, Turkey, in 1948 and more recent accessions have been found from other areas of Turkey. *Iris xanthospuria* is a very intense yellow and its progeny are some of the darkest yellow, verging on orange. This species also has 40 chromosomes.

SHORT SPECIES

The group of shorter species has had no impact on the development of the garden hybrids. However, several of these species are interesting garden plants and have some qualities not found in the larger species or hybrids from them.

Iris graminea is the most widely grown of the short species. This species makes a very dense clump of rhizomes with pretty green leaves and stalks of approximately 15" stems with reddish purple flowers that are just below the height of the foliage. The flowers have a distinct plum scent that is quite delightful. I remember seeing a clump of this iris in Lynn Markham's Massachusetts garden many years ago, a piece of a clump from Bee Warburton's garden. As a native of Austria, it grows well in even cold climates. The variety 'Colchica' has distinctly yellow foliage but is otherwise similar to the species. *Iris sintenisii* is a dark purple flower with the falls white with dark purple lines. Plant habit is similar to *I. graminea* and this makes a charming evergreen clump. *Iris pontica* is very short, up to about 3 to 4" tall and with much taller foliage. It is a pity that *I. kerneriana* is not an easier garden plant as it is an

Vaughn seedling

Vaughn seedling

attractive clear yellow flower of a spidery form on stalks 12 to 15" tall. Some gardeners have good luck with this species and seed from this species is often offered in the seed exchanges.

SMALL AND MINIATURE CULTIVARS

Most spuria cultivars are tall, from 3 to 5' in height and with large flowers. Although these large plants make dramatic landscape effects, they may be out of place in the smaller gardens that many of us have. Similarly, when spuria stalks are cut for use in flower arrangements, the bigger stalks are generally cut off by at least a third.

Several breeders have selected small seedlings that occurred as smaller segregants from crosses of larger cultivars as well as using some of the spuria species that are smaller than the standard spurias. Barry Blyth self pollinated 'Satinwood' and obtained the small golds 'Elves Gold' (Blyth '93) and 'Goblin's Song' (Blyth '93) and the brown 'Leprechaun's Kiss' (Blyth '93). Charles Jenkins has worked in the small spurias extensively and introduced the blue-violet/white bicolor 'Little Frills' (Jenkins '98), cream with large orange yellow signal 'Little Splash' (Jenkins '97), ruffled blue 'Tiny Lou' (Jenkins '90), the cream *I. halophila* seedling 'Elfin Sunshine' (Jenkins '98), violet 'Mini-Trend' (Jenkins '97), and cream-yellow 'Baby Chick' (Jenkins '92). Ben Hager utilized the tiny species *I. spuria* var. *maritima* crossed on to normally-sized spurias to produce the tiny 'Maritima Gem' (Hager '90). Similarly, crosses of *I. halophila* into smaller ruffled cultivars gave Eleanor McCown the beautifully fluted and ruffled white 'Highline Snowflake' (McCown '91). The author used 'Highline Snowflake'

Vaughn seedling

to produce his 'Angel's Smile' (Vaughn '14), an even more ruffled white with gold signal.

All of these small cultivars are selections from the tall species. It would seem to be better to start with the better dwarf species for such hybridizing efforts. Geddes Douglas (1958) first proposed this idea in print and his colleague Paul Cook had attempted crosses between *I. graminea* and *I. sintenisii* with each other and with *I. spuria* subspecies *halophila*. Unfortunately, none of these hybrids were released to the market. Alice White (described in Lenz 1963) obtained a hybrid of one member of the *I. spuria* complex and *I. graminea*. The hybrid had 28 chromosomes, which is consistent with its pedigree. Another possible advantage of using the dwarf species *I. graminea* is to transfer the lovely plum scent to larger-flowered sorts.

Englishman Peter Barr was the first to introduce spuria irises in 1889 and 1899, with the trio of blue-violet hybrids 'A.J. Balfour', 'Lord Wolsely', and 'Premier'. The pedigrees of these irises are not known although they are likely raised from bee set seed, as was the custom of iris nurseries of these days. 'Premier' is still found listed in catalogs and is behind many of the reverse bicolors and striped flowers.

Bertrand Farr imported all of the Barr cultivars to the United States around the turn of the century and was involved in hybridizing all classes of irises. Only one spuria iris was introduced by Farr, 'Mrs. Tait' (Farr '12), a clear lavender blue self with a gold signal. The similarity of 'Mrs. Tait' to the Barr cultivars indicates that one of these was probably the parent of 'Mrs. Tait'.

Vaughn seedling

Sir Michael Foster produced the first planned hybrids, crossing the hybrid 'Monnieri' with an unidentified *I. spuria* type to produce a "Monspur" strain. Based upon the chromosome count of the hybrids, it is likely that some 44-chromosome spuria was used in the cross, probably *I. spuria* var. *halophila* or *notha*. Apparently several of these Monspur clones were offered, with the one known as 'Monspur Cambridge Blue' (Foster '10) the one most frequently seen today and likely the one used in crosses by others. One of the most enduring of the Foster hybrids is 'Shelford Giant' (1907), an *I. orientalis* seedling in similar coloration to its parent, but on a stalk that can grow to 6' tall. These introductions served as a basis for further breeding.

Thomas A. Washington of Nashville, Tennesee, started breeding spurias in the 1920s (Nesmith 1958), using 'Mrs. Tait', a Monspur blue, *I. orientalis* and *I. halophila* to create a unique strain that has distinctly summer green foliage. Unfortunately, he kept no written records of his results so only the recollections of Betty Nesmith, who introduced his strain, allow us some indication as to the parents involved in these Washington hybrids (Nesmith 1958). Chromosome counts indicated that the Washington hybrids did involve some 44-chromosome species or hybrids. This higher chromosome number made crosses onto other strains difficult and only the bronze-red-purple 'Monteagle' (Washington '36) was used much in crosses by other hybridizers. Even with it, the number of seedlings obtained in crosses to other hybrids is small (Muhlestein 1962).

The great iris hybridizer Hans Sass introduced but one spuria, the bright gold 'Sunny Day' (Sass '31). 'Sunny Day' is a very vigorous grower and performs well in climates where many spurias do not, such as New England. As a measure of its popularity, 'Sunny Day' won the Nies award in 1957, twenty-six years after it was introduced into commerce.

Interest in hybridizing spurias now moved to Southern California and stayed until the 1980s. Jemina Branin was the first of these California hybridizers. She imported many of the Barr and bought all the Farr cultivars. Using this base, she created series of hybrids, including white with yellow signal 'Alice Eastwood' (Branin '29), and the golds 'Golden Gate' (Branin '31) and 'Golden State' (Branin '33). 'Alice Eastwood' was used by many breeders and is behind many of the Ferguson introductions.

In this background, two of the most important spuria hybridizers, Eric Nies and Carl Milliken, were starting their careers. Eric Nies started with *I. orientalis* and crossed it with one of the blue 'Monspur' types, in an effort to improve the quality and color of the blue spurias. In the first generation all of the seedlings resembled *I. orientalis*, but selecting first generation seedlings with slight blue tinges and intercrossing them gave a second generation that included much better

blues and, most unexpectedly, a brown (Nies 1947). From this population came the blue 'Azure Dawn' (Nies '43), the first brown 'Bronzspur' (Nies '41), and the lavender-blue blended 'Saugutuck' (Nies '41). Nies strictly followed line breeding, combining the best of these seedlings to create an incredible selection of hybrids that greatly enhanced the public image and interest in these plants. It is very fitting that the top award for spuria irises, the Nies Medal, is named for this outstanding hybridizer. Chief among these later Nies hybrids are cream and gold 'Lark Song' (Nies '46), frilly blue 'Dutch Defiance' (Nies '43), blended lavender 'Two Opals' (Nies '46), brown 'Cherokee Chief' (Nies '51) plus the two very dark browns that were released after his death, 'Black Point' (Nies-Walker '55) and 'Driftwood' (Nies-Walker '57). 'Driftwood', 'Lark Song', 'Cherokee Chief' and 'Dutch Defiance' would all win the Nies Award many years after his passing, indicating the strength of this breeding program and the power of line breeding to recover recessives and combinations of colors. Besides improving the blue colors, Nies gave us the first brown spurias as well as the darker colors and blends. Moreover, the form of these hybrids was much improved, with wider parts, more flaring falls and petal ruffling occurring for the first time. Virtually every spuria iris hybrid introduced subsequently has a Nies cultivar as an ancestor.

Carl Milliken was an important hybridizer of many kinds of irises and daylilies. Although he only introduced four spuria irises, two of them proved to be pivotal breeders. 'Wadi Zem Zem' (Milliken '43) is a huge cream-yellow self that is produced on stalks about 50" tall. 'Wadi Zem Zem' shows extreme resistance to mosaic virus, a scourge of spurias, and was quickly utilized by hybrids to infuse this quality into other hybrids. 'White Heron' (Milliken '48) is a large white flower with a small yellow signal on the falls, carried on very tall stalks. Unfortunately, the pedigrees of these plants are unknown, although Ben Hager has speculated that 'Mt. Whitney' (Milliken '33), a selected *I. orientalis* seedling, may be one of the parents of 'White Heron'. 'Wadi Zem Zem' won the first Nies Award and 'White Heron' the third.

Hybridizer Tom Craig didn't do things a little. Armed with a family of volunteer (?) workers composed of members of his large family, he was able to make large numbers of crosses and huge volumes of seed from each cross. Although a move of the nursery and a flooding (and death) of the spuria plantings ended Craig's hybridizing (Vallette 1961), his 'Big Cloud' (Craig '50), a huge white with a yellow signal was the first of many 'Wadi Zem Zem' seedlings, and 'Blue Valentine' (Craig '50), a yellow and blue blend from Nies's 'Two Opals', are excellent examples that have survived to this day.

From nearby Arizona, Dr. Philip Corliss was a tireless promoter of spuria irises, writing many popular articles, and encouraging the establishment of the Spuria Iris Society.

Vaughn seedling

seedling, named 'Laced Butterfly' (Muhlestein '61), combines the Washington spuria 'Blue Acres' with Nies's 'Two Opals' and is a pastel lavender blend.

Walker Ferguson was one of the most innovative hybridizers of the 1950s through '70s and produced a number of outstanding hybrids in almost all of the color classes. His early hybridization was almost all extensions of the Nies lines, selecting for improvements in form and color (Ferguson 1961; 1964; 1969). However, like fellow breeder Tell Muhlestein, he began by crossing Washington, Milliken and Foster spurias into the Nies strain. These additions would open up both new colors and patterns into these lines. Ferguson's first break was his clean white with yellow signal 'Wakerobin' (Ferguson '59) from a cross of 'Color Guard' × 'Wadi Zem Zem'. 'Wakerobin' would win the Nies Award in 1966. A cross of 'Lark Song' × 'Color Guard' gave the blue-purple 'Thrush Song' (Ferguson '59), which is a much improved version of 'Color Guard', with better form and more blue in the falls. 'Thrush Song' won the Nies Award in 1964. A sibling to 'Thrush Song' that was a whiter version of 'Lark Song' with extra ruffling and eight flowers per stem crossed with 'Investment' (Craig '51) gave Ferguson the widest-petaled spuria of its time, the white with bold lemon signal 'Windfall' (Ferguson '58). 'Windfall' would impart these wider petals to numerous progeny, both for Ferguson and others. The same 'Thrush Song' sibling would give the ruffled white 'Ruffled Moth' (Ferguson '63), which gave rise to the white standards/ yellow bicolor 'Dawn Candle' (Ferguson '65). 'Dawn Candle' would win the Nies Award and proved to be a wonderful parent, imparting ruffling and wide blossom parts to its progeny.

Although he introduced a number of spurias, most were not widely distributed. Some of his later introductions were handled by Fairmont Gardens in Massachusetts and many used the word "butterfly" in the name to promote his idea of renaming the spurias "butterfly irises." Corliss introduced the first grey, brown amoenas, and even horned blossoms in his hybrids; some of these advances have yet to be realized in modern hybrids (Corliss 1958).

Marion Walker inherited the Nies plants and introduced the final plants from the Nies breeding program. Walker also utilized the Nies strain and the Milliken irises to produce many more hybrids, some of which were introduced through Schreiner's Iris garden with their lovely color catalog. Foremost among these introductions are the large white veined pale blue called 'Morningtide' (Walker '56), the brilliant gold 'Oroville' (Walker '71), ruffled white and gold 'Lydia Jane' (Walker '65), and the white with very little yellow signal 'Sierra Nevada' (Walker '74). All of these irises would be used extensively by other hybridizers.

Tell Muhlestein was a great hybridizer of bearded irises and his catalogs were treasure troves of breeding information for budding hybridizers. He turned to spuria breeding in the 1950s after being given collections of some of the newer cultivars (Muhlestein 1962). Crossing Washington's 'Monteagle' with 'Bronze Butterfly' gave the first "red" spuria iris, 'Red Step' (Muhlestein '94). Although only of moderate size and with limited fertility, 'Red Step' is behind almost all present day red spuria irises. Another break in the Muhlestein spuria breeding was the first appearance of lace in the tissue. This

One of Ferguson's most inspired crosses was crossing Nies's 'Two Opals' × Barr's 'Premier' which gave the first of the dark top series from this hybridizer, 'Counterpoint' (Ferguson '62), with dark blue-violet standards and yellow falls strongly veined violet. Directly from 'Counterpoint', Ferguson produced the blue standards/white falls 'Moon by Day' (Ferguson '63) and the blue standards/yellow falls 'Minneopa' (Ferguson '69). The next generation from 'Moon by Day' gave the outstanding blue-violet/ orange-yellow 'Allegory' (Ferguson '66). A later cross of 'Premier' with a seedling gave the very popular 'Blue Spiderweb' (Ferguson '66), with blue standards and white falls finely veined blue, in a spider web pattern. These dark top spurias would be used extensively by other hybridizers, resulting in not only dark tops but a number of cultivars with strongly lined falls.

The other important contributions from the Ferguson lines are the production of the first red and pink cultivars. Neither of these colors existed in the spuria species and even now neither true red or pink spurias have been produced, although we are closer now thanks to this pioneering work of Ferguson. Ferguson first noted a hint of red in a brownish seedling from 'Alice Eastwood' × 'Color Guard'. Crossing this red tinted seedling to the brown 'Driftwood' gave the first of the red spurias, 'Shift to Red' (Ferguson '63). Crossing 'Shift to Red' with Muhlestein's 'Red Step' gave the maroon-red 'Red Oak' (Ferguson '66). 'Fireplace' (Ferguson '67), a violet purple tinted red, is the product of another red-tinted blue seedling from 'Two Opals' × 'Gold Nugget' with

'Cherokee Chief' and 'Counterpoint' and that seedling (62-4) crossed with 'Shift to Red'. 'Fireplace' would turn out to be a progenitor not only of reds, but also pink spurias. 'Pink Candles' (Ferguson '73), 'Transition' (Ferguson '72), and 'La Senda' (Ferguson '72) are all approaches to pink that are descendants of 'Fireplace'. It should be noted that neither the red nor pink spurias of Ferguson are quite those colors but are significant steps towards these colors. Some of these require more imagination to see these colors! Other breeders would use these cultivars in getting cultivars even closer to these colors.

The last great accomplishment of the Ferguson breeding program was in the very dark spurias. Many of these are from crossing some of the dark blues and purples with browns and reds. 'Proverb' (Ferguson '71) is a very dark blue purple with large yellow signals that resembles the Nies hybrid 'Color Guard' in color and distribution but in a much more refined flower. 'Proverb' won the Nies Award in 1977. 'Purple Profundo' (Ferguson '72), a seedling from red breeding, is nearly a purple self, one of the few spurias without much of a signal. 'Crow Wing' (Ferguson '72) is nearly black, but unfortunately a slow grower. Despite this slow growth, 'Crow Wing' has turned out to be an exceptional parent, producing seedlings in delicious dark shades and most seem to be at least adequate growers as well.

Eleanor McCown was one of the most successful spuria hybridizers, winning several Nies Awards and Medals during her hybridizing career. Most of her introductions carry the "Imperial" or "Highline" designations that are her horticultural "stable names." McCown lived in the Imperial Valley of California, where spuria irises were one of the few horticultural plants that succeeded. McCown's first big success in spuria breeding was 'Highline Lavender' (McCown '68). This was one of the first departures in spuria form in which the standards were wider and shorter and the falls were less elongated, but much broader. 'Highline Lavender' proved to be a wonderful parent, siring directly the huge blue-lavender and Nies Medal winner 'Betty Cooper' (McCown '82), the gold infused with brown Nies Award winner

'Violet Fusion'

'Highline Honey' (McCown '78) and the first gold edged with white 'Highline Halo' (McCown '82). 'Highline Honey' was the first of the brown-toned spurias in the new compact form and would be used by many hybridizers across the country. McCown was strongly influenced by Walker Ferguson's breeding lines. In the "pinks," McCown took the Ferguson lines to a much closer to pink color and with much better form in her lavender-pink infused coral 'Highline Coral' (McCown '86). 'Highline Coral' would be another Nies Award winner for McCown. Similarly, she used the Ferguson brown 'Dark and Handsome' to create the dark brown/orange yellow bicolor Nies Award winner 'Adobe Sunset' (McCown '79), and Ferguson's bright gold 'Forty Carats' was the parent of the brilliant orange-gold 'Penny Bunker' (McCown '82). McCown was one of the first to purposively breed for smaller flowers. One of her earliest introductions was the small-flowered but tall white 'Canary Caprice' (McCown '67) but her 'Highline Snowflake' (McCown '91) set the standard for small spurias. 'Highline Snowflake' is a heavily ruffled white with a bright yellow signal that is from *I. halophila* breeding.

Ben Hager was one of the most prolific and successful of all iris breeders and his contributions to the spuria world are in many different colors and plant types. One of Hager's most important contributions was the introduction of several new species into a group that was dominated by *I. orientalis* in its breeding. Hager's first success in this area was 'Elixir' (Hager '64), in which the new species "Turkey Yellow" (now *I. xanthospuria*) was crossed with 'Wadi Zem Zem'. 'Elixir' was the first of the spurias to have significant orange tones, especially in the signal area, and captured the Nies Award in 1971, the first of many for Hager. Unfortunately the most orange-toned of these yellows tended to be small and simple flowers although each generation showed improvement with bright gold 'Eagle' (Hager '71) and the very full-formed and brilliant orange-yellow siblings 'Destination' (Hager '84) and 'Headway' (Hager '86). 'Destination' would win the Nies Award in 1989 and is serving as a parent for even more orange tones. Besides this wonderful group descended from *I. xanthospuria*, Hager also introduced spurias from *I. spuria* var. *demetrii*, 'Megatrend' (Hager '86), from *I. spuria* var. *maritima*, the tiny 'Maritima Gem' (Hager '90), and a trio from *I. spuria* var. *cathalinae*, 'Essay' (Hager '64), 'Neophyte' (Hager '64), and 'Protégé' (Hager '69). Although these plants were less fertile than many of the other spurias, once a second generation is produced, the chromosome counts return to a balanced number and the progeny are fully fertile. Many of the blue spurias to this date tended to fade and the introduction of other sources for blue color was a great help in producing non-fading blues.

Not all of Hager's hybrids involved these species however. Like Eleanor McCown, he was impressed with the progress made by Walker Ferguson in producing better forms and new colors and used these advances in his own breeding. Using the very wide 'Windfall' with his own seedlings, Hager produced 'Archie Owen' (Hager '70) that took the spuria world by storm. Here was a flower with very wide and ruffled flower parts of a clear yellow in nearly a self-colored blossom. It graced the cover of the 1970 Melrose Garden catalog and quickly won the Nies Award in 1973. Although Hager introduced no spurias from it, 'Archie Owen' would prove a useful parent for many other hybridizers.

Hager's red and pink lines also descend from the Ferguson cultivars in these shades but show improvements in form and color. 'Countess Zeppelin' (Hager '87), named for the outstanding plantswoman Helen von Stein Zeppelin, is an unusual shade of red, sort of overlaid with mauve. Although the flowers aren't large the color and form was a big improvement and 'Countess Zeppelin' won the Nies Medal in 1997. 'Zamboanga' (Hager '92) is a more traditional colored red, from the brown side. Its parentage is all-Ferguson cultivars, combining browns, golds and reds. 'Custom Design' (Hager '81) combines the Ferguson purple with Hager's lavender line but is surprisingly a maroon with a prominent gold signal. 'Custom Design' has wonderful flower form and the bright signal sets this flower alive in the garden. Hager's last spuria introduction, 'Stars at Night' (Hager '97) is a seedling from 'Crow Wing' and approaches black in color, with a startling bright yellow signal that adds pizzazz to the flower.

Hager's pinks descend from the Ferguson reds and were the first really pinkish ones, to my eyes. 'First Fruits' (Hager '84), an orchid-pink with a small yellow signal, was the first of these. Crossing 'First Fruits' with 'Perfect Spring' (Hager '85), a lavender descended from the Nies line, resulted in the orchid-violet 'Innovator' (Hager '91), a huge flower with very wide flower parts.

Hager also dramatically improved white spuria irises. His first from these lines is 'Ila Crawford' (Hager '76), the first of these whites to display lots of ruffling and exceptionally wide parts; 'Ila Crawford' won the Nies Award in 1979. It took 16 years before Hager registered 'Ila Remembered' (Hager '92), an 'Ila Crawford' seedling with much wider parts and much more extensive ruffling. Like its famous mother, 'Ila Remembered' captured the Nies Medal in 2000. Most white spurias have a large yellow signal, no doubt from the preponderance of *I. orientalis* in the pedigree of so many of the white spurias. Hager worked for generations to reduce the signal and his 'Fixed Star' (Hager '90) and 'Future Perfect' (Hager '93) have lovely form and minimal yellow signals.

Glenn Corlew and Joe Ghio were both part of the new generation of iris hybridizers from California that experimented some with spurias even though their major interests were in the bearded irises. Corlew's first introduction 'Social Circle' (Corlew '79), a white and yellow bicolor, was the most ruffled spuria of its day and sired the even wider and more ruffled similarly-colored 'Infini' (Corlew '83). My favorite of the Corlew introductions is the very ruffled and compact-formed cream with quince yellow infusions 'Offering' (Corlew '92). 'Offering' reminded me right away of the revolution in form that 'White Swirl' had done for Siberians and 'Clara Goula' did for Louisiana irises. Both Barry Blyth and the author would use 'Offering' as a parent with great results. Glenn's work with the intense yellows gave the siblings orange-yellow 'Flint Ridge' (Corlew '92) and bright but deep gold 'Sentra' (Corlew '93). Both of these had the bigger size that is so difficult to come by in the golds descended from *I. xanthospuria*. Joe Ghio's work was primarily with the dark browns and purples, combining the best of the West Coast hybridizers. 'Ethic' (Ghio '78), a seedling from McCown's 'Highline Lavender', has the wider ruffled form of its parent but in a deeper blue blossom. More dramatic was the very dark brown 'Border Town' (Ghio '84) that combines the dark color with the round ruffled form of its parent 'Ethic'. 'Border Town' gave rise to the mahogany brown self 'Brownstone' (Ghio '93), one of the few spurias that show almost no signal pattern. The more recent Ghio dark purples descend from these earlier dark flowers with blackish purple 'Evening Dress' (Ghio '84) a seedling from 'Ethic' and dark blue-purple with a near black sheen 'Lucky Devil' (Ghio '88), a seedling from 'Border Town'. All of these dark irises from Ghio are good garden plants and have proven very useful as parents.

Like many other iris breeders, Dave Niswonger started breeding tall bearded irises before starting breeding spurias. His breeding program has netted him many awards, including a string of Nies Awards and Nies Medals for his spuria breeding. Many of his spurias carry the stable name "Missouri" for his home state, as he gardens in Cape Giradeau. Like many others, he was fascinated by the work of Walker Ferguson and his lines are clearly built upon this base. Niswonger took up Ferguson's challenge of producing true pinks descended from the pinkish hybrid 'Fireplace'. Niswonger's first hybrid along this line, 'Firemist' (Niswonger '91), has an all-Ferguson pedigree and is sort of a rosy-orchid but of better form than the Ferguson cultivars. The next generation from 'Firemist' crossed to Niswonger's seedlings gave the more well-formed blend of yellow, rose and violet 'Missouri Dreamland' (Niswonger '99) and the mauve-pink 'Rivulets of Pink' (Niswonger '96) that has glints of pink in some lights or growing conditions. The latest offering from Niswonger's pink line, 'Missouri Orchid' (Niswonger '06), has the nicest form and a smooth orchid-pink coloration. Niswonger has laughingly been accused by others of "seeing pink where this is none" but he has made progress in both form and color upon the Ferguson original selections. Niswonger has also pursued the dream of an orange spuria and his 'Missouri Orange' (Niswonger '98) is among

the closest to this color, a golden orange with a deeper signal that approaches true orange, and makes a lovely clump in the garden. 'Missouri Orange' won the Nies Medal in 2009.

Niswonger's dark spurias are also based on Ferguson lines. 'Cinnamon Stick' (Niswonger '83), a maroon brown heavily speckled gold, is a seedling of the very dark and excellent breeder 'Crow Wing'. This popular hybrid won the Nies Medal in 1990. 'Redwood Supreme' (Niswonger '79) is nearly a brown/orange bicolor and descends from both the Ferguson golds and browns. Crossing 'Cinnamon Stick' with 'Redwood Supreme' gave the deep red-violet 'Sultan's Sash' (Niswonger '90), a very well-formed flower and winner of the Nies Medal in 1999. The latest from this line, 'Missouri Iron Ore' (Niswonger '99), is an unusual combination of purple infused red standards over more rust-red infused purple falls. The form of 'Missouri Iron Ore' is very wide and full and it quickly gained the Nies Medal in 2005. 'Missouri Autumn' (Niswonger '97) is a light brown self from 'Redwood Supreme' breeding. It captured the Nies Award in 2009.

One of Niswonger's biggest contributions to the spuria gene pool is bringing in other species (Niswonger 2009). These have especially improved the quality of blue spurias, which tend towards lavender and tend to fade. These first generation crosses to species are often sterile or nearly so because most of the hybrid spurias have a chromosome count of 40 and these species have chromosome counts of 38 or 44. Nevertheless a good many of these hybrids have shown at least some fertility and have proven to be useful parents. Luckily the next generation seems to be much more fertile. Even more miraculously, most are very finished flowers, not typical of crosses to species in other groups. From *I. spuria* var. *notha* crossing came the fine set of blues 'Castor River' (Niswonger '06), 'Eleven Point River' (Niswonger '01), 'Gasconade River' (Niswonger '01), and 'Whitewater River' (Niswonger '01), named for favorite fishing and recreating sites of the hybridizer. My favorite of these is 'Castor River', a vivid blue violet standards over gold falls edged the same as the standards. It has also proven to be an easy parent, setting both seed and having fertile pollen. From *I. spuria* var. *demetrii* came the tall deep blue 'Missouri Springs' (Niswonger '94), the winner of the Nies Medal in 2001, and the only first generation from the species hybrid so honored. Although authorities consider *I. spuria* spp. *klatii* a synonym of *I. spuria* ssp. *musulmanica*, Niswonger has found that these species accessions breed quite differently. From the *klatii* clone Niswonger named two offspring, 'Russian Blue' (Niswonger '83) and 'Russian White' (Niswonger '83). Both of these hybrids are exceptionally tall and have more the wide open form of the earlier species hybrids. However, in the next generation, a seedling from 'Russian Blue', named 'Adriatic Blue' (Niswonger '96), a large flower with very modern form and intense blue standards and gold falls edged the color of the standards, would appear. 'Adriatic Blue' is one of the finest garden plants yet produced and it won the Nies Medal in 2006.

B. Charles Jenkins was trained as a geneticist and spent much of his professional career breeding the grain triticale. In retirement he turned to spuria breeding and introduced more than any other hybridizer to this point. His hybridizing technique was the most different too. In order to create diversity, he deliberately made the widest outcrosses, crossing large to small and without regard to colors or patterns (Jenkins 2009). As a plant breeder he realized that plant breeding is in part a numbers game and he raised relatively large patches of

tall bearded irises. 'Proud Moment' has very wide and ruffled petals and exceptional substance, with blooms lasting for a week. 'Giuseppe' has the widest bloom parts of any spuria to date and was selected from a patch of 3,000 seedlings by Joe Ghio as the best of the group. The name honors Ghio's Italian heritage by using the Italian name for Joseph as the name for this plant. Yellows from this wide outcross campaign include 'Amber Gleam' (Jenkins '93), 'My Gold' (Jenkins '92), 'No Mas Dineros' (Jenkins '08), 'Dandilite' (Jenkins '94), 'Finally Free' (Jenkins '80), 'Alphaspu' (Jenkins '92), 'Butter Ripples' (Jenkins '99), 'Candle Lace' (Jenkins '90) and 'Lady Butterfly'

'Missouri Dreamland'

'Missouri Iron Ore'

'Missouri Autumn'

seedlings in order to increase his odds of finding introducible plants. Of course most of the first generation of such crosses express the dominant traits such as the white/yellow pattern from *I. orientalis* or the yellow self-colored blossoms. However, Jenkins introduced a number of improvements in these color classes. In the white/yellow signal type he introduced 'Popped Corn' (Jenkins '93), 'Lively One' (Jenkins '89), 'Overwhelmed' (Jenkins '08), 'Prime Contender' (Jenkins '07), 'Bali Bali' (Jenkins '89), 'Touch of Lace' (Jenkins '91), 'Proud Moment' (Jenkins '93) and 'Giuseppe' (Jenkins '94). The last three of this group are particularly significant advances. 'Touch of Lace' has petals with tiny laciniations, resembling the lace in

(Jenkins '94). The last four of these are the most significant. 'Alphaspu', as the name implies, is the *first* spuria to bloom. It starts as much as a week ahead of the rest of the hybrids and its bright cheery colors are a welcome beginning to the season. 'Butter Ripples' is a heavily ruffled gold spuria of great height and with a larger number of buds than most. 'Candle Lace' and its seedling, 'Lady Butterfly', are the first modern yellow spurias with lacy petal edges. Both are large flowers on tall stalks.

Besides these advances in the whites and yellows, Jenkins did produce a number of interesting reds and purples, either in the initial crosses or in the second generation where some of the recessive colors and patterns would show up. He also made extensive use of Ferguson's 'Crow Wing' in crosses and recovered a number of amazing seedlings. The most significant of these are 'Universal Peace' (Jenkins '91), 'Zulu Chief' (Jenkins '92), and the siblings 'Falcon Crest' (Jenkins '95) and 'Falcon's Brother' (Jenkins '97). 'Universal Peace' has blue-purple standards over ivory falls strongly veined the color of the standards. This hybrid would prove to be a wonderful parent. 'Zulu Chief' is the darkest of the group; a near black with a glint of red or brown underlying the color. 'Falcon Crest' to me screams Halloween colors of a blackish brown standards and orange-yellow falls strongly veined and edged the color of the standards. It is a slow grower but is so striking it is worth the effort. Its sibling, 'Falcon's Brother' is not as intense a flower but nevertheless very lovely; dark brown standards over yellowish falls with a very fine pattern of dark brown veins. 'Falcon's Brother' is an easy grower. Jenkins honored himself with one of his purple seedlings, the purple with white signal 'Beesea' (Jenkins '93). 'Beesea' is phonetically his initials, B. C. Very clever.

Like Dave Niswonger, Jenkins would introduce many spuria species into his crosses and with **outstanding results**. 'Elfin Sunshine' (Jenkins '98), is an *I. spuria* ssp. *halophila* seedling in a lovely shade of cream-yellow with elegantly ruffled small flowers with nicely branched stalks. This

'Castor River'

'Adriatic Blue'

hybrid blooms early and is a good vigor grower. 'Elfin Sunshine' won the Nies Medal in 2006. (Jenkins's extensive work with small and miniature spurias is described in the section on miniature spurias above.) Pale blue 'Amanda's Eyes' (Jenkins '00), another *halophila* hybrid, is of a similar form to 'Elfin Sunshine', but a larger flower. 'Doris Irene' (Jenkins '03) is an amazingly finished flower for a first generation hybrid from *I. spuria* ssp. *musulmanica*. The flower is a vibrant blue-violet with falls lined slightly deeper and very wide petals, probably because of the sibling to 'Giuseppe' used in the cross. 'Line Dancing' (Jenkins '07) is a seedling from Ghio's brown 'Bordertown' × *I. crocea* and is an unusual dark purple with the falls white with radiating dark purple lines. 'Red Won' (Jenkins '07) is a dark red with an unusual pattern of red veins on bright yellow starburst signal on the falls. The only frustrating thing about the species hybrids of Jenkins is their low fertility. Only 'Line Dancing' has produced seedlings for me although several of the others have produced pods of seed that have failed to germinate.

Floyd Wickenkamp retired to Sun City, Arizona, in 1971 and started growing and later hybridizing spuria irises. His garden was truly in a southwest theme, with huge cactuses intercalated between the spuria plantings, definitely a novel way to display spurias. Wickenkamp's first success was his 'Son of Sun' (Wickenkamp '83), a bright gold that is the result of a cross between Hager's wide-petaled 'Archie Owen' and Ferguson's wide-brown 'Baritone'. 'Son of Sun' was one of the stars of the 1987 American Iris Society convention, winning the President's Cup, for the best iris from the host region. This was the first and only spuria so recognized. It was a landslide winner of the Nies Medal in 1994. 'Sonoran Senorita' (Wickenkamp '89) is also out of 'Archie Owen' breeding and is a large orange-yellow with wide form and ruffles. Many of the darker Wickenkamp spurias descend from that superb Ferguson purple 'Proverb' combined with a number of brass and brown spurias from other breeders. Deep violet 'Love for Leila' (Wickenkamp '86), maroon-brown 'Kaibab Trail' (Wickenkamp '85), dark violet blue 'Cobalt Mesa' (Wickenkamp '86), and blue-violet with brownish signal 'Kitt Peak' (Wickenkamp '87) are some of the first generation progeny that have outstanding form and vigor. The next generation gave rise to other interesting combinations, including the blues 'Sonoran Caballero' (Wickenkamp '89), 'Sonoran Carnival' (Wickenkamp '96), 'Sonoran Nightfall' (Wickenkamp '06), and the huge 'Sonoran Skies' (Wickenkamp '93). The unique striped brown 'Wyoming Cowboys' (Wickenkamp '94), named to celebrate his University of Wyoming alma mater, is the result of combining his line with the orange-yellow 'Headway'. Wickenkamp's hybrids represent an outstanding group of hybrids with excellent form, unique colors and patterns and strong garden growth.

For many years, Don and Bobbie Shepard had one of the largest commercial iris plantings in Arizona and their catalog featured spurias, including the new introductions of Charles Jenkins and Floyd Wickenkamp. With all those spurias it was not surprising that Don would try his hand at hybridizing. My favorite of his introductions is the appropriately named 'Midrib Magic' (Shepard '99), a pale lavender flower with a distinct stripe and falls with a similar darker center line. 'Midrib Magic' is from a cross of the very wide white 'Giuseppe' and dark purple 'Purple Reign'. Other fine spurias from Don's breeding include the violet-lavenders 'Flutter Bug' (Shepard '02) and 'Easter Design' (Shepard '02), and cinnamon-brown 'Our Cindy Ann', a sibling of 'Midrib Magic'.

Anna and David Cadd produced a number of interesting hybrids by combining lines from several different breeders and produced many unusual and beautiful hybrids. Anna was trained in plant breeding so she took the scientific approach to breeding that many lack. Ruffled lavender 'Abalone Pearl' (Cadd '05), white and purple blend 'Air Affair' (Cadd '08), dusky lavender 'Breezy Day' (Cadd '03), bright gold 'California Gold Rush' (Cadd '05), brown and yellow blend 'Kiss of Caramel' (Cadd '02), lavender with bronze signal 'Out of Dreams' (Cadd '04), white-edged golden yellow 'Soul Therapy' (Cadd '04), and lavender edged gold 'Sparkling Cider' (Cadd '02) are outstanding hybrids. My favorite of the Cadd spurias is the strong blue/white reverse bicolor 'Speeding Star' (Cadd '02). This is descended from the original dark top hybrids first produced by Walker Ferguson but has a much more modern form. 'Speeding Star' is a most deserving Nies Medal winner and is quite an interesting parent as well.

Larry Johnson was surrounded by all the wonderful hybridizers in Phoenix and set out to produce his own seedlings. 'Midnight Rival' (Johnson '93) is a very dark purple with a brownish signal on the falls and is an exceptionally vigorous spuria from the pokey grower 'Crow Wing'. It may be my most favorite of the approaches to black in spurias. 'Lemon Dilemma' (Johnson '93) is among the cleanest of the blue standards/lemon falls combination with only the barest of blue surrounding the falls. This is one of the tallest and biggest flowers and makes an outstanding tall clump for the back of the border.

Lee Walker's hybridizing program is a very innovative one, taking the best hybrids from Ferguson, McCown and Hager and using them to create new colors and patterns. An inspired cross of 'Hager's Countess Zeppelin' × Ferguson's 'Pink Candles' gave two pink-toned cultivars with names that celebrate Oregon's favorite fish, 'Salmon Sunset' (Walker '07) and 'Sockeye' (Walker '10). The cross of 'Pink Candles' with McCown's 'Highline Coral', gave what may be the pinkest spuria to date, 'Some Say It's Pink' (Walker '09). Yet another cross with 'Pink Candles', this time with McCown's beautifully formed 'Penny Bunker' gave the cool bronze and gold blend 'Neon Camel' (Walker '05). 'Solar Fusion' (Walker '05) made its public debut at the 2006 American Iris Society convention in Portland and wowed them with its gold blossoms with flushes of bronze and maroon, concentrated at the petal edges. The popularity of this plant sent it on its way to winning the Nies Medal in 2012. 'Red War Clouds' (Walker '10) is my favorite of Walker's hybrids to date, a very even dark red shade with better form than many of this color. This hybrid combines the Ferguson pinks, Hager reds and Jenkins reds in one package and has the best qualities of all these lines rolled into one.

'Speeding Star'

'Some Say It's Pink'

Barry Blyth, the great Australian breeder of bearded irises, became interested in spuria irises as a potential for cut flower potential as they are such superb irises for that purpose. The form and colors in the Blyth hybrids are exceptional and they have set new high standards for the production of spuria hybrids. A self pollination of 'Equality' gave three quality lavender spurias, 'Noble Roman' (Blyth '93/'94), 'Lavender Parade' (Blyth '93/'94), and 'Poet's Love' (Blyth '03). 'Noble Roman' proved to be an exceptional parent, giving rise to the heavily ruffled blue-lavender 'Myths and Dreams' (Blyth '99/'00) and the highly contrasted red-brown with falls brilliantly veined red-brown over gold 'Cinnamon Moon' (Blyth '04/'04), one of my favorites from his breeding. 'Wild at Heart' (Blyth '99/'00) is a very wild flower, an extreme dark top type with smoky violet black standards and bright gold falls strongly veined brown. From 'Myths and Dreams' crossing came the vivid purple with falls veined purple over white 'Bay of Silk' (Blyth '03/'04) and the ruffled lavender 'Dreamcaster' (Blyth '03/'04). Besides these large flowers Barry also selected several small spurias from self-pollinating larger cultivars. Bright gold 'Elve's Gold' (Blyth '93/'94), tan-gold 'Pixie Time' (Blyth '93/'94) and rich brown 'Leprechaun's Kiss' (Blyth '93/'94) are an outstanding group of small spurias. All are floriferous and wonderful landscape plants.

The author has been involved in hybridizing spurias for about 20 years with the aim of producing more round ruffled forms and also miniatures. My 'Banned in Boston' (Vaughn

'Solar Fusion'

'12), a cross of 'Offering' and 'Lucky Devil', combines the compact ruffled form of 'Offering' and the darker purple color of 'Lucky Devil' in a single flower. 'Banned in Boston' has proven to be a tremendous parent. 'Angel's Smile' (Vaughn '14) is a clean white with a bold lemon signal veined orange. The flower is highly ruffled and has a compact form. The plant is on the smaller side, averaging about 30" tall.

Terry Aitken is much more famous for his lovely Japanese and bearded iris hybrids, but he has also made spuria crosses and has produced a number of very nice hybrids. 'Cast of Green' (Aitken '10) and 'Cast of Walnut' ('13) are two tall and large flowered browns, the former with green wash on the falls and the latter a very deep brown with a touch of henna. 'Admiral's Braid' (Aitken '13) has one of the widest petals of any spurias and an unusual color pattern of lavender standards and yellow falls with a braided edge of brownish violet (the "braid" around the falls). Aitken's newest spuria, 'Hot Chili' (Aitken '14) is one of the best of the so-called red spurias; this is one where you can really see the red.

Jim Hedgecock is the *best* promoter of spurias. He is obsessed with spreading the word as to what wonderful garden plants they are. In addition, he rescued the last hybrids from Charles Jenkins and Joe Ghio and named and introduced these plants to the market. Hedgecock has named a few of his own hybrids, including rust red 'Blood of Eden' (Hedgecock '09), intense navy blue 'Mythical Nights' (Hedgecock '09) and dark purple with distinct lines in the falls 'Walk the Line' (Hedgecock '09).

Brad Kasperek is the master of the so-called "Broken color" bearded iris, where the petals are striped and splashed dark colors over a lighter ground color. He has not extended this interest into his spuria breeding, however (Spicker 2013). Kasperek has found that spurias are more satisfactory garden subjects as they bloom late enough that they are not bothered by late freezes that plagued his bearded iris program. 'Ibex Ibis' (Kasperek '12), a medium lavender blue with a large yellow signal is outstanding for its numerous buds and very quick growth. 'Ode to a Toad' (Kasperek '12) is a dark maroon with a vivid orange signal and is one of the brightest of the maroon-reds, which tend to be rather somber. Crossing Niswonger's 'Rivulets of Pink' on Blyth's

'Hot Chili'

'Angel's Smile'

SPURIA IRISES

'Cast of Green'

114

'Art and Soul' combined the best aspect of both, with the wider form of the Blyth line and red-purple with pink flush from the Niswonger line and resulted in 'Wapiti City' (Kasperek '13). Kasperek is growing large numbers of seedlings and it is expected that we will see more spurias from this hybridizer in the near future.

Unlike other iris groups, there has been relatively little work with spurias by the European hybridizers. However, 'Phillippa Baughen' (Baughen '06) is a huge and well-formed clear gold. It won an Award of Garden Merit from the Royal Horticultural Society. In Italy, Augusto Bianco has produced the very wide chocolate brown 'Alice Springs' (Bianco '03) and the unregistered purple over gold bicolor "Touareg." Many of the countries bordering the Mediterranean would be prime areas for growing spurias and it is a shame that they are not being promoted in these areas.

A FEW FAVORITES

Because there are fewer dealers of spuria irises, it is sometimes difficult to find some of the older cultivars and even some of the newer ones are not listed every year. However, the following are worth searching out for your garden.

OLDER FAVORITES

'Sunny Day' (Sass '38) This is one persistent plant. My neighbor in Massachusetts planted this spuria in the early 1950s and in 2002 when she passed away the plant was still there and blooming. That's impressive. The flowers are a little small by modern standards but the golden yellow color is very bright. One of the spurias that grows well even in wet summer and cooler areas.

'Blue Spiderweb' (Ferguson '62) A very neat flower of clear blue standards and white falls veined the same color of the standards. Has proven to be an outstanding parent and is behind many of the "dark top" spurias.

'Shelford Giant' (Foster '07) Okay, *giant* is the operative word here. This can grow to 60" tall and with relatively large flowers with a bold yellow blaze on the falls. It's like a super version of the species *I. orientalis*. Plant this as a clump at the back of the border. This is one you can leave and it just gets bigger and better each year.

NEWER FAVORITES

'Red War Clouds' (Walker '11) Getting unusual colors in the spurias has been difficult and Ben Hager, Walker Ferguson and Charles Jenkins all worked on producing red spurias. While not a large flower, 'Red War Clouds' approaches red from the maroon side and is a very clean, evenly colored flower and is a combination of the efforts of these previous breeders. For a nice garden effect, plant next to a golden orange for a good contrast in the bed and to show off the colors of 'Red War Clouds'.

'Adriatic Blue'

'Banned in Boston'

'Missouri Orange' (Niswonger '02) Ever since Ben Hager introduced 'Elixir', spuria breeders have been trying to increase the size of the so-called oranges and increase the size of the orange signal. This is a step in that direction with medium sized flowers of a deep gold flushed orange in the falls. Very good plant habits.

'Offering' (Corlew '92) This was one of the first spurias that I bought when I resettled in Mississippi. Form is what was important here as it has relatively short-shanked falls that make for a very compact flower. The petals are also nicely ruffled and a pleasing cream with sort of quince texture veining, giving it a cool appearance. Wonderful parent plant too.

'Adriatic Blue' (Niswonger '00) This is one of my favorite spurias of all time. A very clear blue with a bold golden lemon signal on the falls, neatly edged in blue. Very good grower and makes an outstanding clump in the garden.

'Wild at Heart' (Blyth '08) Barry Blyth has introduced a very impressive series of spurias. This to me is his best, a very contrasted dark top type with maroon-purple standards and bright gold falls veined the color of the standards.

'Highline Snowflake' (McCown '94) There aren't many quality small spurias, but this is one. Heavily ruffled flowers in clear white with a gold signal patch on the falls, neatly trimmed in white. Stalks are about 30" tall and this makes a tight clump filled with bloom.

'Banned in Boston' (Vaughn '12) This has the lovely form of 'Offering' but in a flower that has dark blue-violet standards and cream falls that are banded and vein the color of the standards. Has been an amazing parent.

'Falcon Crest' (Jenkins '02) Although this plant is not a fast increaser the flower is such a *wow* that I have to grow this plant. Standards are a solid very dark brown, nearly black, and the falls are a bright orange yellow veined and edged the color of the standards. Its sibling 'Falcon's Brother' is a good bit better grower but not as flashy.

REFERENCES

Bowley, M. (1997) Series Spuriae (Diels) Lawrence. In: *A Guide to the Species Irises. Their Identification and Cultivation.* Cambridge University Press, Cambridge. 172–194.

Corliss, P.G. (1958) Progress in breeding spuria iris. *American Iris Society Bulletin* 150: 97–101.

Douglas, G. (1958) Dwarf spurias. *American Iris Society Bulletin* 150: 101–104.

Ferguson, W. (1961) Spurias for friends and fun. *American Iris Society Bulletin* 162: 52–54.

Ferguson, W. (1964) Hybridizing and growing spurias. *American Iris Society Bulletin* 173: 23–26.

Ferguson, W. (1969) The germination of spuria iris seed. *American Iris Society Bulletin* 193: 91.

Hadley, H.H. (1958) Chromosome number and meiotic behavior in commercial varieties of spuria iris. *American Iris Society Bulletin* 150: 108–115.

Jenkins, B.C. (2009) Some observations of a spuria hybridizer. In: *The Illustrated Checklist of Spuria Irises.* Phoenix, AZ: The Spuria Iris Society. 40–41.

Lenz, L.W. (1963) Chromosome numbers in the spuria irises and origin of garden varieties. *American Iris Society Bulletin* 169: 53–69.

McCown, E. (1969) "Happenings" amongst the spurias. *American Iris Society Bulletin* 193: 89–91.

Mitchell, S.B. (1949) Iris for Every Garden. Barrows and Co., New York.

Muhlestein, T. (1962) Spurias in theory and practice. *American Iris Society Bulletin* 165: 45–49.

Nesmith, E. (1958) The Washington spurias. *American Iris Society Bulletin* 150: 82–83.

Nies, E.E. (1947) Spuria section hybrids. *The Iris Yearbook 1947*: 106–109.

Niswonger, D. (2009) Hybridizing spurias. In: *The Illustrated Checklist of Spuria Irises* (D. Jurn, editor), The Spuria Iris Society. 36–39.

Spicker, S.M. (2013) Talking spurias with Brad Kasperek. *American Iris Society Bulletin* 94(4): 89–90.

Tillie, N.M., M.W. Chase, and T. Hall (2000) Molecular studies in the genus *Iris* L.: a preliminary study. *Annali di Botanica* 58: 105–114.

Vallette, W.L. (1961) *Iris Culture and Hybridizing for Everyone.* Adams Press, Chicago, IL.

'Falcon Crest'

7 SPECIES AND SPECIES HYBRID BEARDLESS IRISES

'Berlin-Cape Connection'

The species (SPEC) class of irises as defined by the American Iris Society includes representatives of groups not included in any of the other classes but also wild or nearly wild accessions of species in another group. For example, the collected form of *I. koreana* called 'Firefly Shuffle' (Probst '11) is registered as a SPEC but so is the Siberian iris 'Forward and Back' (Schafer-Sacks '02). The latter resembles and is bred from the clones of *I. sibirica* so it more resembles the species than a modern hybrid. Species hybrids (SPEC-X) are either from crosses of different species in the wild, such as Ruth Hardy's 'Valley Banner', hybrids that occur in gardens without hand-crossing such as 'Holden Clough', or the result of deliberate crosses between species or cultivars such as the delightful *I. pseudacorus* × Japanese iris hybrid 'Pixie Won' (Copeland '92). There are also bearded SPEC and SPEC-X cultivars that have been registered, although these are not covered in this book.

The establishment of the Founders of SIGNA Medal for SPEC irises and the Randolph-Perry Medal for SPEC-X irises by the Species Iris Group of North America did much to promote the deliberate hybridizing of the species and to create many new hybrids between species. Although Perry started this trend in the early 1900s, the work of Tomas Tamberg, Shimazu, Tony Huber, Jill Copeland, Samuel Norris, and more recently Lech Komarnicki and Chad Harris have greatly added to the kinds of iris hybrids available to our gardens. Not all of the hybrids between different beardless species produce attractive offspring, but luckily, many do. If you want to try something different for your garden, these SPEC-X hybrids are lots of fun. Most interestingly, several of the hybrids produced will grow in areas and conditions where neither or one of the parent species will grow. Thus, we can extend the range where various beardless types of irises may be grown. For example, the so-called CalSibe hybrids, that are crosses of Pacific Coast Native irises and 40-chromosome Siberians, grew well in my gardens in Massachusetts, where the Pacific Coast Native irises were iffy at best.

Because of the huge variety of beardless species and the huge number of potential hybrids that could be created, these classes are extremely diverse. In this chapter, I have divided them by groups so that they may be more easily discussed.

'Do the Math'

I. koreana 'Firefly Shuffle'

WINTER BLOOMING BEARDLESS IRISES

Iris unguicularis, a native of the Mediterranean region, is one of the harbingers of spring in areas where it may be grown, chiefly California and the coastal Pacific Northwest in the United States and similar climates around the world. The flowers are not born on stems, but rather elongated perianths,

ensheathed in bracts. Because of this, trimming the foliage in the fall back to approximately 6" high will ensure that the flowers ascend above the foliage. This species has evergreen foliage and is one of the few beardless irises that prefer dry alkaline soil. In my garden in Oregon, I have a small area near my front porch that is dry because of the overhang of the roof and this soil is made more alkaline by remnants of the concrete base of my porch. The site is protected from the winter so various cultivars of *I. unguicularis* blooms from November to March in all but the coldest years. In very cold conditions (below 20° F), it is advised that blooming plants be covered to protect the delicate blooms. Although this might seem like too much work, the violet blooms, with their delicate scent of violets, are definitely worth the extra work.

There are several cultivars that have been introduced, including the violet wild collected clones 'Mary Barnard' (Anderson '62) and 'Walter Butt' (Anderson '62). Both of these clones came from near Algiers, Algeria, and both clones have been widely distributed and are available from many nurseries. These exhibit the typical pattern of a rather neat violet self with the falls having a prominent signal of white, strongly veined violet. The late Edith Cleaves made crosses between the white form of this species and a large-flowered violet named 'Imperatrice Elizabetta' (a white mottled purple clone) and obtained a number of seedlings that all have the "Winter" stable name. The two white clones that are improvements in form and size over the white form were registered as 'Winter Snowflake' (Cleaves '69) and 'Winter Treasure' (Cleaves '69). Later a purple bitone selection was registered as 'Winter Memories' (Cleaves '82), although it is not known if this clone is in fact from the same parentage as the others in the Winter series. Most recently, Rick Tasco has introduced several improvements in the *I. unguicularis* cultivars from planned crosses. My favorite is the dark violet 'Dazzling Eyes' (Tasco '04) that has a lovely bold patterns of lines on the falls and a dainty silver margin to the edge of the falls. In Oregon, this is one of the last *I. unguicularis* cultivars to bloom, usually in March, along with the earliest daffodils and primroses. The new 'Lavender Moonbeams' (Tasco '14) is a cross of the white form and a clone possibly known as "Marondera." Not only is the flower lighter than the typical violet but the flowers have wider and bigger flowers than other cultivars.

Although *I. unguicularis* has few pests, slugs can ravage the blooms and baiting in winter before the blooms emerge from the leaves is required to produce uneaten blossoms. Because *I. unguicularis* is a Mediterranean plant, it prefers to be dry and baked in the summer months. Addition of crumbled mortar or lime to the soil will improve growth of the plants but avoid much in the way of fertilizers on them. Mine may get a light sprinkle of time-released fertilizer in the spring, but nothing more.

Some authorities recognize two geographical forms as true species, *I. lazica* and *I. cretensis,* the former occupying a different ecological niche (tolerating more shade) and the latter smaller in all proportions than the typical *I. unguicularis.*

"WATER IRISES"

Several species of beardless irises are ones that will not only tolerate but thrive in moist conditions although most of these species are also highly adaptable, performing nearly as well in normal flower border situations. Only *I. pseudacorus* and *I. laevigata* grow best in standing water; the others look best in soil that is constantly moist, not submerged, although they will tolerate such conditions temporarily.

The blue-violet *I. versicolor* is actually an ancient amphidiploid hybrid of *I. virginica* and *I. setosa* var. *interior* and has the most chromosomes of any iris species with 108 (70 from *I. virginica* and 38 from *I. setosa*). It looks like a smaller version of *I. virginica* in many respects with the smaller standards and branched plant habit coming from *I. setosa*. Plants grow from 1 to 3' in height with a few smaller or taller; they bloom with the Siberian irises. *Iris versicolor* is one of the irises of my childhood. It grew wild in swamps, brook and pond edges in many areas of the town where I lived as a child and teenager and was a common wildflower throughout the Northeast United States. Among my fondest memories of my youth are my trips to Maine with Frank and Bee Warburton to visit Currier McEwen's garden. Bee had become fascinated with *I. versicolor* and on these trips we would be scouting for stands of this iris along the roadside. When one was spotted Bee or I would scream "VERSEY!" Frank would pull the car to the side of the road so that we might inspect (and collect) better forms of the species. One of these accessions was named 'Cat Mousam' (Warburton '85), because it was found at that exit on the Maine Turnpike and has the familiar blue violet coloring of the species.

Until Bee began hybridizing *I. versicolor*, there were relatively few forms available, with the reds 'Claret Cup' (Hillson '48) and 'Kermesina' (Perry '01) and the pale blue 'Stella Main' (Main '27) being the only ones of note. Besides collecting wild clones, Bee also grew seed from seed exchanges and from selected seedlings of her friends Sarah Tiffney and Betty Woods, and hybridized from all these approaches to produce a number of superior cultivars. 'Wild Hearts' (Warburton '85), 'Mint Fresh' (Warburton '83) and 'Candystriper' (Warburton '91) would offer good pink tones, the latter two giving a pink look by the application of reddish stripes on a white ground. 'Candystriper' would win the Founders of SIGNA Medal in 2002. Besides these approaches to pink, Warburton introduced the white veined violet 'Whodunit' (Warburton '87) and the violet-rose 'Party Line' (Warburton '88). Marty Schafer and Jan Sacks continued the lines of Warburton, producing the white with blue veins 'Between the Lines' (Schafer/Sacks '91), the long-blooming pale blue with white styles 'Epic Poem' (Schafer/Sacks '04), light blue with dark veining 'Light Verse' (Schafer/ Sacks '04), and the dainty white 'Versicle' (Schafer/ Sacks '98). 'Between the Lines' won the Founders of SIGNA Medal in 2001. Besides these fine plants, other hybridizers have

I. setosa 'All Stripes'

I. versicolor 'Epic Poem'

Vaughn pink
versicolor seedling

lilac 'Enfant Prodige' (Huber '93), violet 'Oriental Touch' (Huber '93) and the backcross of 'Oriental Touch' to *I. versicolor*, 'Belle Promesse' (Huber '93).

Iris virginica is very similar in shape and color range to *I. versicolor*, not surprisingly because *I. virginica* is one of the parents of *I. versicolor*. Although the wild-type plant is a mid blue-violet color, wild variants in white, pinkish, red, and dark purple are known. Ken Durio collected many of these and offered a complete range of these colors in his catalog. In general, cultivars of *I. virginica* are bigger in all proportions than *I. versicolor*, with larger stalks, foliage and flowers. *Iris virginica* is a rapid grower and is one of the few plants that can be used to underplant bald cypress. Fewer cultivars of *I. virginica* have been registered than of *I. versicolor* but the six-falled blue-violet 'Dottie's Double' (Warrell '83), lavender-blue 'Pond Lilac Dream' (Speichert '95), and white-flushed mauve 'Slightly Daft' (Hutchinson '00) are cultivars that are available. All are excellent garden plants for the damper spots in the garden.

Hybrids between *I. versicolor* and *I. virginica* are called *I. × robusta,* and *robust* they are! These are very vigorous garden plants, oftentimes with heavily purple-stained foliage that greatly adds to their garden appeal. 'Dark Aura' (Hewitt '96) has the most dramatic foliage with the foliage dark red-purple in spring and with stalks nearly black as they emerge and flowers of a fine deep violet. Stalks are almost 4' tall. 'Gerald Darby' (Darby '68) is a little paler colored in all parts

Vaughn white *versicolor* seedling

introduced *I. versicolor* cultivars, including the dark red 'Mar Jan' (Bishop '93), raspberry red 'Raspberry Slurp' (Butler '02), rose red 'John Wood' (Wood '98), and the incredibly dark, near black 'Mysterious Monique' (Knoepnadel '86). English nurseryman Galen Carter has introduced several *I. versicolor* cultivars with the "Rowden" stable name. Unfortunately these have not yet reached the United States.

Iris versicolor has been used extensively as a parent to create some unique hybrids. Tony Huber's cross of *I. versicolor* and Japanese iris cultivars is one of the most successful in terms of unique garden plants. These are extremely vigorous plants that have larger flowers than many species hybrids and many have attractive signals. Chief among these hybrids are than 'Dark Aura' and a shorter stalk at 30". Although these first two hybrids were garden plants that appeared spontaneously, 'Mountain Brook' (Kennedy '85) is from a planned cross. It is paler yet than the other two *I. × robusta* cultivars yet no less a fine grower. Jill Copeland has introduced several outstanding *robusta* clones that are the result of planned crosses including the very dark blue-violet 'Wooly Bully'

'Jinen'

(Copeland '06), pansy-violet with white spot 'For Jay' (Copeland '03), and red-violet 'Celia Welia' (Copeland '03). Because of the vigor of these clones, they should be given a good two-foot space when planting.

Ken Durio's hybrid called 'Little Caillet' (Durio '98) is a most beautiful hybrid from a cross of the collected *I. virginica* 'Light Blue' and the tetraploid Louisiana iris, 'Bayou Rouge'. The flower looks like an *I. virginica* "on steroids" with much wider petals and heavier substance but otherwise the color and plant habits of the *I. virginica* parent. I was very privileged to see one of the first blooms of this hybrid at the Society for Louisiana Irises convention in 1996 and Durio offered a plant for the auction. Marie Caillet and I both bid on the plant, raising the price to over $400 in a bidding war. When Marie bid $420 I screamed across the room, "It's yours, Marie!" To honor Marie's bid and endorsement of the plant, Ken Durio named the plant for Marie. Because there was already the Louisiana iris named 'Marie Caillet' he used her nickname "Little Caillet" to honor her. If only I had been a bit more aggressive in my bidding, I might have been immortalized! One of the amazing things was that this hybrid seems to be fully fertile. The only sad part of this tale is that 'Little Caillet' seems to produce mostly its like when self pollinated, as one might expect from an amphidiploids hybrid. Creating hybrids with other colors of *I. virginica* should allow for the full gamut of colors presently found in this species to be present in these hybrids.

Iris prismatica is an Eastern US native that looks like a very small Siberian iris or a very delicate version of *I. versicolor*. Unlike these irises which it resembles, *I. prismatica* makes long slender rhizomes that tend to run. So give this species a bit more room to run or plant it with species where it can go through with no repercussions. Most of the *I. prismatica* clones are blue-violet although even in these many have a bold signal of white on the falls. Red, pink and white variants are also known.

Iris pseudacorus, the European yellow flag, has now spread throughout the world and in many places has been banned as an invasive species. This species can grow up to 5' tall when conditions suit its growth. The stalks generally have twelve or more golden yellow flowers with a pattern of red-purple veins, although the flowers tend to last but a day. In areas where it is still legally cultivated, there are several clones that have improved quality of flowers and plant habit. Light yellow with red purple signal 'Krill' (Copeland '97) and sulfur yellow with red veins 'Seakrill' (Copeland '04) and 'Sushi' (Copeland '13) are popular selections that are less of a brassy yellow as is primrose yellow with violet veins 'Puddle Party' (Vaughn '05). A pair from Dave Niswonger, the nearly white 'Gordonville White'

The Eastern US native *Iris prismatica* makes long slender rhizomes that tend to run. So give this species a bit more room to run, or plant it with species where it can go through with no repercussions.

(Niswonger '94) and 'Gordonville Cream' (Niswonger '94) are not only paler but also tend to be less rambunctious growers as well. Two other varieties worth growing are the double flowered 'Flora-Plena' and the green and white variegated 'Variegata', although the latter has foliage that does turn green as the season progresses.

Hybrids that involve *I. pseudacorus* are for the most part sterile but offer many of the advantages of the easy culture of the species. 'Holden Clough' (Patton '71), a yellow covered in purple veins that give a brown effect, was originally thought to be a hybrid of *I. chrysographes* and *I. pseudacorus* but now it is believed that it is a cross of *I. pseudacorus* with a blue-violet water iris type. Although originally thought to be sterile, 'Holden Clough' can produce some seed. Here's the story of

---

Many of the so-called "eyelash irises" or "pseudatas" irises have a signal patch that forms a lens-shaped structure, with radiating lines from the signal that resemble eyelashes.

---

how the first of these 'Holden Clough' came into being as related to me by Phil Edinger (personal communication, Feb. 7, 2014).

> Okay, the 'Holden Clough' story…Ben [Hager], Sid [DuBose], Gary and moi drove up to Roy Davidson's place for Thanksgiving in 1982, I believe. Soon after arrival, Roy, Ben and I were strolling through the garden when we came upon Roy's large clump of 'Holden Clough'. Roy and Ben immediately got into a "discussion" about the *actual* parentage. It was a no-win conversation, so I busied myself squeezing the many capsules that were supposed to be empty. But no. I found two, as I recall, that had a few seeds in each—the first occasion that seeds had been found on 'Holden Clough'. So…after we all got back to California, Ben went into their commercial field to squeeze capsules on *his* row of 'Holden Clough', and by god he found maybe eight seeds total. I do know that he raised six to flowering. The first one he named for Roy because it was Roy's garden in which the seed potential was discovered. Then a few years later he named the darkest one after moi because I was the first to find the seeds. His crop was much

more interesting than what I raised here: four each from spontaneous pods on 'Roy Davidson' and on 'moi.' The other iris co-mingled with them was the "Gigantea" *pseudacorus* from Lorena [Reid], and *all* seedlings were minor variations on *pseudacorus*.

The yellow with strong brown-black signal 'Roy Davidson' (Hager '87) and the bright gold with brown veins 'Phil Edinger' (Hager '91) that Hager raised from this open pollinated seed on 'Holden Clough' are big improvements on their parent. 'Phil Edinger' would win the Randolph Perry Medal in 2000.

Other hybridizers have also experimented with the 'Holden Clough' family of irises. Tomas Tamberg treated some germinating seedlings from open-pollinated seed of 'Holden Clough' with colchicine and produced the dark brown 'Berlin Tiger' (Tamberg '88). 'Berlin Tiger' received an Award of Merit by the Royal Horticultural Society in 1995. A cross of 'Berlin Tiger' with 'Mysterious Monique' gave the blue-violet 'Appointer' (Tamberg '93). A similar type of cross was probably involved in the two hybrids from Terry Aitken, 'Roy's Lines' (Aitken '02) and 'Roy's Repeater' (Aitken '02), both white with a pattern of dense violet lines throughout the flower. 'Roy's Lines' would win the Randolph-Perry Medal in 2012. Sarah Tiffney was fascinated with the possible pedigree of 'Holden Clough' and carefully self-pollinated it to obtain two progeny, both surprisingly dark red-purple. One of these was named 'Holden's Child' (Tiffney '88) and went on to win the Randolph Perry Medal in 2001. Ben Hager kindly sent me a number of his seedlings from 'Holden Clough' and 'Phil Edinger' to use in further breeding. In the next generation several lemons with bright orange signals appeared as well as some seedlings with brilliant leaf variegation. Unfortunately, these variegated plants proved to be rather slow garden plants and many of these were lost, including one that I had registered as 'Ben's Legacy' (Vaughn '05). Several of the F3 and F4 seedlings from this line strongly resembled *I. pseudacorus* but had flowers that last three days rather than the one typical of *I. pseudacorus*. Fertility in these was much higher than in 'Holden Clough' although not as much as pure *I. pseudacorus* cultivars.

Another important group of *I. pseudacorus* hybrids are the so-called "eyelash irises" or "pseudatas" from cross of *I. pseudacorus* with Japanese irises. The reason for calling them "eyelash irises" is that many of these irises have a signal patch that forms a lens-shaped structure with radiating lines from the signal that resemble eyelashes. Most of these hybrids emerge with very pale yellow to green foliage because of the incompatibility between the plastome (chloroplast DNA) and

Harris *pseudata* seedling

'Lawton Ridge'

'Phantom Island'

the genome (nuclear DNA), leading to poor growth on some of these clones. One of the first of these and one of the most vigorous is 'Chance Beauty' (Ellis '88), a large bright yellow and one with good green foliage. 'Kimboshi' (Ueki '93) has the more typical yellow-green foliage and yellow flowers and 'Sayo-No-Tsuki' (Ichie '94) was the first of these hybrids to show the now more familiar pattern of white with dark purple eyelash eye. The most prolific hybridizer of these eyelash irises is Hiroshi Shimizu. In order to produce these hybrids, Shimizu selected for an improved *I. pseudacorus* type and, from British Iris Society seed obtained the yellow 'Gubijin' (Shimizu '99), which proved to be aneuploid (35 instead of the 34 chromosomes typical of the species), and appears to be a hybrid from the 'Holden Clough' family but with good fertility. Using 'Gubijin' as a pod parent and pollinating it with Japanese iris pollen gave an amazing series of irises with a light yellow to white base color and an unusual signal bold signal on the falls. These include: yellows 'Sunadokei' (Shimizu '10), 'Akimatsuri' (Shimizu '10), 'Rokyu' (Shimizu '11); whites with dark eyelash signals 'Byakuya No Kun' (Shimizu '05), 'Okagami' (Shimizu '08), 'Skokyu No Mai' (Shimizu '11), 'Hanagara' (Shimizu '14); violet to red violet 'Shiryuko' (Shimizu '08), 'Takamagahara' (Shimizu '10), 'Take No Sho' (Shimizu '08), 'Umibotal' (Shimizu '10), 'Yasha' (Shimizu '10), 'Yotsugi' (Shimizu '11); blended colors 'Tsukiyono' (Shimizu '05), 'Yarah' (Shimizu '11), 'Ause' (Shimizu '14), 'Yoru No Akari' (Shimizu '11), 'Kinshkou' (Shimizu '04). Carol Warner of Draycott Gardens has introduced these cultivars to the United States and they are carried by a number of nurseries. Sizes vary from 18 to 38" tall and all are delightful garden flowers. Jill Copeland produced the blue-violet 'Pixie Won' (Copeland '97), a charming blue-violet with gold signals edged near black from a cross of a white *I. pseudacorus* × a six-fall purple Japanese iris seedling. 'Pixie Won' would win the Randolph-Perry Medal in 2005. Bob Bauer and John Coble, prominent hybridizers of Japanese irises introduced two very wide-petaled pastel forms, the soft lemon 'Phantom Island' (Bauer/Coble '13) and the cream with pink edges 'Lawton Ridge' (Bauer/Coble '13). On a visit to Chad Harris's garden in 2013, the variety of "pseudata" types was amazing, from fairly dwarf plants, to plants that were over 4' in height and foliage from very pale to nearly green. Some of these should be coming to the market soon.

The hybrid 'Ally Oops' (Borglum '00) is one of the most vigorous hybrids yet produced and is presumed to be a hybrid between a Siberian iris and *I. pseudacorus*. 'Ally Oops' is a blue with a strong yellow infusion on the falls veined blue. Plant this hybrid and *stand back*. It will quickly fill a spot in the garden. 'Alley Oops' won the Randolph-Perry Medal in 2010.

Iris laevigata is the most water-requiring of the water irises. These have relatively large flowers with the flowers either with three broad falls and small standards or the more full six-fall types. I grow many of mine in a shallow pond next to my patio and they perform beautifully under these conditions. Some cultivars and all of the seedling plants are grown in ordinary garden conditions, with a bit of extra moisture that I would provide for Louisiana irises or daylilies. In Japan, there are many cultivars available that are not in the United States and a whole monograph describes some of these exotic beauties. In the United States, some of the more common cultivars that are available are the six-falled white mottled blue 'Colchesterensis' (Wallace '10), leaf variegated 'Variegata' (Tubergen '16), the reblooming blue-violet 'Semperflorens' (Perry '19), rose-pink 'Regal' (Perry '60), royal purple 'Midnight Wine' (Reid '92), and navy blue splashed white 'Royal Cartwheel'

'Lakeside Ghost'

'Blue Rivulets'

(Reid '81). More recently Chad Harris has started on a planned hybridization program of these lovely irises and his 'Lakeside Ghost' (Harris '12), a blue-white heavily washed and speckled darker blue, and 'Blue Rivulets' (Harris '13), a white with distinct veins cascading from the signal, are big improvements in terms of plant habit and bloom. Harris carefully selects for stalks that don't lean and healthy plants and there should be more interesting colors and patterns in future hybrids.

Iris setosa is one of the parent species of *I. versicolor* and it grows in similar sorts of conditions in the garden although perhaps in drier soils than its child. This species is a pleasing garden plant, sort of like a small branched Siberian iris with no standards and more expanded falls. Not as much work has been done with *I. setosa* although there are several color variants that have been registered. 'Arctic Goldheart' (Reid '94), a white with prominent gold signal, 'Arctic Lavender' (Reid '95), a clear lavender, and 'Arctic Rebloomer' (Lankow '94), in the blue-violet typical of the species but with rebloom, are some of the better cultivars that are commercially available. *Iris setosa* has also been much used in creating hybrids with

Variegated *I. laevigata* foliage

other beardless iris species. The most successful in terms of horticultural importance are the "Sibtosas" that are the result of crosses of garden Siberians with *I. setosa*. These hybrids look much like Siberian irises although they often show very reduced standards. The most successful of these involve tetraploid *I. setosa* seedlings crossed with the best tetraploid Siberian irises. These include the lilac 'Sibtosa Duchess' (Tamberg '02), lavender-pink 'Sibtosa Princess' (Tamberg '98), and blue-violet 'Sibtosa Ruffles' (Tamberg '05).

The cultivars of the water irises are all easy garden plants. Unlike Siberian irises that they resemble, these should be divided after 3 to 4 years of growth. Addition of a time-released fertilizer or compost in the springtime will improve the quality of the stalks and flowers and give larger and more robust plants. For species that will tolerate standing water, their culture is even more simple as their water needs are constantly met and the growth of weeds is almost nil under this condition. In the garden beds, a good mulch of pine or fir bark or something similar will make the growth, watering and weed control in these species much easier.

'Doubly Stylish'

IRIS CRISTATA AND OTHER SMALL CRESTED IRISES

One of the jewels of the Eastern US flora is the small crested iris, *I. cristata*. This species has blue flowers with a distinctive yellow crest on the falls on 3- to 8"-tall stalks. Flowers virtually cover the foliage in peak bloom. *I. cristata* is a denizen of forests and the lightly dappled shade of deciduous trees; it will carpet the ground with its long, thin, rambling rhizomes. Color variants in white and nearly pink are known, as well as all shades of blue from pale to dark navy. One of my favorite plantings at my parents' place in Massachusetts was in a large boulder that had a huge cavity that was filled in with forest humus over the years. A huge clump of *I. cristata* loved this spot and filled it in the entire cavity and the clump was covered in blooms for several weeks. In my Massachusetts neighbor Polly Bishop's garden, clumps of white ('Alba') and blue cultivars of *I. cristata* meandered between stones in a pathway and along and over a dry wall throughout her woodland garden. Anyone with a bit of high shade can produce similar effects. Virtually all of the spring-blooming ephemerals are excellent companions to these irises as are the acid-shade loving shrubs such as azaleas and rhododendrons.

Almost all of the cultivars of *I. cristata* that have been registered are collected clones. The late Don Jacobs, owner of Eco Gardens, introduced a whole series of *I. cristata* clones all with the "Eco" stable name. These include the tiny white 'Eco White Angel' (Jacobs '93), the purple with prominent style crests 'Eco Royal Ruffles' (Jacobs '93) and the very dense-blooming 'Eco Little Bluebird' (Jacobs '93). The late Sam Norris introduced two outstanding collected cultivars of *I. cristata* that are among the extremes of size in this species, the large (3½") flowers are presented on 9" stems of 'Powder Blue Giant' (Norris '97) and the tiny 'Sam's Mini' (Norris '06) with stems only 3½" tall. Marty Schafer and Jan Sacks introduced two fine cultivars, 'Little Jay' (Schafer/Sacks '01), a blue with a signal without yellow in the signal and 'Navy Blue Gem' (Schafer/Sacks '98), a small blue with an amazing density of bloom. Barbara and David Schmeider have long been enthusiasts of species irises and their beautiful wooded property in Concord, Massachusetts, is perfect for cultivation of *I. cristata*. Unlike others, they have raised numerous seedlings, rather than relying on wild selections. Their hybrids are currently the finest, with 'Doubly Stylish' (Schmeider '10), an all-falls type with signals and crests on all of the petals, 'Precious Pearl' (Schmeider '13), an odd pearlescent pale lavender, and 'Dash It All' (Schmeider '13), a navy with a bold U-U shaped signal of bright white edged navy, the three that have entered the trade to date.

'Dash It All'

Although *I. cristata* is a fairly easy garden subject given a spot in moist shade with acid soil, it is a favorite of slugs as well. Be sure to bait early in the spring to prevent damage to the newly emerging foliage and the blooms. A second baiting may be necessary in areas of high slug populations, like the Pacific Northwest. Culture otherwise is fairly simple. Plant these irises shallowly, just below the soil level, and provide a mulch of pine straw or ground conifer bark. Otherwise leave the plants pretty much alone after they are established. Mine may get a little time-released fertilizer in the spring, but are otherwise not given any extra care. Clumps tend to get bigger so they don't wear out their soil like many irises and the clumps become more and more spectacular with age.

Two other crested iris species, *I. lacustris* and *I. tenuis*, are both natives of the United States and are similar-appearing to *I. cristata* but much smaller. *Iris lacustris* is a native of the sandy shaded areas of Great Lakes area and is a good grower in that area but is difficult to grow in other areas of the country. *Iris tenuis* is a native of Oregon and was originally grouped with the Pacific Coast Native irises. It is a difficult plant in gardens even here in Oregon, however.

The other common garden-worthy crested irises require different conditions than *I. cristata*. *Iris tectorum*, the "roof iris" of the Far East, grows in soil and conditions similar to bearded irises, neutral to alkaline well-drained soil, and full sun to part shade. The typical species a pleasing blue-violet but 'Tectorum Alba' (Sprenger '01) is one of the prettiest flowers, a very frilly flat white with gold crests. A more recent collection from the wild is Waddick's 'Woolong' (Waddick '02), a blue-violet with darker spots and flecks. The clones of *I. tectorum* all suffer from the effects of virus and it is wise to keep seedlings growing of the strains to ensure virus-free plants in the garden. The 'Alba Adamgrove Strain' (Tankesley-Clarke '88) is one in which seedlings from 'Alba' have been raised for several generations, slowing the chances for virus infection. Like their bearded iris cousins, *I. tectorum* also appreciates frequent transplanting as their shallow feeder roots quickly exhaust the soil. Addition of alfalfa meal and slow-release fertilizers in the spring keeps the clumps in the best shape.

Several hybrids from crossing bearded irises and *I. tectorum* have been produced. The first, 'Loptec' (Dykes '10) is a pleasing dwarf blue with a combination of beard and crest. Much more well-distributed is the dainty sky-blue 'Paltec' (Dennis '28). As a child I noticed this plant in many gardens, often serving as an edging around bearded iris beds as it formed a nice neat low edge. Other hybridizers have finally started remaking these crosses and it is hoped that we have new examples of these very useful sterile hybrids.

The more tender crested iris species are much more iffy garden plants in all but the warmest areas of the country. *Iris japonica* is worth a try though even in colder gardens. In Salem, Oregon, both Carol Richmond and Judy Nunn grow this shade-tolerant species in their gardens and they are rewarded with long sprays of ruffled lavender blue delicate flowers. A better bet is the form 'Eco Easter' (Jacobs '06), a lovely form that is more hardy and more floriferous than the species. In my Mississippi garden, this plant meandered through the bed and put up endless sprays of pretty blue flowers, generally around Easter time there too.

"CALSIBES"

CalSibes (also written "Calsib") are crosses between Pacific Coast Native Irises (PCNs; their original designation was "California irises," hence the "Cal" part of the names of these hybrids) and Siberian irises. Generally, the Siberian in the cross is one of the 40-chromosome type, although 'Royal Californian' (Lenz '55) and 'Crimson Accent' (Witt '98) are from crosses with the 28-chromosome Garden irises. Although both the 40-chromosome Siberian irises and the PCN irises can be difficult garden subjects outside the few climates where they succeed, the CalSibes are good garden plants over a much greater range of climates. In my Zone 4 garden in Massachusetts, decidedly not a climate for PCN irises, 'Swirling Mist' (Witt

'Cosmic Symphony'

'66) performed like a trooper. It seems that the CalSibes are able to survive with more water than the PCNs and less water than the 40-chromosome Siberians plus greater hardiness and persistence than either parent. Really a happy marriage!

The first CalSibes were the creations of that most creative early iris breeder Amos Perry. These include 'Dougbratifor' (Perry '27) and the very first English Dykes Medal winner 'Margot Holmes' (Perry '27), a red-violet self that seems to be prevalent in crosses of *I. chrysographes* with any PCN mate. After a gap of more than forty years, a group of Pacific Northwest hybridizers began experimenting with the class. They had the benefit of advanced generation of both the 40-chromosome Siberians and a more varied selection of PCNs than did Perry and a greater range of colors and patterns were produced. These new generation PCNs included yellow with red stripes 'El Tigre' (Mahood '70), white with blue veins 'Fair Colleen' (Mahood '66), yellow with violet stitching

'Rubicon'

'Majestic Pearl Violet'

'Starting Calsibe' (Tamberg '83). A grandchild of 'Starting Calsibe' in wine red, 'Sunny Red Wine' (Tamberg '98), represents an improvement upon its grandfather. Dave Niswonger received seed of a cross of 'Starting Calsibe' × a yellow tetraploid CalSibe seedling from Tomas Tamberg and raised the pale yellow veined brown 'Silent Dreams' (Niswonger '97). Bee set seed from 'Silent Dreams' gave Niswonger a nice series of tet CalSibe seedlings. 'Cosmic Symphony' (Niswonger '04), a lavender blue bicolor, and 'Majestic Pearl Violet' (Niswonger '03), were two introductions from this bee pod. Growth of these hybrids has been good even in northern states. Peter Maynard has registered several tet CalSibes with the "Goring" stable name but these have not reached the United States. With the available tetraploids the genetics may be broad enough that a number of interesting hybrids can be produced, with the advantage that the progeny are completely fertile.

"PARDANCANDAS" OR *IRIS × NORISII*

Iris domestica is often sold by nurseries as *Belamcanda chinensis* and is generally offered as a mix of colors (orange with reddish spots, yellows, reddish) or as a pure yellow form known as 'Hello Yellow'. These plants bloom in July-August even in the deep South, with stalks that are highly branched and often bearing hundreds of flowers, each lasting but a day. Flowers remind one of a lily, although the flowers have the basic iris formula of three standards and three falls. After the flowers fade abundant pods are formed. At maturity these pods open to reveal shiny black seeds, arranged in a pattern that resembles blackberry fruit. *Iris dichotoma* has lavender flowers that have

'Fine Line' (Witt '78), bright yellow 'Golden Waves' (Witt '79), white with violet veining 'Carrie Dawn' (Farmer '81), flesh pink 'Half Magic' (Farmer '85), vivid orange 'Lurid Tales' (Farmer '85), bright blue 'Space Child' (Mahood '69), and lavender with deeper spot signal 'Swirling Mist' (Witt '66). These hybrids covered most of the shades found in the 40-chromosome Siberians plus a few unique colors that are the result of combinations with the PCN parent. Flower form and plant habit seem to favor the PCN parent.

Lorena Reid took the 40-chromosome Siberians to new heights and when she combined these with the new PCNs being created by Joe Ghio and others, the CalSibes she created were exceptional. 'In Stitches' (Reid '87), a violet with deeper "stitches" throughout the flower, and the "Pacific" series red-violet 'Pacific Red Velvet' (Reid '95), two violet with black signal, 'Pacific Smoothie' (Reid '93) and 'Pacific Starprint' (Reid '92), and pale lilac with a fall pattern of cream to white, 'Pacific Wildwood' (Reid '03), are all fine hybrids that typify the advancements in colors and form in the CalSibes. Most recently, Carla Lankow has created an amazing red CalSibe that has the appropriate name 'Rubicon' (Lankow '15).

All of the first CalSibes are sterile but Tomas Tamberg crossed tetraploid 40-chromosome Siberian irises (technically these would have 80 chromosomes) and tetraploid PCN seedlings as well as converting normally sterile CalSibe seedlings to fertility by doubling their chromosomes. The first of these hybrids, rosy lavender veined, is most appropriately

'Summer Candy'

'Lots of Fun'

a shape a bit more iris-like, similar in form to some of the crested irises. Like *I. domestica*, the stalks of *I. dichotoma* have flowers that last but a day on well branched stalks and bloom at approximately the same time as *I. domestica*.

In the late 1960s Sam Norris of Kentucky was impressed with the similarity between what was known at the times as *Belamcanda chinensis* (now *I. domestica*) and *Iris dichotoma* (later transferred to a new genus *Pardanthopsis*) and made crosses between the "Avalon" strain of *Belamcanda* and *Iris dichotoma* (Norris 1970). He was surprised at the number of seedlings that resulted from what was purportedly a bigeneric cross and it was dubbed "× Pardancanda" to indicate the bigeneric nature of the cross. Interestingly, nearly 400 seedlings resulted all in shades of violet to purple with copious buds and branching. The flowers opened at 10 a.m. and closed at 7 p.m. each day in the F1. Most amazingly, especially from a bigeneric cross, the hybrids were easily fertile. The F2 of these plants began to show segregation of traits from the parental plants, with yellows, bicolors and others occurring. Plant habits of these are amazing, with up to 300 buds on each stalk. This hybrid complex was named *Iris × norisii* to honor Sam Norris for making this cross. It was Norris's work that also established the close relationships

Seedlings with more desirable colors and plant habits may be retained for planting out in the flower beds or shared with gardening friends.

Named cultivars of *Iris × norrisi* offer a better chance to obtain plants that have specific characteristics and are selected for better colors, form and garden adaptation. George Bush selected the first pure white form from seed supplied by Sam Norris, the hybrid 'Summer Snow' (Bush '79). However, more progress was obtained by careful breeding of these strains by eminent horticulturist Darrell Probst. I was lucky to be part of a group of hybridizers that met each summer at Barbara and David Schmeider's garden to discuss our hybridizing efforts and Probst was among that group. He presented some of the amazing results from his work that subsequently became named cultivars. Several different types of flowers and bloom times were selected from crosses among these seedlings. Some of these open their flowers just before noon and close at about 6 p.m. whereas others don't open until the afternoon but last all evening. Flower forms vary from a form intermediate between the "lily-formed" flowers of *I. domestica* and the more "iris-formed" to forms that are more iris-like, like parent *I. dichotoma*. Colors and patterns have expanded greatly as the result of this hybridization. These hybrids include the pinks 'Bountiful Blush' (Probst '08), 'Cherry Pie' (Probst '08), 'Pink Leopard' (Probst '08), and 'Summer Candy' (Probst '09) and the purples 'Butterfly Magic' (Probst '02), 'Heart of Darkness' (Probst '02), and 'Spooky World' (Probst '02). Marty Schafer and Jan Sacks introduced the Probst cultivars and introduced two cultivars of their own, the reverse amoena 'Soft Spot' (Schafer-Sacks '10) and its boldly patterned purple and white seedling 'Lots of Fun' (Schafer-Sacks '14).

Unlike many beardless irises, the *I. × norisii* hybrids and their parents do not want moist acid soil. Rather, they prefer the same conditions as bearded irises: well drained lighter soil and no mulch. In my garden I have grown the *I. × norisii* hybrids in raised beds, sometimes intercalating them through beds of bearded irises. There they provide color in an otherwise drab bed of bearded irises through the months of July and August. Like bearded irises, they need to be dug and divided every couple years. Fertilizing is the same as for bearded irises, a slow-release fertilizer in spring, supplemented by compost and alfalfa meal around the plants in the fall.

This chapter only gives a brief introduction to the huge variety of beardless iris species and hybrids that are now being offered by nurseries here in the United States. The importation of selected clones from plant expeditions into the Far East and their incorporation into garden hybrids has given us some really outstanding garden plants. Take a chance the next time you see one of these "other" irises offered for sale. You won't be disappointed.

between these species and the eventual classification of these plants back within the genus *Iris*. Recent DNA studies established a close relationship between these plants and bearded irises and their cultural conditions (see below) are similar to these plants. Seed strains of *I. × norisii* have been introduced by several of the major perennial seed companies. Plants from these are pleasing but are quite variable and, like many seed strains, contain many less desirable garden plants. If you are interested in testing whether these plants will grow in your climates, then a package seed will allow you to do a cheap test of these plants.

8 HYBRIDIZING BEARDLESS IRISES

The breeding of beardless irises has been carried on for centuries, starting with the development of the Japanese irises from the wild *I. ensata* in the fifteenth century. These breeders were able to transform the single drooping three-petal flower into a huge variety of forms and colors, long before there was any knowledge of the field of genetics. Hybridizing efforts in the other beardless iris groups has been carried on for a much shorter period of time, but have also produced spectacular results. All of these hybridizers have been able to capitalize upon the work of their predecessors, further refining and expanding upon the types of flowers available to the public. The "History of Hybridizing" sections in each chapter chronicle these developments in each group.

Hybridizing ornamental plants is one of those rare combinations of science and art. As a hybridizer, it is beneficial to have at least a fundamental knowledge of genetics and certainly the very act of transferring pollen to stigma assumes some botanical knowledge. Ornamental plant breeding differs from the breeding of crop plants. In crop plant breeding, quantitative aspects such as yield and vigor are the purposes of the cross. In ornamental plant breeding, although plant health is one of the criteria under evaluation, it is the beauty of the creation that is paramount. Thus, without an artistic appreciation of beauty, all the genetic knowledge is for naught. It is not surprising that some of our most successful hybridizers in many genera are not scientists, but people who are plant fanatics and can recognize improvements in their seedlings.

Another aspect of a successful ornamental plant hybridizer is an active imagination. When making a cross, the hybridizer must have in his head what the combination of the two parental types might produce, or what combination of characters might eventually produce a novel and beautiful flower. This ability is perhaps more rare. Many hybridizers play it safe by crossing like colors and these hybridizers often produce quality hybrids. The truly innovative hybridizer, however, combines existing characters in new ways or introduces unusual germplasm from species into the hybrids. These hybridizers are revolutionaries that truly advance plant breeding. However, I recommend that anyone interested in beardless irises try at least a few crosses. The thrill of seeing a new seedling flower, something that you have created, is a feeling like no other. Much better

'Air Waves', a recessive white PCN useful for breeding

Although it is beyond the scope of this book to delve too much into genetic aspects, the excellent chapter by Kenneth Kidd in *The World of Irises* (1978), as well as the now out of print texts of Crane and Lawrence (1947) and Vern Grant (1975), is recommended reading for anyone interested in breeding any sort of plant.

SELECTING PARENTS

Before one sets out to make crosses, it is good to establish goals for the breeding program. Crossing irises and growing the seedlings is a lot of work so making some decisions early on will help move the program forward. After a goal has been set, obtain a number of parents that are likely to produce the sort of offspring that you want. Growing these parents together in an area of the garden so that comparisons may be made between the prospective parents is also useful. Some may have better growth, branching, or flower qualities than others and growing them in close proximity will sort this out for you. As an example, when I set out to produce a red-black Louisiana iris, I obtained a number of the darkest irises as well as a number of reds to do the crosses. When the irises all bloomed, the only red iris that met my ideals was 'Cajun Cookery' and it was mated with several dark irises. Oddly enough, the cross to 'Jeri' was one I made only because of the plant habit of 'Jeri' as there were many darker irises. However, the combination of 'Jeri' with 'Cajun Cookery' gave 'Red Velvet Elvis', the very color I was seeking and with a nearly perfect plant habit. 'Red Velvet Elvis' went on to win the DeBaillon Medal and was winner of the popularity poll of the Society for Louisiana Irises as well as one of the most popular perennials. Unfortunately not all my ideas worked out as well as that one!

In preparing this book, I was reading the material on many hybridizers and the following quote from the late Eric Nies so summed up the spirit and excitement I decided to include it verbatim (Nies 2009).

"The excitement…the suspense of waiting one or two weeks, watching for an indication of ovary enlarging, the harvesting of the precious seeds, their careful planting, the joy of seeing the tiny seedlings break the soil, the late summer transplanting, and then the great day when the stalk appears. One can hardly wait for the full opening of the flower and when it finally appears, then comes the judgment: Is it good? Well good or bad, it's your very own, and a great joy until something better shows up." That about sums it up, Eric!

Pryor seedling

Other ideas occur more spontaneously. In my garden, the Siberian iris cultivars 'Salem Witch' and 'Blue Moon' grow just feet from each other. 'Salem Witch' has a great pattern of dark purple stripes on a white background on its falls and 'Blue Moon' is a flat type blossom with all the petals exhibiting the small signal pattern of the falls. As I was gathering the pollen from 'Salem Witch' my thought was "Wouldn't it be neat if this beautiful fall pattern was on all the petals?" and then I saw 'Blue Moon', a six-falls or flat type, having the genetic ability to do just that. A cross was made and forty seedlings were rowed out from that cross. Because of the recessive nature of some of these characters it will take longer to achieve my goal of an iris with a beautiful pattern on all six petals. Additional crosses were made between 'Salem Witch' and other flat types so that the various lines may be combined or to see if other combinations of flat parents with 'Salem Witch' might give better progeny.

Pryor seedling

Pryor seedling

Other crosses might be inspired by the pedigrees of irises in your garden. Steve Varner's 'Letitia' is a nice blue-violet flower with a small white signal. The pedigree of this plant is the flat-formed dark purple 'Tealwood' × the blue with prominent white styles 'Mandy Morse'. My mind immediately raced with the idea of producing a flat dark purple with prominent white styles! Every blossom on 'Letitia' was self-pollinated with the hopes that these two recessive traits might be combined in a single flower. Because both traits are recessive, it is necessary to grow larger progenies in order to obtain the double recessive types. Theoretically they should only occur in 1/16 of the progeny, based on independent segregation of two recessive traits.

Besides these more long-term approaches, I normally make some "pretty faces" crosses. That is I might take the best white Siberian I have and cross it with all the best blue Siberians I have or cross the two best yellows with each other. These sorts

of crosses give more predictable results generally but also the progeny are generally quite pretty as well. These sorts of crosses take some of the sting out of a discouraging result from a wider cross or a goal that requires more generations to produce results. When a particularly lovely cultivar blooms, I often do a saturation program of crossing that cultivar to everything in the yard. Well not quite, but to all reasonable mates! If that cultivar turns out to be a particularly fine parent, a fine group of seedlings can result. My own 'Red Velvet Elvis' and 'Beale Street' were used in such a crossing program and the results were quite nice, resulting in several named cultivars. These pretty face crosses should convince garden visitors that you actually know how to hybridize! Some people never venture from the pretty faces types of crosses, but I think they are missing some of the fun of creating something truly different.

Generally it is safest to concentrate on one type of iris or even one color or pattern in a group rather than to cross with abandon in many different areas. My friend Lynn Markham describes this "riding your horse off in many directions," a very apt description indeed! You can make more progress if you follow just a few paths rather than many. I'm talking to myself here too as in bloom season I just find too many tempting things to cross and end up going in fifty different directions. I probably would be ahead of the game if I had stayed close to my first two breaks in the beardless iris breeding, 'Red Velvet Elvis' and 'Beale Street', and bred lines from those flowers. Of course I *have* done that but a number of other things too. However, I'm having lots of fun and creating some nice irises in the process. Every spring as I row out my thousands of seedlings though, I'm thinking I should listen to my own advice more often. Of course when you buy the neighbor's house so that you can expand your seedling area, as I once did, you probably have a problem! If you are just starting in the hybridizing process it might be wise to start on just a couple of objectives. By settling on just a few objectives the chances of obtaining your goals are better as your efforts are less diffused.

Not all irises are equally good parents. Certain irises such as 'Clara Goula', 'White Swirl', and 'Wadi Zem Zem' have sired many beautiful hybrids, although the days for using those particular cultivars are gone. A clever hybridizer searches the yearly registration of new varieties. If an experienced hybridizer is registering good progeny from a particular parent, then it might be wise to use these same parents in your crosses. This will lead to less frustration! When I decide on a particular color or pattern that I'm interested in improving, I'll buy all of the current hybrids of that type and grow them together in an area of the garden. This not only facilitates crossing but also allows one to observe both the strengths and weaknesses of a particular cultivar. In that way, you are less likely to cross flowers with a common fault, such as poor branching or insufficient increase.

In selecting parents, many facets of the flower and plant should be considered. Color is the most obvious but it often blinds us to other characteristics that will also be passed to its progeny. If one parent is a problem grower, then the other parent should have no such problems. The Siberian iris 'Silver Illusion' is a lovely flower, but not a good grower. However, judicious crosses with this cultivar have allowed some of its good qualities to be meshed with a quality plant as well. Some traits such as very poor substance are more difficult to overcome. I suffered through several generations of very ugly and poorly-substanced seedlings from 'Olivier Monette' and 'Bayou Heartthrob' before finding acceptable seedlings. Avoiding these cultivars all together is probably the best approach. Cultivars that have won the top awards in their various classes are often good choices for crosses because numerous judges have seen these flowers so they generally have few if any bad characteristics. For example, my 'Red Velvet Elvis' is a seedling of DeBaillon Medal winner 'Jeri'.

Beardless irises in general produce copious amounts of seed and it is a temptation to grow this seed formed from bee pollinations. I have raised seed from plants such as 'Holden Clough' and 'Phil Edinger' that are nearly sterile and raised interesting progeny. Similarly I have raised seedlings from cultivars that I was unable to obtain in this country but whose genes I would like to use in crosses by purchasing seed from seed exchanges or exchanging seeds with other hybridizers. Bees tend to visit all the flowers on a clump before moving to the next so many of these represent self pollinations so at least some of the progeny will be similar to the cultivar. Species irises are now rarely listed in catalogs and obtaining seeds of these plants through the Species Iris Group of North America, the Society for Pacific Coast Native Irises, and the British Iris Society seed exchanges are great choices for obtaining this source material for introduction into your lines. Oftentimes the seed donated from these species clones is better than the normal forms of these species and thus more desirable for crossing. Moreover, growing seed from these exchanges will give you practice in growing seedlings so that your methodology will be well-established when your own precious hand cross germinates.

I breed many other plants, *Sempervivum* being one of my fondest and of which I have over sixty introductions. They are notoriously difficult to cross as the blossoms are small and the plants must be covered prior to and after pollinations. One prominent grower of the time simply raised bee seed and had good luck creating some very nice plants. He questioned why I would waste time actually making crosses and not letting the bees just cross the finest hybrids and gather the seed. My answer was fairly simple: "The American Kennel Club registers all sorts of wonderful dog breeds and in each group there are clear champions who are clearly lovely animals. Could you then imagine if these breeds were bred at random? Let's say hybrids between dachshunds and huskies were created in this random program. One couldn't conceive of anything good coming from that mating. Dachshund bodies with husky legs and tail and fur that is a composite of both don't sound pretty at all! The indiscriminate crossing of plants is no different. There *might* be some pretty ones, but not all combinations are. Some are just going to be *ugly mutts*." I think that drove the point home, but he didn't change his ways either! This other grower rowed out over 20,000 seedlings each spring whereas I rowed out several hundred. We both had similar numbers of progeny that were eventually named yet I had expended a lot less work growing ugly seedlings and growing only ones that might give the results wanted. My advice to someone breeding beardless irises would be the same: you'll make much better progress making hand crosses than raising bee seed.

MAKING THE CROSS

Unlike bearded irises, beardless irises need to be emasculated and protected to ensure that the cross is not contaminated by insects. Herein are described a few general methods for effective pollinations of beardless irises.

Generally the best stage for attempting a cross is the "late balloon stage," in which the flower is expanded, but not yet open. At this stage of development the anthers have fully matured but have not yet dehisced their pollen. The petals are ready to open but have not, ensuring that no insect has arrived. The anthers may be removed at this stage and stored for use or the pollen may be reamed from the anther with sharp-pointed forceps or the end of a toothpick or a matchstick for immediate use. I have found that Dumont #5 forceps work very well as they have a pointed tip that is useful for opening up anthers that have not dehisced and can be used to apply pollen to the stigmas as well. Pollen that is to be saved for later pollination should be stored in small gelatin capsules or microfuge tubes in the refrigerator. Separating the pollen from the anther should keep the pollen sufficiently dry so that it remains effective throughout the season.

Although some hybridizers do not make the cross at this stage, I have found that crosses may be made at this stage and result in greater than 80 percent takes and Marty Schafer uses

Balloon stage bud on Siberian iris

Siberian flower with petals removed
and anther not dehisced

Fully emasculated
Siberian flower

a similar technique (Schafer 2014). For those not familiar with iris parts, the iris stigma is quite different than the majority of plant stigmas. The style arm has a small lip-like structure towards the end of the bottom side of the style. At this stage, the stigmatic lip is appressed tightly to the remainder of the style and won't open naturally until the next day. The stigma may not be receptive at this stage but by inserting the pollen (or even whole anthers as in the techniques developed by Dunlop and Cole), using the fine forceps to place the pollen on the stigmatic lip, a cross may be made. Many breeders wait until the second day to pollinate the flower as the stigmatic lip has become looser and it is easier to spread the pollen. The main problem with that technique is that the collection of pollen and emasculation of the flower are done on separate days. My memory is sometimes not clear as to which flowers I have readied for pollination. To prevent insects from contaminating the cross make sure that the anthers of the pod parent are removed and that the anthers have not dehisced. Reject any flower where the anthers have dehisced, as there is a great chance that the flower might be self-pollinated. To prevent insect pollinations, either remove the falls or pull the falls back up and secure the flower in its unopened state with small rubber bands, a strip of Siberian iris foliage, or any other thing handy that will keep the flower closed. Some people pollinate all three styles with pollen but I have found that pollinating just one works fine. After the flower parts have withered, you will notice either a swelling of the ovary into a

small green pod (indicating a successful cross) or an aborted pod that will shrivel and die. Within about ten days there will be an obvious green pod and it is wise at this point to remove the remaining spent blossom parts so as to prevent them from rotting your pod. In some cases, I also remove spathe leaves that could potentially rot the pod. This is less of a problem with beardless irises than bearded irises, but it is a good preventative measure.

Jeff Dunlop and Dean Cole invented an ingenious way of pollinating Siberian irises. Anthers which have not dehisced are forced into the stigmatic lip. In this way the anther dehisces normally and completely fills the stigmatic cavity with pollen. As soon as the stigma is receptive pollination is effected. Tetraploid Siberians are more difficult to pollinate than diploid cultivars and this protocol seems to be the most effective way to pollinate these plants.

Dorman Haymon (personal communication) introduced me to a new technique that works very well but is a bit unorthodox for a botanist like me who believes that pollen should germinate properly only from pollen applied at the stigmatic lip. However, I have verified that this method works well and works successfully on flowers with really elaborate style crests where the stigmatic lip is difficult to reach or is compromised because of the ornamentations. The technique takes a little finesse. Hold the style between your fingers and apply a gentle pressure until there is a tiny line of exposed inner tissue at the peak of the style. Too much pressure will

Dunlop and Cole technique of sticking anthers into style arms

Dunlop method of covering flowers to prevent damage from rain

crack open the styles and too little won't allow for enough of an opening. Generally I apply slightly different amounts of pressure to each of the three styles so I'll have the right amount of pressure on at least one of the three styles. Then spread pollen along all of the cavities you have created by opening up the style. In comparison with pollinations at the stigmatic lip, I get a similar percentage of takes and the pods have similar number of seeds. Thus, beardless iris pollen is able to traverse the style arms through an unconventional site of application and result in successful pollinations. In more limited tests, I have been able to use this technique on bearded irises that have limited pod fertility and obtain pods. Many modern Japanese irises have extra frilly almost petaloid style arms and I have been able to get good pods on these rather uncooperative parents by using the squeezing-the-style-arm method. In these flowers, the stigmatic lip is often abnormal and using the cracked style arm method would be one way of pollinating these otherwise uncooperative flowers.

Iris lactea is a fine plant that is able to grow in many adverse situations. Several hybridizers have tried to use it in interspecies crosses and often copious seed is produced. However, the seed is not the result of the pollen parent but rather is the result of apomixis. That is, the seeds are clones of the parent produced by non-sexual formation of the seeds. So far, that seems to be the only iris that has this ability. However, the pollen of *I. lactea* may be used on other species and potentially hybrids could be produced.

Various workers utilize a huge variety of techniques to mark their crosses. The tried and true method is to use stringed cardboard price marking tags and use a soft lead pencil to mark the pollen parent (and the pod parent if this is a seedling in the row that might be confused with another). In very wet and humid climates, these tags often become illegible during the course of the season. Here in the Pacific Northwest, I found many "mystery pollen parents" in crosses marked in this way as the paper tags were biodegradable in this climate. After all the effort going into making a cross, this is something you don't want to face. Metal-stringed plastic tags are more weather-resistant and by writing the cross details with a water-resistant marker is perhaps the easiest solution to this problem. These tags may be washed clean with ethanol and reused from season to season. My new favorite method is to use colored bits of

'Crimson Fireworks'

electrical wire that are cut into about 2″ lengths. After a cross is made I wrap the electrical wire piece and record the cross and the color of wire in a notebook. Suppliers of electrical wire have large selections of colors of these wires so that each pollen parent can be denoted with a different wire. Colored wire tags allow multiple crosses to be made without having to write the same cross name on each tag so are a big time-saver when making multiple copies of the same cross. Record the color of the wire and what the cross is in a notebook. For example, "red and grey striped wire on the terminal blossom of 'Salem Witch' has been pollinated with 'Frilly Vanilly'." This means there will be no confusion when it comes time to harvest the seed.

Jeff Dunlop has come up with a most ingenious method of protecting crosses from rain. As any breeder knows, rain that falls shortly after a pollination almost always ruins the chance for a successful take. He has used a method of covering the pollinated flowers with cups or buckets that are supported on dowels and cover the newly pollinated flower, keeping it dry and protected. In years when rain is a daily occurrence this allows at least some seed to be set.

There are a number of insects that will try to eat the contents of your pod. The worst is the verbena bud moth. Invasion by these pests will result in a pod full of eaten seed; a very frustrating event after all the work that goes into making these crosses. Many ways have been devised to prevent this attack. The easiest method is to cover the developing seed pod with segments of discarded panty hose or silk stockings. By covering these pods, the insect is unable to lay eggs in the pods and the hosiery allows the follow of air and light to reach the developing pod. If pods from bee set seed are destroyed each season, then there is much less chance of this pest being in your garden.

COLLECTING THE SEED, AND PLANTING METHODS

After approximately eight weeks of development, the pod will turn brownish and start to split. The seed may be harvested at this time and spread out in little plastic weighing boats or small plastic dishes so that the seed may dry in a cool place. Keith Keppel dries his bearded iris seed in a discarded mail-sorting cabinet from the post office. It has a huge number of cubbyholes so that each cross may be separated and there is good air circulation. Seed that has been dried will very rarely be coated with mold even if the seed is subsequently transferred to coin envelopes before planting. In treating the seed this way, you have allowed the seed to after-ripen so that the inhibitors have developed in the seed coat and the majority of the seed will not germinate until spring, lowering the chances of it being killed in the winter. An exception to this generality would be if you lived in very benign climates, such as coastal California or along the Gulf Coast; seeds of both spuria and Louisiana irises may be picked as soon as the pod begins to split or turn brown and planted directly. In the case of the Louisiana iris seeds, the corky layer of the seeds may be peeled free of the rest of the seed, further eliminating a barrier to germination. The seeds are then soaked briefly and planted directly in pots. Germination can occur within as little as two weeks. Even in benign climates the young growing seedlings must be protected from any cold. Growing them in protected sites, a cool greenhouse or in a cold frame is required or else the tender young seedlings will be killed. I start many of my seedling pots in a protected area near my garage and the pots of seedlings are further protected by covering with Remay, a fabric that will protect seedlings down to 23° F. When temperatures go lower, a quick trip inside the garage is in order! This last fall, I had very high percentages of early fall germination in several spuria seed lots that were critical to my breeding program. This required constant vigilance and the spuria pots were frequent visitors to my garage during severe cold spells.

If you live in a less benign climate, allowing the seeds to dry and planting them later in the fall, will prevent any early germination so that the bulk of the seedlings will germinate in the springtime. I plant in 6- to 8" pots using a good sterile potting mix. The seeds are put along the surface of the potting medium and an additional inch of potting mix is applied over the top. An aluminum label marked with a soft lead pencil is inserted in the pot; this will be transferred to the field to mark the seedling row so a good quality label is required. The pots are kept moist and allowed to be exposed to the elements. The constant moisture and cooler temperatures will eventually wash out the germination inhibitors present in the seed and allow the seed to germinate in springtime. Seeds of spuria and Louisiana irises are the most difficult to germinate and often the seeds will not germinate the first spring but often will germinate the following spring. Keep the pots in a cool shaded position over the summer and make sure the pots don't dry out completely. In the case of Louisiana irises, removing the corky seed coat will often facilitate germination.

Some hybridizers plant their seed directly into rows into the garden. The huge crop (four coffee cans!) of Siberian seed that Fred Cassebeer produced in order to select 'White Swirl' was planted directly in the field, thus requiring no onerous transplanting. There are problems with this approach, however. Seed must be spaced far enough away from each other that they are not too crowded in the row. For seeds like those of Siberians, that germinate nearly 100 percent, some estimates can be made for what would be a good spacing. However, for seeds like spurias, for which germination is often delayed and erratic, planting seed in the ground could lead to lots of space in a seedling bed with no seedlings. Most importantly, this bed cannot be used for planting out more seedlings because of the chance for delayed germination contaminating future crosses. Alternately, a small area of the garden may be set up in which seeds are planted in tight rows and the seedlings transplanted into garden rows at proper spacing. Seeds will continue to come

Robert Treadway evaluating his crop of Louisiana iris seedlings

up in this area for years after the bed is planted and are pulled out as weeds unless the markers are retained.

One unique technique for encouraging germination is the so-called "toilet tank method." Seeds are wrapped in cheesecloth or muslin bags and placed in the toilet tank so that the seed is in the water but will not be when the toilet is flushed. This cannot be used if you use various treatments that clean, color, and sanitize your toilet water as it will kill your seeds. Seeds are allowed to stay in the toilet for ten days and then transferred to potting soil. In the case of PCN seeds, the seed will germinate almost immediately. Other kinds of iris seeds seem to germinate better after this treatment, although not quite as rapidly as the PCN seed responds. If you find the idea of the toilet tank daunting, an alternate procedure is to dump the contents of the seed packets into individual disposable cups and put a small volume of water over the seed. Change the water daily for a week and then plant the highly moistened seeds directly into potting mix.

ROWING OUT THE SEEDLINGS

After the seedlings have reached 3 to 4" tall, they are ready for being transplanted into field rows in the garden. Prepare the area in the field so that the soil is enriched with organic matter and is easily friable so as to promote the growth of the seedlings. For most of the beardless irises, this should be in an area that receives full sunshine. Pacific Coast Natives, crested irises and some other species require some shade. I plant the seedlings of Siberian irises as close as 4" apart because they make rather tight clumps and nearly 100 percent bloom in the first season. Greater spacing should be used for other irises as they make larger rhizomes, especially the Louisiana irises. By the time the seedlings bloom, the seedling patch would be a tangled mess if the seedlings are planted too closely. Rows 8 to 12" apart allow for good air circulation. Even with this separation, under good growth conditions, the seedling bed will be full at bloom time.

Schafer-Sacks S11-16-10

In order for the seedlings to bloom in one season, the plants should be pushed. They should never want for water. One inch of water per week is a good guide. I also use a foliar feeding of a transplanting fertilizer every two weeks. Using this regime, I get almost 100 percent first year bloom on Siberian, Japanese, and Pacific Coast Native iris seedlings and generally 50 to 70 percent first year bloom on the spuria seedlings. This allows not only for the seedlings to be evaluated more quickly but for the soil to be freed up for planting more seedlings.

As soon as the seedlings are planted, it is wise to make a map of the planting. Many agents (animals, mischievous children, garden visitors) can and do move your markers. A map will make things clear in case of some moving of the markers, accidental or otherwise. In addition, I alternate colors in the rows so that a cross for reds is followed by a cross for blues, for example. This will demarcate the beginnings and ends of the cross in the field even if the markers are disturbed.

EVALUATING THE SEEDLINGS

There is almost no greater thrill than seeing your crop of seedlings bloom; it's like opening presents on Christmas morning! One famous hybridizer couldn't bear the wait, and would open the buds ahead of time! I don't recommend that practice though as often the blossom will rip or not exhibit its true form. Wait the extra few hours for the blossoms to open normally. When the seedlings bloom, one can almost become overwhelmed with all you see. Your first emotion might be one of proud parenthood and that you love them all. Generally sanity returns and you realize that there are both good and bad seedlings in the patch. Compared to bearded iris crosses, the percentage of seedlings that are at least small improvements on their parents is generally in the majority. In some crosses, the number of potential "keepers" is nearly 100 percent. Other crosses show how many of their less pretty ancestors must have appeared as seedlings with poor form, strappy petals and muddy colors the result! Mark any seedlings with orange construction marker flags, plastic markers or paper tags on the bloomstalk. Both flags and tags are even better to ensure that the seedling is saved. I use a numbering system for seedlings that works well for me that consists of a letter and several numbers that recognize the seedling. When I collect the pod of seed I enter that data in my stud book. It is given a code for the year and for the particular cross. For my system I use a letter to denote the year of the cross. For example all the crosses made in 2010 are labelled with an "S" and then each pod is numbered from there, let's say the cross of 'Magenta Madness' × 'Red Velvet Elvis' is the tenth pod to be recorded in my notebook so the seedlings from this cross will be from the S10 series. Individual seedlings that might be labeled for further evaluations are numbered consecutively, e.g., the first seedling is S10-1 and so on. This allows me to know which year the cross was made and which other seedlings are siblings of each other even without referring to my notebook. Others just number the seedlings as they appear each year, e.g., 2015-2. Brief descriptions in a notebook plus digital images are a good way to document your seedlings. Height of the flowering stalk, number of buds and branches, and floral width are useful information to include in your notes as this will be needed if the seedling is to be eventually named and registered with the American Iris Society.

In evaluating the seedlings, the first questions should be: "Is it beautiful?" "Is the form attractive?" "Is it an improvement on its parents?" "Is this a step forward to my goals?" "Does the seedling possess an unusual characteristic that might be useful?" "Does the flower color hold up well over the life of the flower?" "Is it distinctive from other cultivars?" "Does the plant grow well?" If the answer to any of these questions is *no* then you need consider the seedling no further in most instances. Occasionally a seedling will have a "break" of new color, patterns or form that might be worth incorporating into further generations of seedling. Certainly a clear red flower or another similar amazing color break, no matter how poorly formed or weakly-substanced, should be retained for further breeding. It is important that the hybridizer keep a current collection of the best cultivars, especially in colors and patterns of current hybridizing goals, so that they may be used as a yardstick for the evaluation of the seedlings and for potential use as parent with your line.

Another reason for saving a seedling is its genetic potential. Let's go back to the cross I made between 'Salem Witch' and 'Blue Moon', trying to get a *sibirica*-patterned flower that is in the six-falls or flat form. Neither of these characteristics came through in the first generation seedlings. Rather, the seedlings were three-fall types with rather ordinary-looking signal patterns. In order to recover both recessive characteristics, I crossed the best siblings (widest flowers, boldest signals or hints of signals on the standards) from this group with each other. Because only one out of 16 of the seedlings from this cross will contain the combination of flat form and the *sibirica* pattern in one flower (assuming only two genes are segregating), many seedlings should be raised to increase the chances of obtaining the desired results. Although in some plants, that close inbreeding leads to significant loss of vigor, beardless irises are exceptional in tolerating fairly close inbreeding. Besides the cross of 'Salem Witch' × 'Blue Moon', I also crossed 'Salem Witch' with an unrelated flat form, 'Rikugi Sakura', so I also crossed individuals from these two groups of seedlings. Sometimes this multiple approach towards a goal works better than a single path as not all parents are created equal in producing superior offspring.

Bee Warburton used a fairly tight inbreeding program to solidify the form advance of 'White Swirl' into her line of Siberians. For example, after an initial outcross of 'White Swirl' × 'Eric the Red' she crossed the progeny back to 'White Swirl' for three generations before beginning some outcrosses. By doing this, Bee created a line of plants that were uniformly excellent. For example, the first cross gave only one seedling of note, a blue with aqua styles whereas the next generation of crossing the one selected back to 'White Swirl' gave almost 100 percent keepers. Others use a less tight inbreeding scheme, creating related lines of irises so that the lines may share a common parent but also have a bit more genetic diversity. Marty Schafer and Jan Sacks use that sort of approach to breeding. It is a bit riskier in that recessives might be lost if the right sets of plants are not chosen for further intercrossing. One must always be vigilant for weaklings in such a breeding program, but that should be standard practice in any breeding program. Fortunately most beardless irises do not suffer from any severe growth depression by inbreeding, allowing us to recover useful recessives. Moreover, many are diploids so that recessives are much more easily obtained than with tetraploid bearded irises.

In the fall, the selected seedlings should be removed from the seedling bed and given a spot of their own so that they can be evaluated further. At this point you are deciding "Is this a nice flower or one that is so good it should be marketed?" or, "Would I like this flower as well if it were white or plain blue-violet?" are good ones to determine if something is worth naming and introducing to the market. Sending the plants to others whom you trust, to iris society conventions, or to nurseries who might sell the plant is the next step. Reports back from these sources will determine whether others think your seedling has merit. Entry of good stalks of your flowers in local iris shows is another way of assessing the relative merits of your seedling. If the judges give the plant an Exhibition Certificate then five judges have determined that a particular seedling has been deemed worthy. Only a very few plants make the grade each year, probably about one in 1,000 seedlings actually reaching the marketplace. It is probably better to err on the side of not naming, if in doubt. We need quality plants not a bunch of weaklings or look-alikes. I remember as a beginning hybridizer going through Bee Warburton's seedling patch and remarking over the beauty of many seedlings that she not only decided not to name but not to even keep for further breeding. She would then point out what to me seemed like a trivial fault but as she knew, seeing that fault bloom year after year in someone else's garden made it something to be rejected.

Increasingly, hybridizers either knowingly or unknowingly are selecting for a certain type or "look" in the plants. In selecting for plants with superior substance and petal width, many of the beardless irises are starting to look similar. They have the wide rounded form that comes from shortening and widening the falls and broadening the standards. Ruffles are now becoming more than the norm. In daylilies this completely round and ruffled form is described as the "bagel shape" and, although a very pretty look, there is a bit of boredom to having beds that all have a consistent, no matter how lovely, form. Siberian iris breeders have kept the diversity more than other groups so that the classical pendant forms and multi-branched stalks characteristic of *I. sibirica* are still being produced in new hybrids as well as flat and multipetal forms. Part of the reason for this is the buying public and the judging system whereby flowers with these new and improved characteristics are the ones bought and being given the highest awards. It is only natural, as they are spectacular and look modern compared to the previous offerings. However, the excitement that has been sparked by the addition of the Siberian iris 'Snow Prince' into the Schafer-Sacks line gives us hope that more hybridizers will discover different "looks" in their plants by crossing with some varieties with "non bagel" shapes.

Jean Witt (reprinted in Cosgrove 1976) presaged this inevitable development of a "common accepted form" over forty years ago in the early days of the Pacific Coast Native Iris Society. What she says could pertain to all beardless irises:

"Let us deliberately encourage variety in flower form and make it an avowed policy and espouse it as a desirable breeding goal. Evolution has divided the *Californicae* into a number of distinctive species: surely we can find a better objective for our new Society than to press them all back into a single mold."

Witt is still pushing the boundaries of hybridizing, even in her nineties, and is one of the voices of reason in the iris world.

Part of this change is sort of the inevitable changes in flower form that accompany increasing width of petals, ruffling and increasing substance. If you do all these things, you do create a single vision of what a beardless iris flower should be, at least in shape. Another problem with this shape, besides monotony, is the visual impact of the flower in the garden. In the Pacific Coast Native irises, which are generally quite short, this relatively flat shape still allows for a good color display. However, in the taller beardless irises the garden impact of a relatively flat flower is much lower than one with form that is either pendant or semi-flaring falls.

One thing that worries me a bit about beardless iris breeding is the relatively narrow genetic base in some of the groups. For example, in Siberian irises just five cultivars,

'White Swirl', 'Gatineau', 'Caesar's Brother', and 'Tycoon', account for a majority of the cultivars available. Adding 'Eric the Red' and 'Red Emperor' to that list covers many of the others. Certainly the addition of 'Snow Prince' has added a lot of interest but there are lots of older cultivars which have been relatively untouched and could offer the same kind of magic. I have had such fun incorporating some of these older but untapped cultivars with the modern Siberians.

Almost all areas of beardless iris breeding are wide open to newcomers and relatively quick progress may be made. Unlike bearded iris crosses, where many mutts are often obtained, beardless iris crosses tend to give quite nice seedlings. The worst that might happen from making crosses is that you have lots of nice flowers for your own garden or to share with your friends.

TETRAPLOIDS-DIPLOIDS AND CHROMOSOME INCOMPATIBILITIES

Most of the irises described in this book are diploid. That is they have two sets of chromosomes. Crosses between closely related irises with the same chromosome count generally give offspring that are mostly fertile. Examples of this include intercrosses between the three 28-chromosome Siberian iris species or the intercrosses between any of the Pacific Coast Native species. Even when the species involved in the cross have slightly different chromosome numbers, such as in the species of Louisiana irises (40 to 44 chromosomes), mostly fertile offspring are obtained by intercrossing the species. Crosses of species that are less closely related but have similar chromosome counts often are able to cross. For example, the 40-chromosome Siberian iris and the 40-chromosome Pacific Coast Native irises are able to cross readily, but the resulting hybrids are nearly always sterile. Crosses between species with significant differences in chromosome counts or those that are more distantly related are less likely to produce fertile progeny. However, there are notable exceptions to this rule. My best advice is to *try it* if you think the cross might have potential. The work of Tony Huber and Tomas Tamberg took the world of combination of beardless species into exciting new directions. Not all of these combinations give rise to beautiful garden plants but many are.

Some irises have spontaneously gone to higher ploidy levels and others have been changed as the result of conversion of diploids by the drug colchicine or herbicides that act in a similar matter on the spindle apparatus. Briefly, the conversion of diploids (two sets of chromosomes) to tetraploids (four sets of chromosomes), involves treating young growing seedlings with colchicine or a mitotic disrupter herbicide for a time period. In this stage, the cell is able to replicate its DNA, but when the cell tries to divide the spindle apparatus that moves the chromosomes to the poles is disrupted. When the colchicine or herbicide is washed out, the cell is able to divide but, because the number of chromosomes has doubled during the treatment, the newly formed cells reproduce all four sets of chromosomes.

Generally, the seedlings so treated are not pure tetraploids but rather a mixture of diploid and tetraploid tissues called chimeras (Tilney-Bassett 1986). These chimeras are of several sorts. Sectorial chimeras have diploid and tetraploid tissues that occur as sectors, as the name implies. Because tetraploid tissue is about 1.4 times the size of diploid tissue, these often show a mix of sizes of flower parts, so that a third of the flower might have larger parts with the remainder being normally sized. Sectorial chimeras will segregate out both fully diploid and fully tetraploid plants over time. Periclinal chimeras are tetraploid in certain tissue layers but diploid in others. In irises, three histogenic layers occur in the meristem. These layers give rise to all subsequent tissue. In the case of breeding tetraploids, the LII or second tunica layer, is most important because the pollen grains and ovules are formed from cells derived from that tissue layer. Thus, crosses between periclinal chimeras that are tetraploid in the LII layer will give a majority of fully tetraploid seedlings whereas crosses between chimeras that have tetraploid cells only in the LI or LIII will give mainly diploids. These chimeras are stable and may be used for years in crosses. Mericlinal chimeras are a combination of the two types of chimera. In mericlinal chimeras, the tetraploid portions are confined to a single histogen but only a sector of the plant has these tetraploid cells.

Crosses between these chimeras give rise to a mix of diploids and tetraploids, with the crosses between periclinal chimeras with tetraploid LII (or second histogenic layer) giving the highest percentage of tetraploids. That is how the majority of tetraploid beardless irises have arisen. Of course in nature, no one is applying colchicine to make tetraploids, yet tetraploid species do occur, indicating tetraploidy can occur without the influence of man. Many such tetraploid plants were selected as *gigas* (giant) mutants of plants before tetraploidy was understood. Such plants may originate from a doubling of the chromosomes of a somatic cell or by the fusion of two unreduced (diploid) gametes from the parents. McEwen discovered that a Japanese iris seedling of Louise Marx, later named 'Pink Mystery' (Marx by McEwen, '90), is from a cross of two diploids yet is a full tetraploid and crosses easily with tetraploids but not with diploids. The spuria irises are also examples of a probable conversion to the tetraploid

Schafer-Sacks S10-14-1

level but much more anciently. For example, within the various forms described under the cover-all species *I. spuria* there are forms with 22 (diploid) and 44 (tetraploid) chromosomes.

Not all plants that vary in chromosome number vary in whole sets of chromosomes but may contain just one to several more or less than a full set of chromosomes. These are called aneuploids. Tomino (1963) discovered that certain varieties of Japanese irises of the Ise strain contained an extra chromosome (25 chromosomes, instead of the 24 seen in most cultivars) and subsequent studies by Yabuya and colleagues have confirmed this (Yabuya 1991; Yabuya et al. 1989). It is not known what traits are carried on this extra chromosome although these particular cultivars were selected as being especially unique.

There are both advantages and disadvantages to tetraploidy. Because tetraploid cells are bigger the tetraploid flowers also tend to be bigger as well. Flowers tend to have better substance but this can be a double-edged sword. When the pendant formed Siberian iris cultivars were converted to the tetraploid state the increased substance made the falls flare nearly horizontally, giving a most unattractive propeller-shaped flower. In many tetraploid Louisiana and Japanese irises the flowers have so much substance that they refuse to open properly, especially in cooler climates. Fertility of the early generation tetraploids tends to be very low, so that progress in producing tetraploid cultivars can be very frustrating. I remember one year when I crossed literally *every* tetraploid Louisiana iris flower in my garden to obtain just a handful of seed and only a couple seedlings from these crosses germinated and survived to maturity. Of the converted tetraploids, the tetraploid Siberian irises have made perhaps the biggest impact. Besides Currier McEwen, Bob Hollingworth, Tomas Tamberg, Bauer and Coble, Jennifer Hewitt, Jeff Dunlop and Dean Cole have all made significant contributions to this group of plants. Tetraploid Siberians lack the fluttery aspect of many of the diploids but are fine garden plants and newer hybrids have eliminated the propeller look of some of the early tetraploids. Tetraploid Japanese and Louisiana irises are being worked on by a much smaller group of hybridizers. Here are areas ripe for an adventurous new hybridizer.

Besides an increase in substance, the other advantage of the tetraploids lies in their genetic possibilities. In a diploid organism there are only three choices of gene dosage at each allele, that is at the W locus in diploid Siberian irises, the choices of genotypes are WW (blue), Ww (blue, maybe paler than the WW plants), and ww (white). In the tetraploid Siberians there would be five possible genetic constitutions at that locus: $WWWW$ (blue), $WWWw$, $WWww$, $Wwww$, and $wwww$ (white). The genotypes with various combinations of the W and w alleles would allow for perhaps different intensities of blue or even bluer tones. In tetraploid bearded irises, certain colors, such as tangerine pink and the luminata pattern occur that do not at the diploid level or in a very weak form (the beard color only in the case of tangerine). Thus, we might have similar surprises at the tetraploid level with beardless irises too.

MULTIPLE PETALS

Flowers with more than the normal number of petals have been described as early as 300 BCE (Reynolds and Tampion 1983) and many of the beardless iris groups have cultivars that would be described as having extra petals or being fully double. In *Arabidopsis* and other species, the so-called *ABC* genes control petal formation, with mutations in some of these resulting in conversion of sexual parts into petal-like structures (Coen and Meyerowitz 1991; Vishnevetsky and Meyerowitz 2002). Basically, the ABC genes encode for genes regulating the three whorls of structures involved in formation of the flower. Although this model has been well studied in *Arabidopsis* it is not known if similar gene systems control petal formation in irises, although it is still a useful framework to understand how mutations affect the formation of petals. In the case of an iris flower, these three whorls of primordia would correspond to the falls, standards, and the anthers (and possibly styles and ovary). Mutations in the genes involved in this process result in the conversion of one of these structures into another type or the production of an abnormal number of these primordial. For example, the so-called flat Siberian irises have standards which have the same characteristics as the falls; these are described as "identity mutations." Other identity mutations occur in the Louisiana irises that are double because of the conversion of anthers into petaloid type structures. Mutations that affect the number of petals occur when instead of three, petal primordia are produced in a whorl so that more than typical amounts of petals are made. This can range from one more in plants like the Siberian iris 'Fore', to the multipetal Siberian and Japanese irises with more than nine petals. Both dominant and recessive mutations are known in these petal number or petal identity mutations. When flat form Siberian irises are crossed to normally formed forms all of the progeny are normally formed (e.g., the cultivar 'Letitia'), although the flat types do reappear in the next generation. Crosses between flat types produce all flat progeny (e.g., the cultivar 'Steve' from 'Blue Moon' × 'Tealwood'). The flat or six-petal Japanese irises are recessives to the single- or three-petal forms. Conversely, the multipetal Siberian irises are dominant to the non-multipetal types.

Schafer-Sacks S12-41

Marvin Granger discovered a double flowered Louisiana iris that he named 'Creole Can-Can'. This flower makes anthers that are petaloid. Crosses of the double flowers × non-double flowers produce no doubles in the first generation. Rather, these first generation hybrids produce a cartwheel form, in which all of the petals behave as falls and have signals on all the petals. Intercrossing these cartwheels or crossing the cartwheels back to the double forms allows for the recovery of the fully double forms. John Taylor also produced double Louisiana irises but the ones from his lines produce more petals and the anthers are not petaloid. Crosses of the Granger and Taylor doubles produce an F1 of all cartwheel types. Intercrossing these F1 cartwheels produces a series of singles, cartwheels and doubles of both types.

One other mutation that affects the petal morphology in Siberian irises, but not their number but their shape, is called "Spatulate." In these flowers all the petals are long and narrow with the edges rolled up. They are often found in crosses of white Siberian irises that descend from 'Snow Queen' and even the great parent 'White Swirl' can produce this type. I did have one pale blue with spatulate form but their occurrence primarily with whites may indicate a linkage of the white petal color and this form. Generally they are very unattractive flowers but 'Ivory Moonlight' (Spofford '63), in which the petals are overall veined green, and 'Fairy Fingers' (Willott '91), in which the flowers are very small and on short plants, give acceptable looking flowers with this form. In general, however, such forms are not attractive.

GENETICS OF FLOWER COLOR

Flower color is the most obvious characteristic in any flower and one of the areas in which we have some knowledge of the inheritance of these traits. Most of the groups seem to follow a model based upon studies of the Siberian irises. The spurias, however, are quite different.

The genetics of Siberian iris flower color is fairly simple. Blue-purple is dominant to all other colors, as one might expect, because the wild type plants of all three 28-chromosome Siberians are that color. Crosses of blue-purples to clear whites give all blue seedlings. Thus, blue-purple is dominant to clear white. The F1 hybrids of these crosses are often more towards true blue than the blue-purple parent and often a lighter shade of blue as well. Oftentimes, these pale blues will show slips of white, revealing the recessive genes present in this plant. The clear whites produce flavones that are pigments that cause a "blue-ing effect," perhaps by complexing anthocyanins and other molecules. Crossing the F1 hybrids from blue × white crosses results in a 3:1 ratio of blues: whites, indicating that only one gene causes the production of clear white. We can diagram this as follows:

$$\text{Blue-purple } (WW) \times \text{Clear white } (ww)$$
$$\downarrow$$
$$\text{First generation (F1) blue purple } (Ww)$$

$$\text{F1 blue-purple } (Ww) \times \text{F1 blue-purple } (Ww)$$
$$\downarrow$$
$$\text{3 blue-purples } (WW, Ww)\text{: 1 clear white } (ww)$$

Crosses of reds to blue-purples give all blue-purples and these oftentimes have a bit of a red tinge. Intercrossing the first generation seedlings from this cross gives the expected 3:1 segregation of blue-purples to reds. We can diagram this as:

$$\text{Blue-purple } (CC) \times \text{Red } (c^r c^r)$$
$$\downarrow$$
$$\text{F1 blue-purple } (Cc^r)$$

$$\text{F1 blue-purple } (Cc^r) \times \text{F1 blue-purple } (Cc^r)$$
$$\downarrow$$
$$\text{3 blue-purples } (CC, Cc^r)\text{: 1 red } (c^r c^r)$$

Pink and *sibirica* type milk whites are also recessive to blue-purples in the same matter as the reds. Crosses of reds with pinks or *sibirica* whites gives all reds whereas cross of pinks with *sibirica* whites gives all pinks. Thus, all of these color choice genes are due to the control of the single gene C and that there is a dominance relationship between these alleles in the order blue-purple $(C) \rightarrow$ red $(c^r) \rightarrow$ pink $(c^p) \rightarrow$ *sibirica* type milk white (c).

Crosses between milk whites and clear whites give all blue seedlings and in the second generation the seedlings segregate out in the ratio of 9 blue-purples: 3 *sibirica* type whites; 4 clear whites. We can express that using the following diagram:

$$\textit{Sibirica} \text{ type milk white } (cc\,WW) \times \text{Clear white } (CC\,ww)$$
$$\downarrow$$
$$\text{F1 blue-purple } (CcWw)$$

$$\text{F1 blue-purple } (CcWw) \times \text{F1 blue-purple } (CcWw)$$
$$\downarrow$$
$$\text{9 blue purples } (CC\,WW,\ Cc\,WW,\ Cc\,Ww)\text{:}$$
$$\text{3 } \textit{sibirica} \text{ whites } (cc\,Ww,\ cc\,WW)\text{:}$$
$$\text{4 clear whites } (Cc\,ww,\ CC\,ww,\ cc\,ww)$$

Milk-whites (cc WW) and clear whites (CC ww) are complementary, that is they both lack an enzyme or factors that are required to produce blue-purple color but they are different factors. By crossing the two, the two factors required for anthocyanin production are brought back together. The clear whites are said to be epistatic to the milk whites as any genotype that is *ww* will be clear white, regardless of what genes are present at the *C* locus. Clear whites have no trace of anthocyanin but instead accumulate flavones, a colorless pigment that is a precursor molecule to anthocyanins, indicating that the *W* locus is involved somewhere in the anthocyanin pathway, upstream of the production of anthocyanins (Vaughn and Lyerla 1978).

Mutations at the *C* locus appear to affect the kind of anthocyanin as well as its quantity. Red, pink and milk white flowers all have the more red pigment malvidin in addition to delphinidin, the common blue pigment ubiquitous in irises. Red Siberian irises contain the pigment malvidin in addition to delphinidin, and this confers the redder color to these varieties. Pinks contain just malvidin but in smaller quantities (Vaughn and Lyerla 1978).

Here's a summary of these genotypes and the corresponding color:

Blue-purple: CC WW or CcWw
Red: $c^r c^r$ WW or $c^r c^r$ Ww
Pink: $c^p c^p$ WW or $c^p c^p$ Ww
Milk white: cc WW or cc Ww
Clean white: any combination of alleles at the c locus plus ww

One of the exceptions of this genetic model has been the behavior of the Siberian iris 'Red Emperor'. In crosses of 'Red Emperor' to blues there were some red progeny (Tiffney 1967) and Gladys Wiswell's 'Carrie Lee' is a very light red from crossing the clear white 'White Empress' × 'Red Emperor'. 'Red Emperor' was reputed to be from *I. chrysographes* (Kellogg 1959) but 'Red Emperor' crosses easily with other 28-chromosome Siberian irises. Moreover, the red gene from 'Red Emperor' appears to be similar if not identical with that in other Siberian irises as crosses of 'Carrie Lee' × 'Sugar Rush' gave all red progeny and a seedling from 'Red Emperor' inbreeding crossed with an inbred from 'Eric the Red' produced all red progeny. Self pollination of 'Carrie Lee' did allow the recovery of the recessive white so the cross does appear to be as indicated in its registration. Recent information courtesy of Jean Witt indicates that 'Red Emperor' is in fact an 'Emperor' seedling so at least half of the pedigree is a garden Siberian. The branching habit of 'Red Emperor' does indicate that there must be an *I. sibirica* type parent that was mated with 'Emperor' as 'Emperor' itself is two-budded.

Since the pigment and genetic studies of Vaughn and Lyerla (1978), Siberians have developed much stronger yellow color that has spread throughout the petals, rather than being confined to the signal. These yellows started with the McEwen attempts to extend the yellow signal into a broader area of

the signal and eventually throughout the flower. The addition of the carotenoid yellow pigments allows for the combination of yellows and the blue and red pigments. Brown, truer red and salmon shades are produced by combining blue, red and pink anthocyanin pigments in the epidermis with yellow pigments in the sub-epidermis. Not all of these overlays are successful in terms of attractive colors, especially if the overlaying or underlying colors are applied unevenly.

Inheritance of flower colors in *I. versicolor* appear to be under similar control to that in the Siberian irises (B. Warburton, personal communication) and from limited crossings of the author, the *I. virginica* color variants may be explained by a similar genetic model.

Whites in the Japanese irises appear to be similar to the clean white Siberian irises and white color is controlled by a single gene that is recessive to the wild-type blue-purple. Inheritance of the other colors is less clear, partly because the Japanese irises are of such mixed ancestry that the genetics has not been as easy to clarify as in the highly inbred Siberian irises. Some hybridizers have remarked that certain Japanese iris crosses will give a complete range of colors found in the Japanese iris colors.

In Louisiana irises there are two kinds of white irises, although distinguishing the two types is difficult. White mutants from *I. giganticaerulea* (e.g., 'Her Highness') are complementary to those from *I. nelsonii* (e.g., 'Clara Goula') so that crosses between them give all blue-violet progeny. Thus, these two types of white Louisiana irises are due to different complementary genes, similar to the situation in Siberian irises. Yellow Louisiana irises are simply white irises but with the presence of carotenoid pigments. As in the Siberian irises, the red Louisiana irises contain the reddish anthocyaninidin malvidin. When the reddish purple pigments overlay a yellow base, the effect created is quite red, certainly the reddest colors to be found in the genus iris.

Inheritance of the flower colors in the spuria irises is much different than the other beardless irises, which is maybe not surprising considering the recent DNA studies indicating that spurias are not as closely related to the core *Limniris* group. Eric Nies documented his early crosses and show the complex inheritance of flower color in this group. In the F1 of the cross between *I. orientalis* (white with yellow signal) × the blue-violet 'Monspur' (itself a hybrid of *I. monnieri* × a blue-violet member of the *I. spuria* complex) all of the progeny were of the *I. orientalis* color and pattern. Nies chose two of these that showed a glimmer of blue color and intercrossed them to produce a F2 that included whites with yellow signals, all yellows, blues and a single brown. The brown was the result of both recessives, blue and yellow occurring together, resulting in a brown. Although the *I. orientalis* pattern behaves as a dominant, pale yellows or creams (like the cream 'Offering') can be crossed with other colors and the other colors will be expressed in the progeny. For example, the cross of cream 'Offering' with the blue-purple 'Lucky Devil' gave all blue-purple progeny. Segregations in some of these crosses indicate that, instead of the simple 3:1 F2 segregations of traits that are found in the other beardless iris diploids, the ratios reflect tetraploid segregations (35:1 vs. 3:1 in the F2) of these traits. Dave Niswonger (2009) made similar observations on the odd segregations in his crosses to recover pinkish flower colors, as many factors segregated in ratios that reflected non-simple inheritance. Similarly, Hadley (1958) observed chromosome configurations called quadrivalents in meiotic squashes of spuria pollen mother cells, indicating four homologous chromosomes. As for the Siberian irises, when carotenoid pigments are overlaid with anthocyanins other colors may be produced, sometimes interesting blends or colors are produced. For example, when blue-purple overlays yellow, the flowers are brown. The pinks and reds are from similar combinations but different sorts, amounts, or distributions of the two classes of pigment.

Patterns in iris flowers are of several types. There are many veined patterns, such as in *I. sibirica* derivatives, that have white falls strongly veined blue-violet. Crosses of the veined Siberian irises to non-veined types give plants with some indication of a white signal with some veins but not as extensive as in the veined parent. The F2 from these plants gives a wide segregation of these types from fully self-colored blossoms to veined types typical of *I. sibirica*. Although these data indicate that the pattern is heritable, the number of genes involved, or the effects of genes that might modify the extent of the pattern is not known. Some of the patterns appear to be under control of controlling elements, similar to the ones described first by McClintock in maize. The Louisiana iris 'Finders Keepers' is a white with irregular splashes of blue on the flower. When 'Finders Keepers' is crossed to white *I. brevicaulis* strains, all the progeny are splashed but crosses to blue-violet types give all blue violets. This is similar to the inheritance of plicatas in bearded irises where the patterned flower is dominant to one type of white but recessive to blue-violet self-colored flowers. There are similar sorts of splashed patterns in the Japanese irises such as in 'Grape Fizz' and 'Trance' and in the Siberian irises 'Neat Splash' and 'Suji Iri' that may be under similar genetic control.

Details of the genetics of the 40-chromosome Siberians are much less well known. One of the interesting peculiarities of this group is that crosses of blue types with yellows instead of resulting in solid colors, results in heavily speckled progeny, even though the parental types show no signs of these patterns. Speckled patterns are known to be controlled by controlling elements like the splashed patterns described above. In other genera such speckled patterns are due to the differing control of pigment synthesis in the two parental lines so that each tries to exert its influence, resulting in a patchwork of colors.

QUANTITATIVE INHERITANCE

Not all characteristics are inherited simply. Characters such as petal width, height of stalk, flower size, numbers of buds and branches, and flowering times are characters that appear to be under control of multiple genes. For example, a cross between a short and tall Siberian iris, the progeny in the F1 might be somewhat in between the two parents. In the second

Schafer-Sacks S11-23-12

generation, plants are obtained that are the full gamut of types in a Poisson distribution that centers around the size of the first generation progeny.

Bloom shape is even more complicated because of genes controlling petal identity, width and length of the petals, presence or absence of ruffling, substance of the petals and many other factors. Because these flower characteristics involve so many genes, it is much more difficult for the breeder to anticipate which of these characteristics will appear in the progeny. Generally, crossing irises with good basic shape will pass on these characters to a majority of the seedlings. However, this is where the ancestors to the parents you have used in your cross will show up in the worst possible ways.

In particular, I remember a row of spuria seedlings where I had used two parents that were both from crosses of species to modern cultivars. Neither parent had what would be called bad form, but of course the genes from the parents were there lurking waiting to be expressed in the next generation. The seedlings displayed all sorts of awkward forms that were odd combinations of all the form defects of the species and some new ones! Needless to say, there were no introductions from that cross!

In contrast, I crossed the same two parents with the very well-formed 'Offering' and all of the progeny had lovely form. Very neutral flowers colorwise with very good form, such as 'Offering', are ones I go back to time and again as parents as they are essentially a "blank canvas" where I can express other colors and patterns but also be confidant that whatever I produce will have fine form. Bee Warburton described this once to me as "Whites are not so important for their whiteness but for allowing the expression of the other parent. In addition, they often contain an array of other useful recessives that appear in later generations." She did repeated backcrosses to 'White Swirl' to combine that form into all of her lines. Later, she used 'Wing on Wing' and her own 'Bellissima' in crosses, knowing that they had the same genetic goodies as 'White Swirl' but had improved form and branching.

THE FUTURE

In Graeme Grosvenor's wonderful book on irises he ends with some very fanciful "Photoshopped" photos that illustrate some of the more fanciful combinations that might be possible in the irises of the future. Sea foam greens mixed with pinks, black and orange, and other sorts of wild edged patterns. All very fun and I'm sure many of these will be accomplished, although maybe not in my lifetime. Remembering what beardless irises were in 1964, when I first started, the iris colors and forms have gone through improvements by leaps and bounds. My list of "things to accomplish" in each group I think are perhaps more attainable, maybe even short-term goals.

SIBERIAN IRIS GOALS

As I look at the Siberian irises that I knew as a child and those available today, there are vast improvements in virtually every color. The blues are closer to true blue. The reds, now especially those with a yellow underlay, are much closer to red than the old wine reds. The pinks have become not just lavender but actually a respectable pink. When these pink tones are overlaid on yellow backgrounds, very attractive salmon and apricot colors have been produced. Further refinement will bring these colors into cleaner and more even colors. Although there has been much progress in yellow garden Siberians, many of the yellows are not color-fast and/or are much deeper on the falls. Currier McEwen named a cultivar 'Dreaming Orange' in 1987 and frankly we are still dreaming of that color! A similar statement could be made for his 'Dreaming Green'. We know from our experience with yellows that, if a flower has a bit of a certain color, we can expand that color so it occupies more of the petal by selective breeding. We do have a few brown Siberians now such as 'Jerry Murphy', where blue-violet overlays yellow, creating a brown effect. Considering all the lovely shades of brown and copper in the bearded irises, this could be a fruitful area.

More surprisingly, we seem not to have markedly advanced towards very dark flowers despite the large number of quality dark purples that have been available ever since 'Caesar's Brother'. Possibly by combining the very darkest purples with some of the darker yellows will result in some overlaid colors that more approach black. The new varieties 'Bat Wing' and 'Black Joker' hint at that possibility. Amoenas in yellow and pink are available already but more surprisingly one in blue hasn't appeared since the old English variety 'The Gower'. Similarly, blues with white styles, which were present in Cleveland's 'Silver Tip' and Spofford's 'Mandy Morse', many years ago have not appeared in any modern cultivar. Bee Warburton's 'Deep Shade' set a high bar for a darker flower with light styles many years ago, but progression towards white styles on dark purple have not appeared. The *sibirica* pattern of dark veins on a white ground have enjoyed a resurgence with the appearance of 'Banish Misfortune' and 'Shakers Prayer'; 'So Van Gogh' adds a bit of a yellow ground color. I would love to see that pattern in red or pink. The dappled and atoll patterns that were developed by Steve Varner and Bee Warburton have been extended into other colors. These patterns are popular and could be more developed in the darker shades as well as red or pink.

Siberian irises are in general very healthy plants. Branching and bud count are much improved with four buds becoming more the norm in newly introduced cultivars. 'Salem Witch' regularly produces sixteen to nineteen buds per stalk in my garden and it seems to pass on a large number of buds to its progeny. A more modern flower, 'Where Eagles Dare', often has nine buds. Coupling this high bud count with rebloom will ensure the popularity of Siberian irises as garden plants.

No one has really pursued Siberian irises in warmer climates, where they tend not to do well. There are some exceptions, though. 'Caesar's Brother', 'Velvet Night', 'Ruffled Velvet' and 'Lights of Paris' are all plants that perform admirably in warm climates. I had crossed 'Ruffled Velvet' and 'Velvet Night' while living in Mississippi and raised a crop of approximately one hundred seedlings, all of which burgeoned in that climate. Thus it might be possible to create a "Southern-happy" strain.

LOUISIANA IRISES

The progress that Louisiana irises have made from the swamps of Louisiana to the fine wide and ruffled creations we have today is nothing short of a miracle. Had Louisiana irises had the same long history as the Japanese irises there is no telling what sort of irises that could have been created. Still, there is room for improvement.

Pinks still really aren't anywhere near as pink as the bearded or Japanese irises in those colors. John Taylor's 'Dancing Vogue' is still the closest of the introduced varieties. I have approached this through the orchid-pink lines of Granger and although quite lovely, are no nearer to pink than their parents. Lighter or white styles on darker flowers have not progressed as much even though 'Mac's Blue Heaven' gave us a very nice navy flower with white styles and a plant that is also a useful parent. The ice blue shades have proven difficult. Many of these have poor substance or plain forms or both. My 'Aqua Velva' (Vaughn '14) is the first that covers most of these defects although a bit more ruffling would be nice. Crosses of yellows into solid colors often give flowers that are banded in lighter shades and there are some outstanding varieties in the market with these colors. Yellow Louisiana irises have some of the most advanced forms of any color class so it should be possible to produce haloed types in many colors and with excellent forms. The tetraploid Louisiana irises have attracted much less attention and it is possible that many interesting things could result from these lines.

The Louisiana plant could use a bit of a makeover. Many gardeners won't grow them because they produce such large clumps. 'Kristen Nicholas' is a nice red flower and the rhizomes are short enough that it makes for a very compact clump. Unfortunately most of the ones that make compact clumps don't have the size or ruffling of the most advanced Louisiana hybrids. Mating the two types may result in the necessary

Schafer-Sacks S11-16-11

combination of smaller rhizomes with large ruffled blossoms. Buds on the lower positions on the stalk often don't open properly. I consider this a severe fault that I never use these cultivars in crossing.

PACIFIC COAST NATIVE IRISES

The PCNs are such beautiful flowers but in most climates they are not the most wonderful plants. In many climates few or none of the cultivars can be grown successfully. Some attempts have been made by breeders that live in less favorable climates to obtain seed from breeders that grow the most current cultivars. In that way seedlings might be selected that perform in these adverse climates yet have all the modern attributes. Some other varieties that grow very well in diverse climates, such as 'Canyon Snow', might be useful in crossing to modern cultivars to increase the "garden-ability" of the PCNs.

Of the other colors and patterns, the only colors that have not been achieved in pure forms are the reds and pinks, although much progress has been made in each of these color classes. Similarly, the patterns in the PCNs are very well developed, especially all the permutations of the 'Valley Banner' pattern. Creating ground colors of bright yellows and apricots with the various patterns might produce some very interesting effects.

SPURIA IRISES

Hybridizing spuria irises seems to have stalled a bit compared to the other beardless iris classes. Part of this has been the loss of so many great hybridizers (Hager, McCown, Jenkins, and Wickencamp) that are impossible to replace. The other problem is the relatively slow maturation and increase of spuria irises compared to other beardless irises. However, there are several hybridizers taking up the challenge of breeding these plants and some very interesting flowers are now entering the market.

In spurias, extending the color range has been a challenge. There are very good whites with yellow signals, yellows of all shades, browns and some blues or purples. Reds and pinks are not close to true shades of either color although they are definitely closer than what was available 20 years ago. Truer and more color-fast blues have become possible by bringing in genes from the blue species that has been pioneered by Dave Niswonger. Unfortunately, many of these first generation hybrids have reduced fertility, although the few seedlings that are obtained generally have close to full fertility. Striped and dark standards with light fall color patterns are present and are very popular. Developing these into new color combinations and improving the form of these cultivars is definitely on the "to do" list for these plants. Miniature cultivars now exist in almost all of the colors available in the full sized varieties.

Forms of the newer spurias have also improved. In the past the spurias had rather widely separated petals, leading Phillip Corliss to suggest the term "butterfly irises" for spurias. The more modern look is wider and shorter petals although I do like the look of the spurias which have wide upright standards as well as they are showier in the landscape. Most spurias are not highly ruffled and even fewer have laciniations to the petals that resemble the lace in bearded irises. Addition of these petal form modifications into all colors and flower types will greatly enhance the beauty of the spuria flower.

Branching and bud count are also areas where improvements might be seen in the future. In many areas of the country, a good spuria stalk has four buds. While this gives a fairly long bloom because of the heavy substance of the individual flowers, more buds would clearly be an improvement. Phillip Corliss produced cultivars with 12 to 14 buds on gracefully branched stalks using principally the Nies strain, so the genes are there to produce such stalks in our modern cultivars. Some cultivars derived from *I. notha* have more expanded branches, which sometimes look like clumsy arrangements of blossoms rather than an improvement in branching pattern; however, some happy medium in which the flowers are more separated from the spathe but not so widely branched as to look like a witch's broom would be good.

JAPANESE IRISES

One would think that a plant group with a several hundred year hybridizing history could not be improved upon. *Wrong!* Although Japanese irises have some lovely wide blooms, the color range is a bit stymied because of the absence of yellows. Not only would this give good quality yellow irises but it would also open up all the colors from overlaying red, pink and red-purple over yellow. Some progress has been made, in extending the yellow signal and also in creating cream whites. The Japanese iris breeders have the example of what has happened to the Siberian iris flowers in just a relatively few years of extending the yellow signal color into both yellow amoenas and full yellow flowers. A similar comment could be made for the Japanese irises with green in the flower. Up to now the green is limited to the signal, although the signals on some of these flowers are larger than in most cultivars and some white cultivars have green veins that might be exploited in a breeding program.

Max Steiger many years ago tried to select for Japanese irises that would grow in higher pH soil, which is generally death to Japanese irises. Out of many thousands of seedlings, most perished, but a few did survive this rather extreme treatment. Unfortunately, these plants were lost during an illness of the hybridizer.

SUMMARY

I think that what I have listed here for the various groups are all easily obtainable goals. Most of these goals are ones that I've used in my own hybridizing in these groups. Any gardener who has grown more than a few of any of these plants will see all sorts of potential avenues for improvement. Get your tweezers ready! You will have such fun. To spur you on, I have included images of some of the most recent selected seedlings from Heather Pryor and Marty Schafer, as well as a Siberian registered but not yet on the market from Jeff Dunlop. Enjoy this peek into the future!

Schafer-Sacks S12-41-5

REFERENCES

Coen, E.S. and E.M. Meyerowitz (1991) The war of the whorls: genetic interactions controlling flower development. *Nature* 353: 31–37.

Hadley, H.H. (1958) Chromosome number and meiotic behavior in commercial varieties of spuria iris. *American Iris Society Bulletin* 150: 108–115.

Kellogg, W. (1959) Siberian irises. In: *Garden Irises* (L.F. Randolph, ed.). Ithaca, NY: American Iris Society. 259–264.

Nies, N. (2009) *The Eric Nies Chronicles*. Special publication, American Iris Society, 44.

Niswonger, D. (2009) Hybridizing spurias. In: *The Illustrated Checklist of Spuria Irises* (D. Jurn, editor), The Spuria Iris Society. 36–39.

Reynolds, J. and J. Tampion (1983) *Double Flowers*. New York: Van Nostrand Reinhold.

Schafer, M. (2014) I can't wait for spring. *The Siberian Iris* 12(6): 5–14.

Tiffney, S. (1967) The Siberians of Elizabeth Scheffy. *The Siberian Iris* 2:240–242.

Tilney-Bassett, R.A.E. (1986) *Plant Chimeras*. Arnold, London.

Tomino, K. (1963) Studies on the genus *Iris* in Japan especially cytotaxonomy of the genus and breeding of *Iris ensata* Thunberg. Bull. Lib. Art. Dep., Mie Univ. 28: 1–59 (in Japanese with English summary).

Vaughn, K.C. and T.A. Lyerla (1978) Flavonoid genetics of the 28-chromosome "Siberian" iris. *Theoretical and Applied Genetics* 51: 247–248.

Vishnevetsky, M. and E.M. Meyerowitz (2002) Molecular control of flower development. In: *Breeding for Ornamentals: Classical and Molecular Approaches* (A. Vainstein, editor). Kluwer, Dordrecht, The Netherlands. 239–252.

Yabuya, T. (1991) Aneuploidy of ornamental species. In: *Genetics and Breeding of Ornamental Species* (J. Harding, F. Singh, and J.N.M. Mol, editors). Kluwer, Amsterdam. 39–52.

Yabuya, T., H. Kikugawa, and T. Adachi (1989) Karyotypes and chromosome associations in aneuploid varieties of Japanese garden iris, *iris ensata* Thunb. *Euphytica* 42: 117–125.

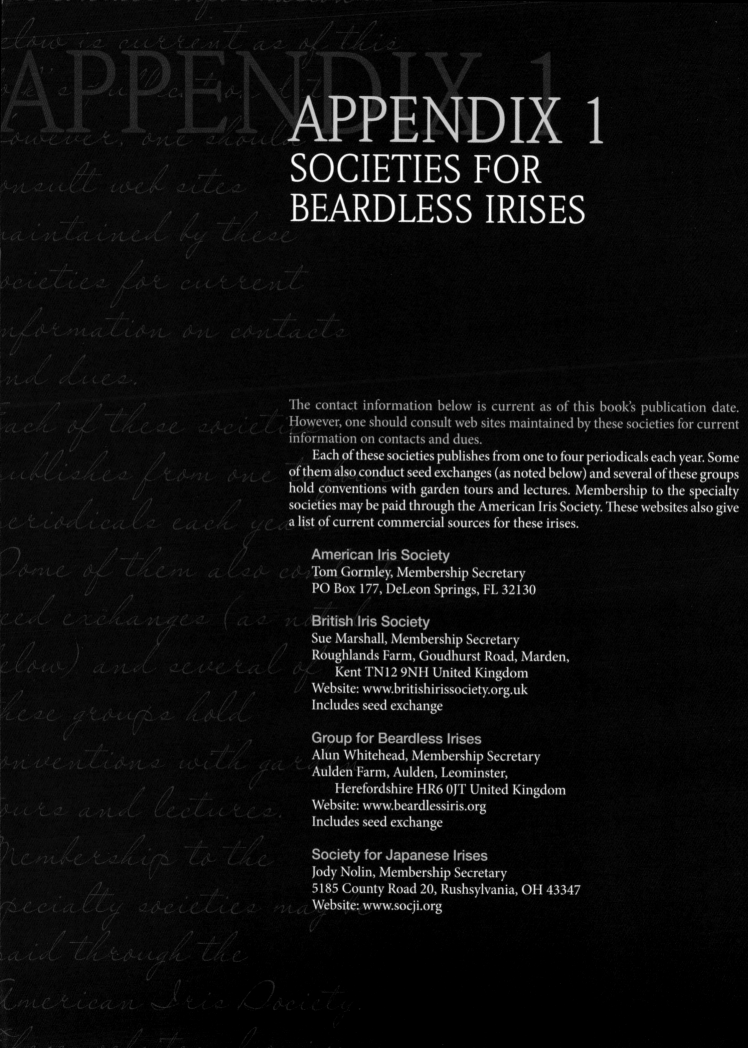

APPENDIX 1
SOCIETIES FOR BEARDLESS IRISES

The contact information below is current as of this book's publication date. However, one should consult web sites maintained by these societies for current information on contacts and dues.

Each of these societies publishes from one to four periodicals each year. Some of them also conduct seed exchanges (as noted below) and several of these groups hold conventions with garden tours and lectures. Membership to the specialty societies may be paid through the American Iris Society. These websites also give a list of current commercial sources for these irises.

American Iris Society
Tom Gormley, Membership Secretary
PO Box 177, DeLeon Springs, FL 32130

British Iris Society
Sue Marshall, Membership Secretary
Roughlands Farm, Goudhurst Road, Marden,
    Kent TN12 9NH United Kingdom
Website: www.britishirissociety.org.uk
Includes seed exchange

Group for Beardless Irises
Alun Whitehead, Membership Secretary
Aulden Farm, Aulden, Leominster,
    Herefordshire HR6 0JT United Kingdom
Website: www.beardlessiris.org
Includes seed exchange

Society for Japanese Irises
Jody Nolin, Membership Secretary
5185 County Road 20, Rushsylvania, OH 43347
Website: www.socji.org

Society for Louisiana Irises
Ron Killingworth, Membership Secretary
10329 Caddo Lake Road, Mooringsport, LA 71060
Website: www.louisianas.org

Society for Pacific Coast Native Irises
Kathleen Sayce, Membership Secretary
PO Box 91, Nahcotta, WA 98637
Website: www.pacificcoastiris.org
Includes seed exchange

Society for Siberian Irises
Susan Grigg, Membership Secretary
195 Trotters Ridge Drive, Raleigh, NC 27614
Website: www.socsib.org

Species Iris Group of North America
Rodney Barton, Membership Secretary
3 Wolters Street, Hickory Creek, TX 75065
Website: www.signa.org
Includes seed exchange

Spuria Iris Society
Nancy Price, Membership Secretary
32009 S. Ona Way, Molalla, OR 97938
Website: www.spuriairis.com

APPENDIX 2
FURTHER READING

These wonderful books on irises have been used in part by the author in creating the text for this book. Many of these books are out of print but can be borrowed from libraries or purchased from used book dealers on the Internet. Nothing is more fun than curling up with a great gardening book on a cold winter evening, where gardening itself isn't possible but "gardening in your mind" is.

GENERAL BOOKS ON IRISES

Austin, C. (2005). *Irises: A Gardener's Encyclopedia.* Timber Press, Portland, OR. This contains the British perspective on irises, from a prominent nurserywoman. Covers all irises briefly, with long lists of illustrated recommended cultivars.

Grosvenor, G. (1997). *Iris: Flower of the Rainbow.* Kangaroo Press, Kenthurst, NSW, Australia. Amazingly good photographs are the highlights of this book, as are some fanciful predictions of irises for the future.

McKenny, E.P. (1927). *Iris in the Little Garden.* Little, Brown, Boston. A charming book that is a pure pleasure to read, and McKenny's sense of how to use irises in the garden is spot on even today.

Mitchell, S.B. (1949). *Iris for Every Garden.* Barrows, New York. Sydney Mitchell was the irisarian for whom the Mitchell Medal was named. He had enthusiasm for all sorts of irises and his book is a very pleasant read. His suggestions for garden design and companion plants are still good ones.

Price, M. (1966). *The Iris Book.* Van Nostrand, Princeton, NJ. A great book for beginners that covers all irises in brief form. Beautifully written. If you want a general introduction to irises, this is the book for you.

Randolph, L.F. (1959). *Garden Irises.* The American Iris Society, St. Louis, MO. This was the first comprehensive book on irises and contains lots of valuable information on chromosome counts and species hybrids not printed in other sources.

Vallette, W.L. (1961). *Iris Culture and Hybridizing for Everyone.* Adams Press, Chicago, IL. Although the discussion of beardless irises is rather brief, the discussions of hybridizing, selecting seedlings, and naming your offspring are very extensive and very useful.

Warburton, B.A. and M. Hamblen (1978). *The World of Irises.* American Iris Society, Wichita, KS. This is a compendium of the results of experts in all aspects of irises. Although the cultivars mentioned are not the most recent, there is much wonderful information on culture and hybridizing that is timeless.

BOOKS ON SPECIFIC GROUPS OF IRISES

Caillet, M., J.F. Campbell, K.C. Vaughn, and D. Vercher (2000). *The Louisiana Iris: Taming of a Native American Wildflower.* Timber Press, Portland, OR. A very comprehensive account of the Louisiana irises, covering the species, development of hybrids, hybridizing, and garden uses.

McEwen, C. (1990). *The Japanese Iris.* University Press, Hanover, NH. Currier's wonderful account of the Japanese irises, done with Currier's usual attention to detail.

McEwen, C. (1996). *The Siberian Iris.* Timber Press, Portland, OR. A very comprehensive volume that goes into great detail on treating seedlings with colchicine, which is useful to all of those attempting these techniques.

BOOKS ON IRIS SPECIES

Species Group of the British Iris Society (1997). *A Guide to Species Iris: Their Identification and Cultivation.* Cambridge University Press, Cambridge, England. A volume of collected chapters written by experts on each of the various species of irises. Besides the rather dry botanical descriptions, the authors describe garden uses and cultural conditions for each species.

Waddick, J.W. and Z. Yu-tang. (1992). *Iris of China.* Timber Press, Portland, OR. Dr. Waddick explored China collecting iris species and bringing back a number of these to the United States for the first time. This book covers these unusual species. Based upon their habitat in China, some prediction of how these species might fare in cultivation is given.

GENERAL INDEX

SPECIES INDEX

HYBRIDIZER INDEX